THE MARTYRS

GOD'S GENERALS

The Martyrs

God's Generals

Roberts Liardon

Whitaker House

Boldface type in the Scripture quotations indicates the author's emphasis.

God's Generals:
The Martyrs

Roberts Liardon Ministries
P.O. Box 781888
Orlando, FL 32878
www.robertsliardon.com

ISBN: 978-1-62911-731-7
eBook ISBN: 978-1-62911-733-1
Printed in the United States of America

Whitaker House
1030 Hunt Valley Circle
New Kensington, PA 15068
www.whitakerhouse.com

LC record available at https://lccn.loc.gov/2016039072

4 5 6 7 8 9 10 11 12 **W** 28 27 26 25

DEDICATION

I dedicate this book to my ancestor, Wilhelm Heckardt.

Wilhelm Heckardt was born in 1498 in Dresden, Saxony, Germany, and grew up in a wealthy and influential family. Like most Saxons at that time, he was raised Roman Catholic, but just before his father died and he inherited his father's title and vast estate, a man named Martin Luther nailed his 95 Theses to the door of the Wittenberg Castle Church. Wilhelm was swept away with the revelation that *"by grace you have been saved through faith"* (Ephesians 2:8), and it changed the course of his earthly life as well as his eternal life.

Wilhelm's family wealth and prestige could not save him from the Roman Catholic Church's persecution of the new Protestants, so he fled Germany. Because he was very educated and could speak the English language fluently, he moved to England and anglicized his name. Now called William Hacker, he failed to "blend in" with the religion of Britain, which at that time (under Henry VIII) was staunchly loyal to the

Roman pope. Instead, true to his new nature in Christ Jesus, William went about telling everyone he met about being saved by faith.

Having lost all his financial assets when he immigrated to England, most of the people William preached to were not wealthy or influential. However, he had a few wealthy patrons who bought Bibles for him to distribute and allowed him to preach in their castles. When the pope began pressuring Cardinal Wolsey for money to complete St. Peter's Cathedral in Rome, the cardinal gathered up Protestant "heretics" and tortured them to gain the names of any wealthy believers. He would then have them burned at the stake and confiscate their wealth for the pope's building fund.

William Hacker was imprisoned and tortured but refused to give up the names of those who had helped him. He was put on the rack and stretched until his joints were pulled apart. When that didn't work, hot coals were applied to his spine until the flesh peeled away. At that point he was babbling and nearly unconscious. All he was saying was, "Yes, yes, yes." They would ask him if a certain nobleman was one of his benefactors, and he would say, "Yes, yes, yes."

After the cardinal's men had William's "testimony" concerning these "heretics," they executed his benefactors, sending their wealth on to Rome. William was released, and shortly thereafter, in 1528 in London, he died from the effects of the torture.

This book is dedicated to the many who, like William, have laid everything down for Jesus Christ, even to the point of persecution, torture, and death. Let us be pierced in our hearts that we should do no less for the One who was pierced for us!

CONTENTS

FOREWORD

The *God's Generals* library has become a literary treasure chest of church history's spiritual giants—a powerful resource that inspires faith and imparts wisdom. My friend and fellow evangelist, Roberts Liardon, has done the digging and painstaking excavation; we get to share the treasure. Now his latest installment, *The Martyrs*, in my opinion, has become the collection's most important volume. Let me explain why.

As a missionary evangelist to Africa, I have had the incredible privilege of knowing Christians who gave their lives for the gospel. Some of these died only moments after giving public testimony to their conversion on our platform. I have also known family members left behind by martyrs. Many of our team members have several times escaped martyrdom by the breadth of a hair. Others have given their lives in the work, and all of us are ready and willing to do the same.

So a book like this is very dear to me. It helps connect two worlds within the body of Christ. Western Christians need the veil removed that often hides what is "normal" Christianity to the rest of the world. Indeed, most Christians today live outside of North America and Europe. More to the point, most of the church's history—our history—had to grow and prosper in very hostile territory. Many of our brothers and sisters had to suffer pressure, rejection, discrimination, beatings, torture, death, and loss of loved ones simply because of their faith in Christ and their loyalty to the gospel. That is the reality—and it is an ongoing reality.

Contrary to what some believe, the time of the martyrs has not ended. More people have given their lives for the gospel in the past century than in all previous church history combined. Today the remaining unreached places in the world are dangerous and hostile to Christianity. To reach them will require a generation willing to pay the ultimate price.

Revelation 12:11 describes those who overcame the enemy "*...by the blood of the Lamb, and by the word of their testimony; and they loved not their lives unto the death.*" This unwavering fidelity to the name of Christ, even in the face of persecution, suffering and death, will be a key to the victory of the church in the last days. And this reality is playing out, even now, throughout the world.

In a day when Western Christianity too often ignores the cross to appeal to consumers, Roberts' book gives us a dose of reality we badly need.

And it's a dose the Bible requires us to take. Scripture calls us to remember those who have suffered for their faith. (See Hebrews 11:1–12:3.) It tells us to allow their examples not only to inspire us, but also to instruct us wherever we live. If those courageous witnesses valued God's kingdom more than their own well-being, so can we. If Jesus was worth it all for them, He can be worth it all for us, too!

The martyrs remind us that this world is not our home. God's eternal kingdom is our destiny, worthy even now of all our affections and ambitions. Life on earth is a short sojourn. Jesus will return. The dead will rise, and all will stand before the judgment seat of Christ. We cannot allow our Christian freedoms and wealth to hypnotize us into the practical denial of the age to come. It is not enough to claim comfortable biblical orthodoxy while we live rooted in this world. Jesus died to give us *eternal* life.

Besides Scripture, what better way to keep an eternal perspective and stay spiritually sober than to read about the martyrs? Roberts Liardon provides us with the perfect source for their stories. Naturally he had to select certain examples to represent the many. But you will find here a book teeming with amazing accounts of saints spanning the ages who put Jesus and His gospel above their own lives.

Right out of the gate, Roberts confronts us with martyrdoms that occurred recently in today's global conflict. Then he goes back to New Testament days, tracing the stories of martyrs chronologically back to our own day. In fact, after reading this book I felt like I got a bird's eye view of Christian history. But don't let that statement fool you. This book is not a boring textbook. It informs like a history book, but it reads like a thriller. Roberts' exceptional story-telling skills and easy prose will keep you engaged from paragraph to paragraph, and page to page. Yet the intense drama and breathtaking action are real. These stories are true, impeccably researched and well-documented throughout.

So I wholeheartedly commend this book to you. It is like an updated *Foxe's Book of Martyrs* for a new generation. Every Christian should read it and take it to heart. We only get one chance to live for Jesus in this world, and He is worth it all.

—Daniel Kolenda
President and CEO, Christ for all Nations

INTRODUCTION

"The Blood of the Saints Is the Seed of the Church"

In the last two thousand years, the Christian church has grown from twelve uneducated apostles in Judea, to one hundred and twenty anointed disciples in an upper room, to thousands of converted Jews and Gentiles in the Middle East, to hundreds of millions of people from nearly every tribe and nation on earth. Jesus Christ's true church, filled with believers who have been born again by the Holy Spirit, has grown in spite of every tactic Satan has used to try to destroy it. Jesus promised that He would be the One to build His church and that *"the gates of hell shall not prevail against it"* (Matthew 16:18 ESV). He is keeping His promise.

One of the most amazing ways the body of Christ has grown through the centuries is following the martyrdom of faithful witnesses to Jesus Christ. Tertullian, a church leader in the second century, wrote a prophetic word: "The blood of the saints is the seed of the church." That word and the shedding of blood for Christ's sake have remained true through two thousand years of Christian history. Wherever there is martyrdom in Jesus' name, there is a blossoming of church growth in the body of Christ. *"I assure you and most solemnly say to you, unless a grain of wheat falls into the earth and dies, it remains alone [just one grain, never more]. But if it dies, it produces much grain and yields a harvest"* (John 12:24 AMP).

It's All About Being a Witness!

Being a martyr is all about being a witness for Jesus. What was the original meaning of the word "martyr"? Taken from the Greek word *martur*, it was originally translated as "witness." Initially, a martyr was someone who witnessed an important event and then spoke publicly about what they had seen. Today's dictionary describes a witness as "an individual who is personally present to see or perceive something; a spectator or eyewitness."

A witness cannot not just make up his own story! That would be a false witness. A true witness must report facts and life events just as he or she saw them. Of course, if there is more than one witness to an event, it gives it even more credibility.

Jesus knew all about the importance of needing witnesses to prove something was true. He said to the disciples, *"And the Father himself, which hath sent me, hath borne witness of me"* (John 5:37 KJV). In Jewish law, a minimum of two witnesses was required to validate any testimony. Jesus knew this law and the importance of having witnesses. Jesus assured His disciples, *"I am He who testifies about Myself, and the Father who sent Me testifies about Me"* (John 8:18 NASB). The night before His crucifixion, He told the disciples, *"But when the Helper comes, whom I shall send to you from the Father, the Spirit of truth who proceeds from the Father,* ***He will testify of Me. And you also will bear witness****, because you* *have been with Me from the beginning"* (John 15:26–27).

It is God's eternal plan to use human witnesses to spread the gospel message.

It is God's eternal plan to use human witnesses to spread the gospel message of Jesus Christ throughout the whole world. This is why it was so crucial for the disciples to understand the importance of being His witnesses. Jesus' final command to them was to go forth in the power of the Holy Spirit and witness. *"And you shall receive power when the Holy Spirit has come upon you; and* ***you shall be witnesses to Me*** *in Jerusalem and in all Judea and Samaria, and to the end of the earth"* (Acts 1:8). Jesus wanted to make His point crystal clear: a Christian's life was all about being a witness.

Witnesses Become Martyrs

Sixty years after Jesus ascended to heaven, the apostle John wrote a letter reinforcing the Lord's command to be a witness. John wrote: *"What we* ***have heard****, what we* ***have seen with our eyes*** [witnessed], *what we* ***have looked at*** *and* ***touched with our hands*** *concerning the Word of Life* [Jesus]*...****what we have seen and heard we proclaim to you also****, that you may have fellowship with us; and indeed our fellowship is with the Father and with His Son Jesus Christ"* (1 John 1:1, 3 NASB). Nothing was more important to the early apostles: their call was to be bold witnesses, to proclaim what they had seen and heard about Jesus Christ from Jerusalem to Judea and then throughout the whole earth.

By the time John wrote this letter, it was approximately AD 97. The other eleven apostles and thousands of disciples had already been brutally killed by Nero and other foreign leaders for their faith. Being a witness for Christ had taken on a whole new meaning. The word "martyr" no longer referred to those who simply witnessed for Jesus but those who were willing to die rather than deny Him.

We Know Who Wins This Battle!

It has been centuries since the Western Christian church has experienced the brutality of martyrdom for the Christian faith. For most Western Christians, martyrdom is something of the very distant past. Thanks to digital media and the rise of globalism, however, Christian martyrdom, which had taken place in "dark corners" for centuries, is now thrust into our field of vision. Kidnappings, beheadings, and mass murders of Christians are painfully depicted on gruesome internet videos. Islamic extremists and political rebels flaunt their violence against Christian communities. In countries in the Middle East, Asia and Africa, whole villages of men, women, and children have been massacred by sword, gun, and fire in the name of hatred. Organizations like Voice of the Martyrs and Open Doors have worked tirelessly to bring the tragedy of persecuted Christians around the world to our attention.

Satan has renewed his effort to brutally wipe God's people from the face of the earth.

Today, the spirit of the antichrist roams through the earth filling men and women's hearts with hatred for the followers of Christ, just as he has done since Christianity was born. Satan has renewed his effort to brutally wipe God's people from the face of the earth. He will use any means or ideology available to him to do the job.

But there is good news! We know who wins this battle! Because of Jesus dwelling within us, we know that the ultimate victory is ours. The Word of God reassures us, *"You are from God, little children, and have overcome them;* ***because greater is He who is in you than he who is in the world****"* (1 John 4:4 NASB). The followers of Jesus will overcome this world and the true enemy, Satan, *"by the blood of the Lamb and by the word of their testimony"* (Revelation 12:11).

Honoring Christian Martyrs from the Past and Present

In *God's Generals: The Martyrs,* I would like to shed some light on our Christian history, sometimes long-forgotten. Whenever possible, I have quoted directly from the original text of the martyrs' experiences—their words are more powerful than anything I could have written. There is no way I could ever cover even one percent of all of the faithful Christian martyrs' lives. Sharing a few of their stories is my attempt to honor them all. (At times, I have related some of the graphic details of their deaths so we can understand how much they sacrificed for Christ.) I am certain that the Father knows the name of every single martyred man, woman, and child, and that He has blessed them with their ultimate reward—eternal honor in heaven.

Today's martyrs and the millions who have gone before them echo the apostle Paul's cry: "*I have been crucified with Christ; it is no longer I who live, but Christ lives in me; and the life which I now live in the flesh I live by faith in the Son of God, who loved me and gave Himself for me*" (Galatians 2:20).

PERSECUTED CHRISTIANS ON THE WORLD STAGE

1

PERSECUTED CHRISTIANS ON THE WORLD STAGE

(AD 2000–today)

Orange jumpsuits on a sandy beach, twenty-one dark-haired men kneeling, heads bowed, black clad militants standing above them, swords in hand, the blue Mediterranean Sea roiling in the background.

This infamous image was emblazoned on hearts and minds worldwide as people watched the news flash across their screens. Minutes later, these nameless captives were simultaneously beheaded and the gruesome act was videotaped and broadcast across the earth. This is the face of Christian martyrdom in the twenty-first century...and it has gained the world stage.

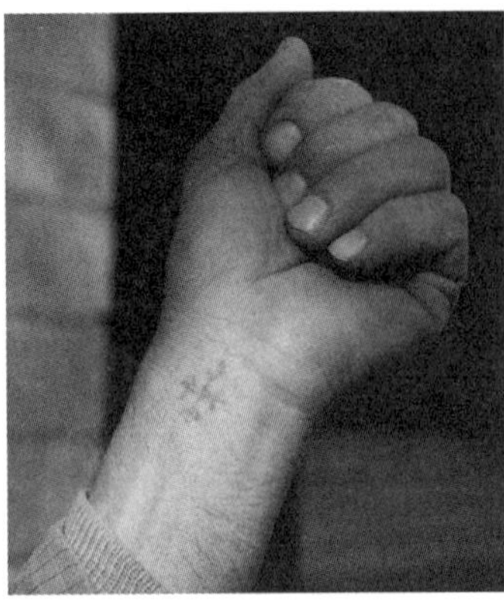

A Coptic Christian in Egypt shows the cross tattoo on his wrist.
Joel Carillet\Thinkstock

On January 3, 2015 at 2:30 a.m. in the city of Sirte, Libya, masked gunmen raced from house to house beating viciously on front doors before rushing in. They pulled frightened men from their beds, grabbed their arms, and searched for the traditional tattoos that marked them as Coptic Christians—Christians from the Egyptian Orthodox Church. Fourteen men were pulled from their homes, taken to an undisclosed location in Libya, and imprisoned along with seven other Christian hostages who had been kidnapped a week earlier.[1]

On February 15, 2015, after five weeks of imprisonment, the twenty-one were beheaded for their faith on a beach near Sirte.

Christians Targeted

The Coptic Christians kidnapped in Sirte had been working there for months on end, sending their incomes home to feed extended families. In the rural areas of Egypt, the economy is poor and work is hard to find, so scores of Egyptian husbands and fathers leave their impoverished towns to work in the more prosperous, oil-based economy of Libya.

These twenty-one workers were not singled out for being Egyptians in Libya's hostile countryside, however. They were targeted by radical Islamists for being followers of Jesus Christ.

1. Sophia Jones, "ISIS Boasted Of These Christians' Deaths. Here Are The Lives They Lived," *The World Post*, February 18, 2015, updated March 3, 2016, http://www.huffingtonpost.com/2015/02/18/isis-christians-killed-_n_6703278.html.

The caption on the video labels the captives as "the people of the cross, the followers of the hostile Egyptian Church." Egypt has been the home of a Christian minority since the days of the early apostles. St. Mark, who wrote the Gospel of Mark, likely brought Christianity to Egypt in the first century, during the reign of Nero. The Coptic Church traces its roots all the way back to Mark! Coptic Christians, who make up 15 percent of Egypt's population of 80 million, have survived Roman persecution, Turkish conquerors, and modern Arabian conflicts, but now they face a new enemy—the rise of Islamic terrorism.

Islamic terrorists often appear indiscriminate in their violence, killing anybody and everybody in their path: in 2014, journalist James Foley was similarly beheaded, soon followed by fellow reporter Steven Sotloff. Most recently we have the horrific killing of innocent families celebrating on Bastille Day in Nice, France, by an Islamic radical driving a semi-truck. I would never claim that the death of Christians should be condemned more than the other cruel murders that the jihadists commit.

However, it is vital that we understand that Islamic militants *do* have a reason behind their terrorism. The militants are committed to the deaths of all followers of Jesus Christ—as well as anybody of Jewish faith or descent, or any belief that has a root in Christianity. True believers, however, will never die in vain.

And *that* is precisely what makes what happened on that beach on February 15, 2015, so vitally important.

Their Families Mourn

As the facts unraveled in the week after the release of the gruesome video, the Egyptian government identified twenty of the men as Egyptian citizens and Christians, thirteen from the small farming village of Al-Our, Egypt, one hundred and fifty miles west of Cairo. The tight-knit village was filled with loud weeping and grief the week the video surfaced, over the husbands, brothers, nephews, and friends who were killed.

Hani Abdel Messihah, thirty-two years old, was a husband and father who loved his four children more than anything and had traveled to Libya to provide for them. His wife, Magda, described him as a gentle man full of laughter who loved God and took great care of his family. "There was a prayer in anything [Hani] said," Magda explained of her devout husband.[2]

A Coptic monk holds up the Coptic cross.
Mark Fischer\Flikr

Yousef Shoukry, twenty-four years old, was, according to his brother, a quiet young man who simply wanted to find a job and start a family. He had hoped that Libya could provide him with the finances he needed to launch his life. When his mother begged him not to go, Yousef answered with the courage of his faith, "I have one God; He's the same here and there." Although it was difficult, Yousef's brother forced himself to watch the video of Yousef's execution. "I saw that he had strength in his last moments," his brother said quietly.[3] Like the others, Yousef did not cry or scream as he approached death, but only murmured, "O Lord Jesus."

Maged Suleiman Shahata, forty-five years old, was born into poverty and couldn't find a way out for himself, his wife, and their three children, all living together in one room. Maged traveled to Libya, determined to make the money to give his family a future. It wasn't long before he had earned enough to help his oldest daughter attend college. Maged's brother mourned his death but said he wasn't consumed with hatred for the executioners. He acknowledged that the men were now

2. Ibid.
3. Ibid.

safe where no danger could reach them. "'We are proud that they went to the Father in the sky,' he said with a warm smile."[4]

In honor, here are the names of the other seventeen identified Coptic Christians: Towadros Yousef , Milad Makeen Zaky, Abanub Ayad Atiya, Kirollos Shokry Fawzy (Kirollos Bashree Fawzy), Bishoy Astafanus Kamel, Malak Ibrahim Sinweet, Girgis Milad Sinweet, Mina Fayez Aziz, Samuel Alham Wilson, Samuel Astafanus Kamel, Ezat Bishri Naseef, Loqa Nagaty Anees, Munir Gaber Adly, Esam Badir Samir, Malak Farag Abram, Sameh Salah (Sameh Salah Farug), and Girgis Sameer Maglee.

"Their God Is My God!"

You'll notice that so far, I have only listed twenty names. Although twenty of the martyrs were identified as Christians by their families, friends, and churches, number twenty-one was not.

Who, then, was the twenty-first martyr?

His name was Matthew Ayairga; he was from Chad, and, like the others, he had come to Sirte to find much-needed work. Unlike the others, however, Ayairga was not a Christian when he was first captured. No one knows why the ISIS militants kidnapped him with the rest. But as Ayairga spent five weeks with the Coptic Christians in prison, his heart was eternally changed.

On the video, an ISIS militant asks Ayairga, "Do you reject Christ?" His resolute response was, "their God is my God."[5]

Egyptian Christians believe that Ayairga would have had a much better chance at life had he embraced Islam, or at least denied that he was a Christian. But instead, he boldly proclaimed a faith in the God of his companions.

---

4. Ibid.

5. "What made a non believer Chadian citizen die for Christ," Bombay Orthodox Diocese, February 22, 2015, http://bombayorthodoxdiocese.org/what-made-a-non-believer-chadian-citizen-die-for-christ-along-with-his-20-coptic-christian-friends/.

This is what makes the martyrdom of these twenty-one Christians both so terrible and so important: it is a picture, gruesome and in-our-faces, that forces of evil are doing all they can to darken the world with violence and to specifically target followers of the cross. *Yet,* it is also a powerful confirmation that they are no match for the witness of Christ through the death of His followers.

The Growth of the Church

Memorial to the 21 martyrs at a church in Jerusalem.
Chetanya Robinson\Flikr

Ayairga's confession was not the only positive report after the ISIS brutality.

"In the month and a half while the people were kidnapped, the whole congregation was coming to the church to pray for their return, but in their prayers later on, they asked that if they died, they die for their faith, and that's what happened. The congregation is actually growing, psychologically and spiritually," one of Al-Our's pastors, Father Makar Issa, explained soon after the men had been slain.[6]

6. Jared Malsin, "Christians Mourn Their Relatives Beheaded by ISIS," *TIME Magazine*, February 23, 2015, http://time.com/3718470/isis-copts-egypt/.

Also, one week after the video was released, 1.65 million tracts entitled *Two Rows by the Sea*, with a photo of the Islamic militants marching the orange-clad Christians down the beach, were published by the Bible Society of Egypt. "We must have a Scripture tract ready to distribute to the grieving nation as soon as possible," the head of the Society, Ramallah Atallah, told his staff.[7] Christ's message was circulated throughout the nation of Egypt, reaching the hurting and lost once again with the message of salvation.

Two Rows by the Sea tract.

As we remember these believers martyred for their faith, Jesus' words from the Sermon on the Mount are a clear reminder of God's eternal promise:

> *Blessed are those who are persecuted for righteousness' sake,* ***for theirs is the kingdom of heaven****. Blessed are you when they revile and persecute you, and say all kinds of evil against you falsely for My sake. Rejoice and be exceedingly glad,* ***for great is your reward in heaven****, for so they persecuted the prophets who were before you.*
>
> (Matthew 5:10–12)

Profound Unrest in Syria

Syria was once the birthplace of many flourishing Christian communities. Since the civil war that has been raging since 2011, however, the country has been ripped apart and nearly destroyed by the fighting—in

7. Jayson Casper, "How Libya's Martyrs are Witnessing to Egypt," *Christianity Today*, February 23, 2015, http://www.christianitytoday.com/ct/2015/february-web-only/how-libyas-martyrs-are-evangelizing-egypt.html.

both the natural and spiritual worlds. Human forces are fighting for and against the Syrian government on the physical battlefield while the spiritual forces of God's kingdom and Satan's fight on the supernatural fields. Here is a heartbreaking report from a country that is experiencing thousands of these stories monthly.

Twelve-Year-Old Syrian Boy Crucified for His Faith

Man carries the body of a child in war-torn Aleppo, Syria.
Freedom House\Flikr

In early August 2015, twelve Christians near the city of Aleppo, Syria, were captured by ISIS militant forces. Their leader was a pastor and missionary who, along with his twelve-year-old son, had planted nine churches in the countryside surrounding Aleppo. Taken to an unnamed village, the pastor and son, along with two other Christian workers, were paraded before a crowd. Pushing the father to the forefront, the Islamic militants demanded that he renounce his faith in Jesus Christ and return to Islam, or die. When he refused, they dragged his son before the horrified crowd of relatives and neighbors and, as his father watched, they began to slice the ends of the boy's fingers off.

Still strong in their faith in the Savior who had hung on the cross for their salvation, the father and son refused to renounce Jesus. Both, along with the two other Christian captives, insisted that nothing could separate them from the love of God through His Son, Jesus Christ. They would not renounce their faith.

Losing all patience, the murderers brutally beat the four Christians before crucifying them in the middle of the village. According to a Christian Aid worker, "They were left on the crosses for two days; no one was allowed to remove them."[8] The four were crucified beside signs that proclaimed them *infidels*.

Eight More Die for Christ

That same day, the eight remaining Christian captives were taken to another site in the same village and commanded to renounce Christ and His church or die. Courageously, the eight Christians stood on their faith in Jesus Christ as Lord and refused. The two female captives, aged twenty-nine and thirty-three, were publicly raped while the crowd was forced to watch. Then, as the captives faced death, their grieving relatives reported, "Some were praying in the name of Jesus, others were praying the Lord's Prayer, some just lifted their heads and commended their spirits to Jesus. One of the women looked up and seemed to be almost smiling as she said, 'Jesus.'"[9] All eight were then beheaded and their bodies hung on crosses as a menacing threat to the Syrians of Aleppo.

"We're Ready to Stay"

What was the response of the Syrian church? Tom Doyle, Middle East director for a global ministry and author of the book *Killing Christians*, shared that in Syria today there is a team of church planters that has decided to risk everything to stay rather than deserting the suffering Christians who can't escape. They have recently recruited fifteen more Christian disciples to join them. "We're ready to stay, we're ready to suffer, we're ready to die here in Syria for Jesus."[10]

There are Christian pastors resolutely remaining in Syria in spite of the turmoil, the threats, the bombings, the destruction, and death.

---

8. Brooke Singman, "Boy 12 Among Dozen Tortured and Crucified," FOX News, October 7, 2015, http://www.foxnews.com/world/2015/10/07/boy-12-among-dozen-tortured-and-crucified-by-isis-in-latest-atrocity-says-aid.html.

9. Ibid.

10. Monica Cantilero, "Syria Church Growing," *Christianity Today*, August 12, 2015, http://www.christiantoday.com/article/syria.church.growing.as.christian.leaders.risk.lives.amid.isis.persecution.pastor/61695.html.

They told Open Door ministries, "We're in a big harvest. God is waking up a sleeping church.... The Muslims coming to faith are ready to die for their new beliefs; that is a different kind of Christianity." Thousands have lost their lives in the civil war and tens of thousands have fled the country. But still people are receiving the salvation message of the Messiah in Syria today.

God is waking up a sleeping church.... The Muslims coming to faith are ready to die for their new beliefs.

"What attracted me is the loving environment of the church," said one Syrian believer from a Muslim background. They are grateful that so many leaders are staying to take care of the Christians that remain. "We, under the Lord's grace and through His strength, have decided to stay and carry on."[11]

Two thousand years ago, the apostle Paul and the Christians who served God beside him knew exactly what this kind of persecution meant. They witnessed it and experienced it firsthand. Paul spoke strong words of encouragement to his fellow believers to stand with bravery no matter what the future held.

> *I eagerly expect and hope that I will in no way be ashamed, but will have sufficient courage so that now as always Christ will be exalted in my body, whether by life or by death.* ***For to me, to live is Christ and to die is gain.*** (Philippians 1:20–21 NIV)

From South Korea to Iraq

In the spring of 2004, waving good-bye to his extended family, Kim Sun-il boarded an airplane in Seoul, South Korea, bound for the

11. Florence Taylor, "God is Waking Up a Sleeping Church," *Christianity Today*, March 11, 2016, http://www.christiantoday.com/article/syrian.pastor.god.is.waking.up.a.sleeping.church.more.people.becoming.christians.than.ever.before/81695.html.

war-torn lands of Iraq. He was joining the Gana Trading Company, a South Korean business in Fallujah, Iraq, as an Arabic interpreter.

The devout Christian man had an additional purpose, however. A few years earlier, Sun-il had received his undergraduate degrees in both English and Christian theology, and continued on to graduate school to study Arabic in the hopes of becoming a Christian missionary. Now, just four months after graduating, the thirty-three-year-old Sun-il was intending to use every opportunity to establish relationships with the Iraqi people. He arrived on June 15, 2003, in the midst of the US invasion and war with Iraq.

US Navy patrols the streets of Fallujah.
This picture was taken a few months after Kim Sun-Il was killed.
U.S. Navy Seabee Museum\Flikr

Eleven months later, Kim Sun-il was kidnapped in Fallujah by an Islamic terrorist group. They cited his Christian beliefs as the reason for choosing him as their captive. He was held as ransom, not for money, but for political pressure. His captors demanded that South Korea reverse their commitment to send 3,000 troops to the Iraqi battlefield. The government in Seoul would not agree to the terms. On May 30, 2004, after three weeks in captivity, Kim Sun-il was videoed bowing before his captors in an orange jumpsuit. He was beheaded by the Islamic terrorists as an act of vengeance, and the video was sent to network broadcasters as proof of the execution.

US soldiers recovered Sun-il's body on a road leading to Baghdad, and it was flown back to South Korea for burial. As mourners flocked to the funeral in his hometown of Pusan, they praised God for the steadfastness of the young man who believed his faith in Christ could make a difference in the world. Sun-il's brother, Jin Kook, told the congregation that his family had forgiveness in their hearts for the Iraqi people just like Sun-il would have wanted. Young missionaries in South Korea, instead of being intimidated by the execution, have continued to reach out to the unsaved nations around them with the eternal gospel of Jesus Christ.[12]

> *I consider that our present sufferings are not worth comparing with the glory that will be revealed in us.* (Romans 8:18 NIV)

British Aid Worker Killed in Afghanistan

In most Middle Eastern cultures, women from Western nations are frowned upon or considered immoral. Yet, many Christian women serve in those same nations unselfishly to help their suffering people. Some have lost their lives.

On October 20, 2008, Gayle Williams walked briskly down the busy cobbled street in Kabul, Afghanistan. It was nearly 8:00 a.m. and she had a full day of work ahead of her. She thought fondly of the children she would see throughout the morning hours, young innocent victims of the Afghan Wars, disabled but still full of the energy and joy of childhood. Working as an occupational therapist, her job was to encourage and train each of her young patients as they worked their way to recovery.

12. Associated Press, "South Korean Beheaded in Iraq is Buried," *Los Angeles Times*, July 1, 2004, http://articles.latimes.com/2004/jul/01/world/fg-funeral1.

As Gayle stepped from the curb and walked toward her home office, she was faintly aware of a motorcycle engine growing louder as it approached the street corner. Suddenly, without warning, the motorcycle made an abrupt stop beside her. Two men jumped off and began firing at the unsuspecting woman. Within moments they sped away, leaving Gayle Williams lying on the sidewalk in a pool of blood.[13] The thirty-four-year-old Christian aid worker died immediately from her gunshot wounds...but she was alive in Christ forever.

Suddenly, without warning, the motorcycle made an abrupt stop beside her. Two men jumped off and began firing at the unsuspecting woman.

Serving Children

Gayle Williams was an adventurous British woman whom people referred to as full of life and laughter. She was born and raised in Zimbabwe, but moved to London with her British mother as a young teenager. She held citizenship in both countries. Growing up, Williams always knew that her life should count for something. She attended school to become an occupational therapist and then decided that her talents and her heart should be used helping those in the greatest need.

In 2005, Gayle joined a non-governmental organization that provided aid to the Afghan people. Working in the politically torn country, she treated the children with compassion and a cheery smile for two and a half years until she was gunned down by Taliban militants. A Taliban spokesman said she was targeted "because she was working for an organization which was preaching Christianity in Afghanistan." He

13. Jenny Percival, "British aid worker shot dead in Afghanistan," *The Guardian*, October 20, 2008, https://www.theguardian.com/world/2008/oct/20/afghanistan-internationalaid-anddevelopment.

added, "Our [leaders] issued a decree to kill this woman. This morning our people killed her in Kabul."[14]

The president of the organization denied that Williams' primary mission was to convert Muslims to Christianity: "They [the Taliban] will make any excuse. They probably saw there was a Christian organization operating in Kabul and thought, 'This is how we can kill it.' *We are Christians*. That is what gives us the motivation to go into a dangerous and difficult country to try to help. But she was not involved in proselytization."[15]

"She Is Definitely with Him"

When Gayle's mother was contacted in London and told of her daughter's death, she grieved and yet she knew the passion of her daughter's life—what she had lived and died for. "Gayle was serving a people that she loved, and felt God called her to be there for such a time as this. We know her life was blessed and she was a blessing to all those around her. No one could have asked for a more humble daughter with a more loving heart. She died doing what she felt the Lord had called her to do and now she is definitely with Him."[16]

Gayle's mother and sister, Karen, attended the funeral in Afghanistan and then held a memorial service for her back in London. A prayer walk for the Williams family and colleagues was arranged for November 8, 2008, in London in Gayle's honor, and the prayer team stopped to pray in front of the embassy of each country where Christian believers still face persecution. They recognized the truth that prayer is the primary weapon against the attack on Christians throughout the world today.

---

14. "UK charity worker killed in Kabul," BBC News, October 20, 2008, http://news.bbc.co.uk/2/hi/south_asia/7679212.stm.
15. Percival, "British aid worker shot dead."
16. Caroline Gammell, "British aid worker: Gayle Williams' mother pays tribute," *The Telegraph*, October 21, 2008, http://www.telegraph.co.uk/news/worldnews/asia/afghanistan/3233628/British-aid-worker-Gayle-Williams-mother-pays-tribute-to-daughter-shot-in-Afghanistan.html.

And pray in the Spirit on all occasions with all kinds of prayers and requests. With this in mind, be alert and always keep on praying for all the Lord's people. (Ephesians 6:18 NIV)

"Six Americans Slain on Medical Mission"

Walking briskly through the forest high in the Hindu Kush mountains of Afghanistan, the Christian medical team was returning to their headquarters in Kabul. It had been a successful three week mission providing much-needed eye care to isolated Afghan villagers. The ten member team, six Americans, one Briton, one German, and two Afghans, worked with the International Assistance Mission (IAM) a non-profit Christian aid organization serving in Afghanistan since 1966. Tom Little, the team leader, was an American ophthalmologist who had been working in Afghanistan for over thirty years. His service in the war-torn Asian country had survived both the Soviet invasion and the bloody civil war of the 1990s.

The beauiful Hindu Kush mountains,
where the medical missions team was working.
Afghanistian Matters\Flikr

The team stepped out of the woods and into a clearing where their vehicles had been parked for weeks while they hiked into the isolated villages. Famished from the walk, they settled into a grassy field to eat their lunch. Suddenly, several gunmen with long red-dyed beards burst into the clearing, shouting orders in Pashto for them to stand and put their hands in the air. Pushing the unarmed team members away from their vehicles with the butt of their rifles, they marched the seven men and three women into the forest, lined them up execution style, and shot them one by one. The only survivor was a Muslim Afghan driver who pleaded for his life by reciting verses of the Qur'an.[17]

"She Fell in Love with the Afghan People"

The Taliban accepted full responsibility for the executions, insisting that the group had been "spying for the Americans" and "converting Muslims to Christianity." Among the dead was 32-year-old Cheryl Beckett from Knoxville, Tennessee, who had been working in Kabul for five years to better the lives of young mothers and their children. She was invited on the eye care mission trip to serve as an interpreter to the impoverished women in the mountain villages. Her father praised Cheryl as a strong Christian woman "who had a heart of compassion to meet the needs of those around her" and "who fell in love with the Afghan people."[18]

We know that Cheryl and her fellow Christian workers lives were not sacrificed in vain. The Word of God reassures us, *"Therefore, my dear brothers and sisters, stand firm. Let nothing move you. Always give yourselves fully to the work of the Lord, because you know that your labor in the Lord is not in vain"* (1 Corinthians 15:58 NIV).

---

17. Associated Press, "Afghan medical mission ends in death for 6 Americans," NBC News, August 7, 2010, http://www.nbcnews.com/id/38604010/ns/world_news-south_and_central_asia/t/afghan-medical-mission-ends-death-americans/#.V4fujmlTFgU, accessed July 25, 2016.
18. Lydia X. McCoy, "Slain aid worker Cheryl Beckett remembered," *Knoxville News Sentinel*, August 22, 2010, http://www.knoxnews.com/news/local/slain-aid-worker-cheryl-beckett-remembered-ep-407842771-358566481.html.

Christians Attacked on Easter Sunday

Children's voices squealed in delight as they ran around the grassy knolls of the community park and took turns riding on the playground swings. Peals of laughter rose from small groups of chattering mothers, dressed in saris the colors of the rainbow. In the crisp evening in Lahore, Pakistan, on March 27, 2016, over one hundred families celebrated Easter—Resurrection Sunday—with a play time in the park.

Without warning, the laughter turned into screams of agony and fear as a bomb suddenly exploded in the middle of the park. Mothers and fathers ran frantically, calling out the names of missing children. In the chaos, the wounded and dying cried for help as they lay in pools of their own blood. When the carnage was over, sixty-nine Pakistanis lay dead on the ground, victims of a jihadist attack on Easter, the Christians' holiest Sunday of the year. Although some Muslims lost their lives in the explosion, the Pakistani Taliban admitted to targeting Christians celebrating their holy day.[19] The global war against Christianity is intense. It is time for the entire Christian church to stand up and take notice!

1500 Years of Middle Eastern Conflict

We can see from these stories that the Middle East in the twenty-first century is an epicenter of violence. Jay Sekulow, President of the American Center for Law and Justice, put it this way: "The brutality is unspeakable, with nearly one million Christians slaughtered or displaced in the last few years in the Middle East."[20]

The events in the Middle East today are not happening in a vacuum. There has been 1500 years of conflict between Islam and Christianity. In the seventh through ninth centuries, following Mohammed's death

19. Sophia Saifi, "Deadly Blast Kills Christians on Easter Sunday," CNN, March 28, 2016, http://www.cnn.com/2016/03/27/asia/pakistan-lahore-deadly-blast.
20. Peter Chiaramonte, "Beheadings, imprisonment made 2015 worst year for Christian persecution," FOX News, March 8, 2016, http://www.foxnews.com/world/2016/03/08/beheadings-imprisonment-made-2015-worst-year-for-christian-persecution-report-finds.html.

(AD 632), Muslim armies invaded the Middle Eastern cities with large Christian populations—Damascus, Antioch, Jerusalem—killing tens of thousands of Christians and taking as many captive as slaves. The Islamic armies continued moving west, overrunning Italy and Spain, killing or oppressing Christians who refused to embrace Islam.

In the tenth through twelfth centuries, Christian armies retaliated, routing Jerusalem and later Constantinople during the Crusades, killing tens of thousands of citizens, including Muslims, on sight. (Of course we question how much of that killing was done by those who really understood Christ's plan of salvation and forgiveness.)

In the later Middle Ages, the armies of Islam retaliated once again, retaking lands captured by the Crusading armies, and killing tens of thousands of Christians who opposed them in cities like Aleppo, Antioch, and Constantinople. Centuries of bloodshed filled the Middle Eastern lands, and while Western cultures may have a short memory, Middle-Eastern cultures do not forget previous generations. They have a long memory that easily reaches back to the brutality at the time of the Crusades.[21]

Now, we have arrived at the twenty-first century. Christians are eager to point out that, at its very foundation, Christianity is a gospel of peace and salvation, and that many of the Crusades weren't in line with Jesus' commands of love and forbearance. Unfortunately, that gospel of peace is not accepted, particularly by Islamic jihadists today.

Radical Hindus and the Orissa Massacre

Even though jihadists permeate the news, Islamic radicals are not the only people in the world that persecute and execute Christians. Satan has used many different people groups to persecute Christians in the past, and he does the same today.

21. See James Pinkerton, "The Ancient War Between the Judeo-Christian West and Islam," *Breitbart,* September 21, 2014, http://www.breitbart.com/national-security/2014/09/21/the-ancient-war-between-the-judeo-christian-west-and-islam/.

On August 25, 2008, Hindu mobs, incited by the death of a radical nationalist leader, descended upon the towns in Orissa province in eastern India with a vengeance. Hundreds of radical Hindus attacked Christian villages without mercy for weeks on end. As the violence escalated, it spread to more than six hundred villages; some sources estimate that five hundred Christians were murdered, many hacked to death by their machete-wielding countrymen. Thousands more were injured as they attempted to flee.

As frenzied mobs ran through the villages brandishing torches, five thousand Christian homes were destroyed and three hundred churches lay in ruins.

As frenzied mobs ran through the villages brandishing torches, five thousand Christian homes were destroyed and three hundred churches lay in ruins, burned to the ground. Fifty thousand displaced Christians were forced to flee to refugee camps where there was little food or shelter. One tragic story was of the gang rape of a Catholic nun, Sr. Meena Barwa, who was then marched naked through her village to be mocked and ridiculed.[22]

In India, where Christian missionaries have been accepted for two hundred years, many moderate Hindus and Western foreigners were shocked by the level of violence. *The Times* of London called the Orissa massacre "the worst anti-Christian violence in India since independence [in 1947]."

The Christian Church Is Growing Rapidly in India

How has this increased persecution affected the Christian church in India?

The Mission Society, a ministry that supports Christian missionary work around the world, reported that there is significant growth in the Christian church in India today, especially among middle- and

22. John L. Allen, Jr., *The Global War on Christians* (New York: Image Publishers, 2016), 5.

upper-caste Indians and the younger generation. "With more than 71 million claiming Christianity, India is now the eighth largest Christian nation in the world," Dick McClain, president and CEO of The Mission Society, explained. Despite the persecution in specific regions of the country, thousands of Indians are still coming to Christ.

"The Spirit of God is blowing across the land in fresh ways as many 'Christward movements' are occurring," *Christian News* reports. "In these movements, people may not be moving toward the 'Church' or 'Christianity' as we know it, but they're moving towards Christ." The article concludes, "The need of the hour is to 'understand the times' (1 Chronicles 12:32), 'interpret the times' (Luke 12:56), and serve appropriately in 'such a time as this' (Esther 4:14)."[23]

How Long, Lord?

Unfortunately, we know that this chapter on Christian martyrdom in the twenty-first century does not end here. Flip to chapter twelve for a snapshot of all regions of the world today and their persecution of Christians. We could probably add a new story to the book every day and not be finished. Even as I write these words, another news story comes across the headlines: Jacques Hamel, an eighty-five-year-old priest in northern France, had his throat slit—on the altar!—by two men who were ISIS militants. A witness shared the priest's last words before he was murdered. Twice he declared, "Get away, Satan! Get away, Satan!"[24] Jacques Hamel understood that his battle was not just against terrorists but with the enemy of the cross—Satan.

The increase in stories of martyrdom that comes across our radar regularly forces two questions to rise in our minds: how long has this been going on? And how long will it last?

23. Garrett Haley, "Report: Christian Church Growing at a Rapid Rate in India," *Christian News*, December 2, 2013, http://christiannews.net/2013/12/02/report-christian-church-growing-at-a-rapid-rate-in-india/.
24. Associated Press, "Funeral Mass for Murdered French Priest: Attackers Were 'Satan,'" FOX News, August 2, 2016, http://www.foxnews.com/world/2016/08/02/funeral-today-for-french-priest-killed-in-normandy-church.html.

First, we know that martyrdom for the gospel of Jesus Christ began on the cross when Jesus sacrificed His own life *"that whoever believes in Him should not perish but have everlasting life"* (John 3:16). Jesus told us that a servant is not greater than his master. And that there would be those who would suffer for His name's sake.

So how long will it last? In the book of Revelation, John wrote of the martyrs who asked the Lord the same thing, "How long, O Lord?" The Lord's answer was clear: There will be Christians in this world who will be called to sacrifice their lives as witnesses for Christ until the Lord Jesus Christ returns in His glory. (See Revelation 6:9–11.)

Mocking God's People

We know that today—throughout the world—Satan has once again launched an all-out attack—a global war—on God's people; he has many weapons in his arsenal and we need to be aware of them all.

Mockery and ridicule are two of Satan's fiery arrows heading straight for the heart of the persecuted Christian. Look at the amount of derision that Christians face in the world today. We need to remember that mockery and ridicule have always been strong weapons in Satan's arsenal of flaming arrows set to destroy our faith. This is especially true in an age where we are so secure in our own abilities. We must all remember that Christ Himself was scorned on our behalf. He was mocked by lowly soldiers as the "king of the Jews;" He was crowned with a false crown of thorns and spit upon by men who were unbathed, unlearned, and unholy. Yet He was the very Son of God.

Christian, depend upon it; you will be ridiculed in this world by the enemy of your soul. God has intentionally chosen the foolish things of this world to confound the wise. Humiliation, mockery, torture, death—these are four primary weapons that Satan uses to persecute God's saints. Even if he can't get to you with torture and death, Satan will use humiliation and scorn to tempt you to deny Christ or to hide Him in the public areas of your life. Where you go, what you watch, who you spend time with, what you wear, what you drink. Satan attempts to whittle away at our testimony for Jesus pressing us to avoid the jeers of the world that we are different, set apart, strange.

We must never forget—we have been *chosen* to be different: "*You are a chosen generation, a royal priesthood, a holy nation, His own special people, that you may proclaim the praises of Him who called you out of darkness into His marvelous light*" (1 Peter 2:9). We are set apart to bring glory and honor to Jesus, our Lord and King. May we never forget it! As we look back through the centuries in the chapters of this book, we will see that the heroes faced the mockery of the world and paid the ultimate sacrifice of their lives...but they counted it all loss for the gain they found in Jesus Christ.

> *But whatever gain I had, I counted as loss for the sake of Christ. Indeed, I count everything as loss because of the surpassing worth of knowing Christ Jesus my Lord. For his sake I have suffered the loss of all things and count them as rubbish, in order that I may gain Christ and be found in him, not having a righteousness of my own that comes from the law, but that which comes through faith in Christ, the righteousness from God that depends on faith—that I may know him and the power of his resurrection, and may share his sufferings, becoming like him in his death.*
>
> (Philippians 3:7–10 ESV)

TURNING THE WORLD UPSIDE DOWN

2

TURNING THE WORLD UPSIDE DOWN

(AD 1–100)

"Look! I see the heavens opened and the Son of Man standing at the right hand of God!"... And they stoned Stephen as he was calling on God and saying, "Lord Jesus, receive my spirit." (Acts 7:56, 59)

Stephen the Faithful

There he is, the blasphemer! We have heard him speak blasphemous words against Moses and against God!" A throng of Jewish men and women, enraged by the shouts of the accusers, raced down the cobblestone street and viciously grabbed at Stephen's outer cloak. "Here he is! Let's take him to the council to be judged!" (See Acts 6–7.)

Dragging Stephen through the streets of Jerusalem, the revilers stumbled up the steps of the outer courts of the temple. Men and women, caught in the mindless heat of hatred, moved as a human wave toward the council's meeting place, the Hall of Hewn Stones, built into the north wall of the Temple Mount. They shouted feverishly for the leaders to open the doors.

The council, or Great Sanhedrin, met daily in the Hall to settle the spiritual and civil disputes of the Jews. Centuries after Moses' seventy handpicked elders administered the laws of the Jewish people, these seventy Pharisees and Sadducees would judge the life of young Stephen. The high priest ruled the council and was referred to as *nasi*, or "prince." Along with the other seventy elders, they held the highest religious authority in Jerusalem, just as in the time of Moses. The Sanhedrin had the power to impose the death sentence with no higher court of appeal.[25]

Marching Stephen across the cold stone floor, the angry mob thrust him in front of the council

Marching Stephen across the cold stone floor, the angry mob thrust him in front of the council, where false witnesses heatedly stepped forward and testified, "*This man incessantly speaks against this holy place and against the Law; for we have heard him say that this Nazarene, Jesus, will destroy this place and alter the customs which Moses handed down to us.*" (Acts 6:13–14 NASB).

As one body, the council members turned to face the young man, the power they held over him reflected in their glares. They were already well-acquainted with Stephen by his reputation—he was an ardent follower of Jesus of Nazareth and was stirring up the Jews by doing

25. Shira Shoenber, *Ancient Jewish History: The Sanhedrin*, Jewish Virtual Library, www.jewishvirtuallibrary.org/jsource/Judaism/Sanhedrin.html.

"great wonders and signs among the people" in Jesus' name (Acts 6:8 NASB). The multitudes recognized Stephen as a disciple *"full of faith and the Holy Spirit's power"* (6:8 TLB). He laid hands on the sick and they were healed; he prayed for the people's needs and they were answered; he had led many Jews to Jesus their Messiah. The council was determined—he had to be stopped.

The Stoning of Stephen.
Photos.com\Thinkstock

Expecting fear and trembling from Stephen, the leaders were astonished to see the young disciple gazing at them as though enveloped in a cloud of peace, his face *"like the face of an angel"* (v. 15 NASB). The high priest stood abruptly in anger. With his blue and purple ephod hanging stiffly at his side, he shouted at Stephen, "Are these accusations so?"

He and the council were greeted with Stephen's Spirit-inspired opening, *"Hear me, brethren and fathers,"* (7:2 NASB) followed by a full witness to the good news of Jesus Christ. With Jesus as his only Advocate, Stephen preached an anointed sermon relating God's history with His chosen people, culminating with their stiff-necked rejection of the true Messiah of Israel. *"You men who are stiff-necked and uncircumcised in heart and ears are always resisting the Holy Spirit; you are doing just as your fathers did"* (7:51 NASB).

The spiritual leaders stood in fury, the crowd gnashed their teeth in anger at the young disciple, but Stephen kept his eyes of faith focused on Christ: *"Being full of the Holy Spirit, he gazed intently into heaven and saw the glory of God, and Jesus standing at the right hand of God, and he said, 'Behold, I see the heavens opened up and the Son of Man standing at the right hand of God'"* (v. 55 NASB). His accusers were *"cut to the quick,"* by Stephen's passionate words, but instead of falling to their knees in repentance, they responded with cruel vengeance. *"They cried out with a loud voice, and covered their ears and rushed at him with one impulse. When they had driven him out of the city, they began stoning him"* (v. 57 NASB).

With murder in their hearts, his accusers cast off their outer cloaks at the feet of a young Pharisee named Saul and laid hands on the sharpest stones on the roadway. Blood coursed down Stephen's cheek and arms and pooled on the ground where he stood, but they *"went on stoning Stephen as he called upon the Lord and said, 'Lord Jesus, receive my spirit!' Then falling on his knees he cried out with a loud voice, 'Lord, do not hold this sin against them!' And having said this, he fell asleep"* (vs. 59–60 NASB).

A Powerful Model

The day Stephen died, the martyrdom of Christians began in earnest, and, according to the apostle John's Revelation, it will continue until the moment the number of martyrs is completed.

> *When He opened the fifth seal, I saw under the altar the souls of those who had been slain for the word of God and for the testimony which they held. And they cried with a loud voice, saying, "How long, O Lord, holy and true, until You judge and avenge our blood on those who dwell on the earth?" Then a white robe was given to each of them; and it was said to them that they should rest a little while longer,* ***until both the number of their fellow servants and their brethren, who would be killed as they were, was completed.***
>
> (Revelation 6:9–11)

The details of Stephen's martyrdom became a model of courage and faith for the persecuted Christians in the early centuries. The Acts of the Apostles, written by Luke, was read by first, second, and third century converts as they faced Jewish and Roman persecution. Stephen's strong witness to his faith and the overwhelming presence of the Holy Spirit during his martyrdom emboldened the early Christians to stand faithfully for Christ. They held a conviction that they could be overcomers in the name of Jesus Christ, and that the Lord Himself would anoint them with the Holy Spirit's power to endure horrific torture and death at the hands of those determined to wipe Christians from the face of the earth.

God Won't Waste a Drop of Blood!

Stephen's martyrdom also launched a new era of growth to this early faith not yet called Christianity. Believers in Jesus fled Jerusalem in fear of retaliation from the Jewish authorities. As they scattered throughout the Middle East, the gospel spread across the Adriatic Sea to Antioch, Syria.

> *Therefore, those who were scattered went everywhere preaching the word.... Now those who were scattered after the persecution that arose over Stephen traveled as far as Phoenicia, Cyprus and Antioch preaching the word to no one but the Jews only. But some of the men from Cyprus and Cyrene, who, when they had come to Antioch, spoke to the Hellenists* [Jews who lived as Greeks], *preaching the Lord Jesus. And the hand of the Lord was with them and a great number believed and turned to the Lord.* (Acts 8:4; 11:19–21)

And the church of Jesus Christ grew.

From Jerusalem, Peter and James sent Barnabas to check out what was happening in Antioch. When Barnabas arrived and saw *"the grace of God"* upon the people and the powerful evangelism, he rejoiced. *"And* [he] *encouraged them all that with purpose of heart they should continue with the Lord.... And a great many people were added to the Lord"* (Acts 11:23–24). The church of Jesus Christ was exploding! And in this city of Antioch, these disciples were first called Christians. (See Acts 11:26.)

Stephen laid down his life for the gospel of Jesus Christ and, as a result, Christianity spread throughout the Mediterranean countries. We can be certain of this: God will not waste a single drop of the blood of His saints that is shed in Jesus' name.

James, the Son of Thunder

> *Now about that time Herod the king stretched out his hand to harass some from the church. Then he killed James the brother of John with the sword.* (Acts 12:1–2)

Statue of James in Granada, Spain.
Sedmak\Thinkstock

James, the brother of John, was referred to as James the Greater by the disciples. He was well-known as one of the twelve original apostles, was one of the strong-willed sons of Zebedee, was nicknamed a "Son of Thunder," and was privileged to be present with Jesus on the Mount of Transfiguration and in His agony in the garden of Gethsemane. Yet the Bible contains only one short sentence about James' martyrdom for Christ. Herod Agrippa, the newest Herod to the throne in Judea, began to arrest a number of the disciples, including James. And then, with little explanation, the book of Acts simply records that Herod *"killed James the brother of John with the sword."*

According to the Gospels, James had been included with his brother, John, and with Peter in every major event in Jesus' earthly ministry. Together these three apostles had ministered with the Lord and to the Lord. They loved Jesus and were loved by Him. But for each Christian believer, the time we live on this earth and the ministry that we are called to fulfill is a decision that belongs to God alone.

Peter was chosen to preach the first call to salvation on the day of Pentecost, and his sermon ushered thousands of new Christians into the church. For several decades after, he traveled throughout the Middle East and beyond, spreading Jesus' teachings. James' brother, John, the beloved disciple, was given the Revelation of Christ on the island of Patmos and spent years writing his gospel account and three epistles, while discipling believers in the city of Ephesus. It is believed that John lived to be over one hundred years old.

But God's plan for James was much shorter; his time of ministry limited. For just a few years, James preached in Judea and served in church leadership there before he became the first of the twelve apostles to be martyred (c. AD 45). James didn't even have the opportunity to give an eloquent witness as Stephen did. However, without a doubt, James received his reward with Christ in heaven.

"Peter, Follow Me"

> *"When you were younger, you girded yourself and walked where you wished; but when you are old, you will stretch out your hands, and another will gird you and carry you where you do not wish." This* [Jesus] *spoke, signifying by what death he would glorify God. And when He had spoken this, He said to* [Peter], *"Follow Me."*
>
> (John 21:18–19)

View from a boat on the Sea of Galilee.
alefbet\Thinkstock

The early morning sun was breaking over the watery horizon; the Sea of Galilee had produced no catch through the long, dark night. Simon Peter, along with Thomas, Nathaniel and the sons of Zebedee, had been fishing throughout the night and, despite their backbreaking effort, had caught nothing.

A lonely figure on the beach called out to them in the morning mist, "Children, you do not have any fish, do you?" When they answered "No," he called again, "Cast the net on the right-hand side of the boat and you will find a catch." They cast, and the fish were flowing into the net in such overwhelming numbers that they couldn't even heave the net on board.

A reckless Peter, sweaty from the exertion of his labor, hastily pulled on his outer garment and threw himself into the sea, shouting as he fell, "It is the Lord!" Peter—always reckless and yet always ready to repent and faithfully follow the voice of his Master.

That morning, Jesus asked Peter to show his love by feeding the Lord's flock. But Jesus also warned him of the consequences of following His call. The disciple would stretch out his hands and, much as Jesus had just weeks before, be led by his enemies to his death. Jesus concluded with the familiar words that were etched into Peter's heart after three years with the Savior, *"Peter, follow Me."*

Willing to follow His Savior, Peter championed the cause of Christ for the next thirty-five years, preaching the power of Christ's gospel to save and deliver. As one of the original twelve apostles, he served as a church leader and evangelist, traveling through portions of the Middle East and witnessing to the lordship of Jesus Christ. But as Christ warned His disciple, Peter's road held conflict and fatal persecution.

God's Kind of Honor

The New Testament doesn't give us the details of Peter's death as it does with Stephen and James. What we know of Peter's martyrdom and the death of the remaining apostles comes from the accounts of early church historians, such as Origen of Alexandria, Egypt (ca. 185–254), and Eusebius Pamphili of Caesarea, Israel (ca. 260–341). Eusebius was a Roman historian and a Christian scholar who became the bishop of Caesarea in AD 316 and wrote the most vital book on early church history in existence, *The Ecclesiastical History of the Christian Church*.

Circus Maximus.
lachriss77\Thinkstock

According to Origen and Eusebius, Peter and the other apostles divided the work of evangelizing the world. Peter took Pontus, Galatia, Cappadocia, and Bythnia (located in modern-day Turkey near the Black Sea). Eventually, he traveled to Rome where he continued to preach the gospel and encourage the Roman Christians before being arrested by Nero's guards.

Origen wrote that when Peter was sentenced to death by Roman crucifixion, he protested—not about dying for Christ, but about being unworthy to die in the same manner as his Lord. He requested to be crucified hanging upside down! Peter's martyrdom took place ca. AD 66, while Nero was still persecuting the Christians.

According to the early accounts, Peter was crucified in Nero's Circus Maximus and was buried nearby on what was called Vatican Hill. Initially, the grieving Roman Christians marked Peter's grave simply with a red rock. A few years later, a small shrine or tombstone was erected over the site. When Emperor Constantine I embraced Christianity, he built the first St. Peter's Basilica between AD 319 and 333 in memory of the apostle's life and martyrdom. In the sixteenth century, the current St. Peter's Basilica in Rome was erected over the old site, constructed in part with stones from the destruction of the Roman Colosseum.

Great halls and churches are beautiful structures for those who remain. But the greatest honor for the apostle Peter, the humble servant who wished to be crucified upside down as worship to the Lord, will last long after this earth fades away; his greatest reward is to reign with Jesus Christ through eternity. Peter spoke of this honor in his first epistle: *"That the proof of your faith, being more precious than gold which is perishable, even though tested by fire, may be found to result in praise and glory and honor at the revelation of Jesus Christ"* (1 Peter 1:7 NASB).

Paul's Road to Eternity

Seething with hatred for the "traitor Jews" who followed Jesus, Saul, *"still breathing threats and murder against the disciples of the Lord"* (Acts

9:1 ESV), left Jerusalem for Damascus. Tucked into his clothing was the letter of condemnation signed by the High Priest that would lead to the arrest of any disciples found in Damascus. With each step of the journey, Paul's disgust of the "heretics" grew, and he found himself dwelling on the purity of his own Jewish lineage.

Suddenly, a blinding light seared across Saul's vision and he fell from his rearing horse into the middle of the road. Drowning out the sounds of frightened animals and shouting travelers was heaven's voice meant for Saul alone: *"Saul, Saul, why are you persecuting me?"*

Those seven words rocked the very foundation of Paul's self-righteousness, for in his heart he knew—this was the Lord. In the book of Acts, Paul describes the rest of the scene:

> *So I said, "Who are You, Lord?" And He said, "I am Jesus, whom you are persecuting. But rise and stand on your feet; for I have appeared to you for this purpose, to make you a minister and a witness both of the things which you have seen and of the things which I will yet reveal to you. I will deliver you from the Jewish people, as well as from the Gentiles, to whom I now send you, to open their eyes, in order to turn them from darkness to light, and from the power of Satan to God, that they may receive forgiveness of sins and an inheritance among those who are sanctified by faith in Me."* (Acts 26:15–18)

The story of Saul, renamed Paul after meeting Jesus on the road to Damascus, is a familiar one to Christians. But rethink the meaning of this act in the context of martyrdom. When Jesus knocked Paul off of his horse that day, He had a very specific mission in mind for Paul's life. What was that mission? It was all about being a witness. Why did he face such persecution in all of the cities he traveled to throughout his missionary journeys? He was being a witness to the life, death, and resurrection of the Lord Jesus Christ.

Stirring Up the Crowds

Very few men in the Bible could stir up the crowds the way the apostle Paul could—but not always with assured safety! Thousands of people in Italy, Greece, and Asia Minor turned to Christ because of Paul's bold witness. Paul never preached a soft gospel. He was as bold as a lion in declaring the salvation in Jesus Christ available to both the Jew and the Gentile. He aroused jealousy and anger in both the Jewish and pagan leaders.

A great part of Paul's ministry describes his remarkable cheating of death. From Antioch to Lystra, Iconium to Thessalonica, angry mobs searched for Paul, took him captive, and dragged him through their cities threatening his life. In Lystra, the Jews *"having persuaded the multitudes, they stoned Paul and dragged him out of the city, supposing him to be dead"* (Acts 14:19). In Iconium, they plotted to stone him and he fled the city at the last moment (see Acts 14:5–7); in Philippi, he was beaten along with Silas and imprisoned before being miraculously set free (see Acts 16:22–24); in Thessalonica, he was accused of being one of those men *"who have turned the world upside down"* barely escaping the plot against him in the dead of night (Acts 17:6, 10). Paul was beaten, scourged, stoned, and left for dead, but by God's grace in each

Sculpture of Paul.
filipe_lopes\Thinkstock

city he got up in renewed strength to preach the message of eternal salvation in Jesus Christ.

Throughout his years of ministry, Paul encouraged crowds in the synagogues and in the streets to turn from the kingdom of darkness to the kingdom of light. Wherever he went, he preached in the power of the Holy Spirit, performed miracles of healing, changed lives, and repeated the message of Christ. Paul traveled and preached throughout the Mediterranean basin. He made at least three missionary journeys where he suffered persecution but saw the fruit of his labor as faith in Jesus Christ spread throughout Asia Minor and into Europe.

In spite of being warned not to go, Paul returned to Jerusalem:

> *A certain prophet named Agabus…took Paul's belt, bound his own hands and feet, and said, "Thus says the Holy Spirit, 'So shall the Jews at Jerusalem bind the man who owns this belt, and deliver him into the hands of the Gentiles.'" Now when we heard these things, both we and those from that place, pleaded with him not to go up to Jerusalem. Then Paul answered, "What do you mean by weeping and breaking my heart? For I am ready not only to be bound, but also to die at Jerusalem for the name of the Lord Jesus." So when he would not be persuaded, we ceased, saying, "The will of the Lord be done."* (Acts 21:10–14)

Once Paul reached Jerusalem, he went directly to the synagogue to preach about Jesus; there, the Jews who hated him quickly captured him and dragged him to the Roman authorities.

"You Must Witness at Rome!"

Paul would have been released by the Romans because they found no guilt in him. But God had other plans for this Apostle to the Gentiles. The Lord appeared to Paul once again, this time in the Roman barracks in Jerusalem: "*The following night the Lord stood by him and said,*

'Take courage, for as you have testified to the facts about me in Jerusalem, so you must testify also in Rome'" (Acts 23:11 ESV).

For two years in Rome, Paul was merely under house arrest and free to preach the gospel whenever he had the opportunity. At the end of the book of Acts, Luke writes, *"For two whole years Paul stayed there in his own rented house and welcomed all who came to see him. He proclaimed the kingdom of God and taught about the Lord Jesus Christ—with all boldness and without hindrance!"* (Acts 28:30–31 NIV).

Bible scholars believe that Paul was released after these two years and continued on his missionary journeys, perhaps traveling as far as modern-day Spain and France before returning to Rome where he was again arrested, imprisoned, and sentenced to die. Now locked in a prison cell, Paul wrote what would be his last letter, the second letter to Timothy, before he was executed around AD 67. In the letter to Timothy he admitted it was his time to go: *"For I am already being poured out as a drink offering, and the time of my departure is at hand"* (2 Timothy 4:6).

Because Paul was a Roman citizen, the apostle was beheaded rather than crucified, according to Eusebius, at a place called Tre Fontane in Rome. The Basilica of St. Paul Outside the Walls, constructed by Emperor Constantine I, stands over the location of Paul's grave.

Paul's triumphant words before his martyrdom should be our words as well: *"I have fought the good fight, I have finished the course, I have kept the faith; in the future there is laid up for me the crown of righteousness, which the Lord, the righteous Judge, will award to me on that day; and not only to me, but also to all who have loved His appearing"* (2 Timothy 4:7–8 NASB).

James: Hurled from the Temple

> *James, a bondservant of God and of the Lord Jesus Christ, to the twelve tribes which are scattered abroad: Greetings. My brethren, count it all joy when you fall into various trials.* (James 1:1–2)

Within two years after word reached Jerusalem of Paul's death, the Jewish Sanhedrin turned their persecuting gaze on "James the Just," the leader of the Jerusalem church. James was the Lord's brother and the writer of the epistle of James. Although he was not one of the original twelve apostles, he was a gifted leader and the bishop of Jerusalem for over thirty years. James personally experienced the *"various trials"* and painful persecutions that he wrote about in his epistle. We don't have a record of James' death in the Bible, but Eusebius' history does give an account of his martyrdom.

James the Just was a man of fervent prayer, "frequently found upon his knees begging forgiveness for the people, so that his knees became hard like those of a camel." [26] The fruit of James' prayers was that scores of Jewish believers embraced Jesus as the Messiah.

Furious at his success, the scribes and Pharisees took matters into their own hands. The Sanhedrin "turned against James, the brother of the Lord...and leading him into their midst, they demanded that he should renounce faith in Christ in the presence of all of the people...but with a clear voice and great boldness, James spoke out before the whole multitude and confessed that our Savior and Lord Jesus is the Son of God."[27]

There were tragic consequences for the Jews following James' martyrdom.

In an outrage, the Jewish leaders dragged James to the top of the temple spire and "threw down the just man and then cried to each other, 'Let us stone James the Just!' [since the fall did not kill him]. And so James died a martyr and the church of Jesus Christ grew in boldness among the Jews."[28]

26. Eusebius, *Ecclesiastical History,* Vol. 2:23:10–17, Christian Classics Ethereal Library, http://www.ccel.org/ccel/schaff/npnf201.iii.vii.xxiv.html.
27. Ibid.
28. Ibid.

There were tragic consequences for the Jews following James' martyrdom. Eusebius concludes his report: "James became a true witness—both to Jews and Greeks—that Jesus is the Christ. And immediately after Vespasian besieged them."[29]

Jesus' Prophecy Was Fulfilled

The Roman emperor Vespasian sent his son, Titus, and his armies to Jerusalem to crush the Jewish rebellion. Immediately after James was martyred, the Roman attack began. During that year, AD 70, Jerusalem was overrun and the temple was utterly destroyed without a single stone remaining "one on top of the other."

Jesus' prophecy to His disciples had been fulfilled:

> *Jesus left the temple and was walking away when his disciples came up to him to call his attention to its buildings. "Do you see all these things?" he asked. "Truly I tell you, not one stone here will be left on another; every one will be thrown down."* (Matthew 24:1–8 NIV)

The Bitter Destruction of Jerusalem

One year later, in AD 71, Emperor Vespasian and Titus held a gala victory celebration in the streets of Rome. Among the parade floats depicting Rome's victory over Judea, the Romans displayed their spoils of war: the sacred treasures of the Jewish temple and the prisoners of war bound in chains. Josephus, the Jewish historian, was present that day and described the victorious celebration held in front of thousands of cheering Roman citizens. As Vespasian and Titus, crowned in laurel wreaths, looked on with the haughty pride of Roman domination,

> spoil in abundance was paraded past them. None of it compared with that taken from the Temple in Jerusalem, a golden table many stones in weight and a golden lamp stand, similarly made,

29. Ibid, 2:23:18.

which was quite unlike any object in daily use. A center shaft rose from a base, and from the shaft thin branches or arms extended, in a pattern very like that of tridents, each wrought at its end into a lamp. There were seven of these lamps, thus emphasizing the honor paid by the Jews to the number seven. A tablet of the Jewish Law was carried last of all the spoil. The procession was completed by Vespasian, and, behind him, Titus. The procession ended up at the Temple of Jupiter on the Capitol.[30]

The Old City of Jerusalem.
mbears\Thinkstock

It was a final blow to the demoralized Jews, witnessing the Roman victors offering the sacred temple treasure as spoils to their false god. It

30. "Rome Celebrates the Vanquishing of the Jews: AD 71," EyeWitness to History, 2008, www.eyewitnesstohistory.com.

was a bitter day in Jewish history. God's chosen people had paid a frightful price for rejecting their Messiah.

Many of the Jewish leaders and elite were exiled, killed, or sold into slavery. Those who survived annihilation fled Israel and scattered throughout the Roman Empire in what is now known as the Great Diaspora. The Jews remained a people in exile until their miraculous return to an Israeli homeland two thousand years later in the twentieth century.

Apostles Preach in Power Until Death

Far away from Jerusalem, the other apostles were sharing the gospel message throughout most of the known world. Because of their witness, the church of Christ spread from the city, throughout the villages, and into the rural countryside in every country in which they traveled. In the end, they gave their lives while fulfilling their calling. According to early church writings, the following is the fate of the other apostles.

Andrew was the first to lead his brother, Simon Peter, to Jesus, "We have found the Messiah!" he told Peter. (See John 1:41.) Andrew preached in modern-day southern Greece, Ukraine, and southern Russia. As a result, he is considered the patron saint of both Greece and Russia.

According to early records, in AD 60, while Andrew was ministering in the seaport city of Patras, Greece, he baptized the wife and brother of the governor, Aegeus. The governor was so angry that he ordered Andrew's death by crucifixion. Andrew was reportedly crucified on a cross in the shape of an X on November 30 of that year. The X-shaped cross has become the symbol of Andrew and appears on the Scottish national flag, called the Saltire, as a reminder that Andrew is the patron saint of Scotland as well.

According to Scottish history, centuries after Andrew was slain, some of his bones were moved to the western seacoast of Scotland, to a town named Kirrymont. They were buried in the great medieval cathedral and the town was renamed St. Andrews in the apostle's honor.

Philip the apostle, not the evangelist, is the one who asked Jesus when they would see the Father. Jesus responded, *"He that hath seen me hath seen the Father"* (John 14:8–9 KJV). Philip preached the gospel in Phrygia (Turkey) before being tied to a pillar and stoned to death at Hierapolis.

Bartholomew preached in present-day Armenia, Turkey, northern Iraq and Iran, and India. It is recorded that he was skinned alive and then beheaded near present-day Baku, Azerbaijan, on the shores of the Caspian Sea.

Thomas Didymus, otherwise known as doubting Thomas, fulfilled his gospel call in India. Thomas preached throughout the southern tip of India, beginning in the western area of Kerala. He later traveled to Madras (modern Chennai), a beautiful seacoast city on the Bay of Bengal. In Madras, Thomas was speared to death on a hill outside of the city, a location renamed St. Thomas Mount in his honor. The Basilica of the National Shrine of St. Thomas in Chennai, India, has been built over his burial site.

Matthew, the writer of the Gospel, is believed to have preached and died by the sword in Ethiopia. James, son of Alpheus, known as James the Less (so he wouldn't be confused with James the son of Zebedee), preached in Palestine and in Egypt, where he was martyred.

Remember, the apostles were eyewitnesses to Jesus' life on this earth. It was their mission to bear witness to this truth to as many people as possible while they were still alive. They were willing to lay their lives down for the Christian faith because they had been greatly privileged to see Christ's death and resurrection with their own eyes. They knew without question that He had died for the sins of the world and had risen again so that we could live with Him through all of eternity. And they would be faithful witnesses to Him until the end.

Nero: The Spirit of Antichrist

It was a hot summer evening in the city of Rome, July 19, AD 64. Roman citizens walking through the western valley beside the Palatine hills gazed at the Circus Maximus, the mammoth chariot stadium looming up ahead. The Circus had been built six hundred years earlier, and, during the lavish Roman festivals, it resounded with the thunder of hooves and the celebration of one hundred thousand cheering Roman citizens.

On this July night, however, all was quiet until the cry "Ignis! Ignis," or "Fire! Fire!" shattered the darkness. The wooden merchant shops lining the Circus Maximus had burst into flames. Moving swiftly, the fire spread throughout the Roman capital, destroying houses, temples, and palaces of the rich and poor alike.

The city of Rome was a raging inferno for six days as thousands desperately struggled to flee the flames or lost their lives trapped in the inner city. Brave men and women who attempted to fight the fire were prevented by bands of looters. In the end, ten of Rome's fourteen districts were in charred ruins. How could such a tragedy have occurred? And where was the Emperor Nero while his city was destroyed in the flames; was he really playing the fiddle, as tradition would have it, as he watched Rome burn?

Just about everything we know of the great Roman fire is from the writings of the aristocrat and Roman historian, Tacitus. Nero was a cruel and ambitious ruler and Tacitus, along with many of the elite of the city, was disgusted with him. It was Tacitus who wrote that Nero fiddled merrily as the imperial city went up in flames, although historians have disputed whether the account of the fiddle was only a rumor Tacitus created out of hatred for Nero's despotic rule!

Months earlier, Nero had revealed his expansive plans to tear down a third of the city and build an elaborate series of palaces named Domus Aurea or Neropolis in his honor. When the emperor laid his plans before the Roman Senate, they objected vehemently. Shortly after, the fires of Rome raged.

Rumors flared everywhere! Nero had been the cause of the fire! Not only had these citizens lost their homes and much of the capital city, but their eight-hundred-year-old temple to Jupiter had been destroyed as well. The populace was in turmoil. The emperor had to redirect the accusations and anger of the Roman citizens. Nero needed a scapegoat. And he found one—right in his own palace.

In his letter to the Philippians written from prison in Rome, the apostle Paul acknowledged the followers of Jesus Christ living in the royal household. "*Greet every saint in Christ Jesus. The brethren who are with me greet you. All the saints greet you, especially those of Caesar's household*" (Philippians 4:21–23 ESV). Nero was well-aware of his Christian servants and began his accusations starting with his own house. After arresting these men and women, he sent out his palace guards to round up all of the Christians they could find in Rome to throw into prison.

The First Mass Execution of Christians

The innocent Christians were accused not only of the fire but also of every wicked deed imaginable; they were labeled criminals by the Romans and sentenced to be tortured and put to death. Tacitus, although Roman and not a supporter of Christians in general, describes Nero's plot and the horrific mass executions of Rome's Christians:

> *The innocent Christians were accused not only of the fire but also of every wicked deed imaginable.*

> To get rid of the report [that he had started the fire], Nero fastened the guilt and inflicted the most exquisite tortures on a class hated for their abominations, called Christians by the populace. Christus, from whom the name had its origin, suffered the extreme penalty during the reign of Tiberius at the hands of one of

our procurators, Pontius Pilatus, and a most mischievous superstition, thus checked for the moment, again broke out not only in Judaea, the first source of the evil, but even in Rome, where all things hideous and shameful from every part of the world find their centre and become popular. Accordingly, an arrest was first made of all who pleaded guilty; then, upon their information, an immense multitude was convicted, not so much of the crime of firing the city, as of hatred against mankind.[31]

The head of Emperor Nero.
Tonygers\Thinkstock

By AD 64 the Romans had turned punishment and death into a form of amusement for the public. It wasn't enough just to execute people accused of crimes. The Roman authorities used cruelty and mockery as an entertainment for the masses. We imagine, or have seen depicted in movies, that the hungry animals released into the Circus Maximus would have immediately attacked prisoners in the arena, but humans were not their usual prey. In order to insure the beasts would attack, and to make a mockery of the prisoners, the Romans dressed the Christians in the skins of dead animals and then watched as the lions or wild dogs viciously tore them apart.

31. Tacitus, *The Annals*, translated by Alfred John Church and William Jackson Brodribb, available at http://classics.mit.edu/Tacitus/annals.11.xv.html, accessed April 20, 2016.

Hundreds of Christians were crucified by Nero's guard. Hundreds more were lit and burned as torches in Nero's gardens in viciously inhumane ways that are almost unimaginable to us today. While still alive, they were wrapped in linen mantles that were coated with oil or pitch, attached to wooden stakes and hammered into the ground throughout Nero's palace gardens. Tacitus writes that after lighting the Christians as torches, Nero himself appeared as a charioteer riding a chariot throughout his royal gardens raising his arm as a Roman victor.

What gave those early Christians the strength to endure such inhumane torture and death? Anointing! They were anointed by God, given the unconquerable belief that Jesus Christ was standing with His arms outstretched in love just on the other side of the curtain between earth and eternity—welcoming them into His heaven.

Be Assured, God Is Not Mocked

Besides Tacitus, other Roman historians were also convinced that Nero was the culprit behind the Great Fire. In spite of protests from the Senators, Nero went ahead and built his Domus Aurea, an elaborate network of villas and pavilions in a park complete with a man-made lake, in the heart of the Roman city. In the vestibule of the Domus Aurea, Nero arrogantly erected the Colossus of Nero, a one-hundred-foot bronze statue of himself.

Modern-day view of the Colisseum from the direction of the Domus Aurea.
Tonygers\Thinkstock

A short time later, Nero paid for his brutality and self-glorification. *"Do not be deceived; God is not mocked; for whatever a man sows, that he will also reap"* (Galatians 6:7). Within two years of the Domus' completion, the Senate and the Roman elite deserted him. Nero was forced to flee Rome and made the decision to commit suicide in a villa outside of the city. Nero was too afraid to kill himself, so he commanded one of his guards to kill him. Nero died on his own sword on June 9, AD 68. His successor, Emperor Vespasian, added bronze "sun rays" to the head of the Colossus of Nero and turned it into a statue in honor of the sun god Sol. The Roman people rejoiced at Nero's death.

Unfortunately, the persecution of Christians did not die with Nero's cruel reign. But neither did the church of Jesus Christ! Throughout the empire, from city to village to rural countryside, as Christians lost their lives thousands more rose up to take their place, steadfast in their love for Jesus Christ and one another.

> *We give thanks to God always for all of you, constantly mentioning you in our prayers, remembering before our God and Father your work of faith and labor of love and steadfastness of hope in our Lord Jesus Christ.* (1 Thessalonians 1:2–3 ESV)

ON THE ROAD TO GLORY

3

ON THE ROAD TO GLORY

(AD 100)

Ignatius of Antioch

"All the pleasures of the world, and all the kingdoms of this earth, shall profit me nothing. It is better for me to die in behalf of Jesus Christ than to reign over all the ends of the earth."
—Ignatius of Antioch[32]

The road to Rome was long and dusty, the guards hot and sullen as they made another weary stop in their 1,500 mile journey from ancient Antioch to the Roman capital. This time they

32. Ignatius, *The Epistle of Ignatius to the Romans* (Orthodox Ebooks), 152.

stopped in Smyrna, a flourishing Roman city on the coast of the Aegean Sea where they could rest their travel-weary bodies for several weeks before boarding a final ship for Rome.

Remains of ancient Roman road through Antioch in modern-day Turkey.
Creatista\Thinkstock

The surly guards glared at the man whom they were transporting in chains to the Emperor Trajan. What a nuisance these Christians were, they grumbled as they slammed the jail door behind Ignatius, the fearless bishop of Antioch.

Just a few weeks earlier, Ignatius stood before the Roman authorities and a furious mob in the city courts of Antioch, the fourth-largest city in the Roman Empire. The Christian community was growing very quickly in this prosperous Syrian city, and the pagan citizens were becoming agitated by these "strange believers and their Christian God." Accusing the Christian leader, Ignatius, of disrupting society and breaking Roman law, the authorities arrested him in order to silence his teachings and to spread fear through the rest of the Christian community.

"Renounce your faith in Jesus Christ or die!" was the threat. Refusing to deny his faith, Ignatius was sentenced to appear before the Emperor Trajan, who wanted to interrogate the Christian leader before throwing him to the wild beasts in the newly built Roman Colosseum. The pagan citizens of Antioch roared their approval and Ignatius began his road to martyrdom.

Sentenced to the Beasts

Ignatius *Theophorus* (which translates God-bearing) was born in Antioch in ancient Syria (modern-day Antakya, Turkey) around the year AD 50. As a young man, he traveled throughout the western Mediterranean cities including the infamously pagan city of Ephesus, home to the Temple of Artemis (Diana) and one of the seven wonders of the ancient world. It was also a thriving center for early Christianity and the home church of the apostle John during his final years. In Ephesus, Ignatius was blessed to be one of John's disciples and to study the life, death, and resurrection of Jesus Christ directly under the beloved apostle himself. In the dark, sin-eroded world of Ephesus, Ignatius' powerful Christian teachings and fearless evangelism encouraged the entire Christian population.

By the year AD 89, Ignatius was ordained as the overseer or bishop of Antioch, Syria, which also had a growing Christian community. Antioch's Christian church had been founded fifty years earlier when the disciples fled from Jerusalem after Stephen was martyred. Ignatius was a strong leader—sharing the apostle's teachings, standing up against the early heresies of the church, and spreading the gospel of Christ throughout Syria.

Early in the year AD 107, Ignatius' Christian influence became too much for the Roman elite in the city. He was arrested, brought before the governor, and ordered to renounce his faith. Three times he was asked to deny Christ; three times he adamantly refused, so he was condemned as a "Christian agitator." Rather than executing Ignatius in

Antioch where he was so well-loved, he was sentenced to be taken to Rome, first to appear before Emperor Trajan and then to die in the Colosseum, fed to the animals.

"I Fight with Wild Beasts"

Ignatius' guards were so cruel to him on the journey, he referred to them as ten ferocious leopards: "From Syria even unto Rome I fight with beasts, both by land and sea, both by night and by day, being bound to ten leopards, I mean a band of soldiers, who, even when they receive benefits, show themselves all the worse."[33] But in spite of the guards' cruelty, Ignatius was still permitted to meet with Christian visitors in every city along the way.

Icon of Ignatius.
Boris Zatserkovnyy\Thinkstock

When the Roman guards stopped to rest in the seaport of Smyrna before sailing to Rome, the Christians of Smyrna and nearby Ephesus flocked to the prison to encourage Ignatius. His greatest spiritual refreshment came from his friend, Polycarp, the bishop of Smyrna. These two godly men—Polycarp and Ignatius—were among the last alive who had personally walked with Jesus' apostles. Together they glorified their Savior for the privilege to proclaim His name among the Roman people. (Forty years later, Polycarp would also face martyrdom in the arena.)

33. Ibid., 151.

During his journey, Ignatius wrote five letters to the churches of Asia Minor, one letter to the church at Rome and a final letter to Polycarp. Miraculously, all of these letters have survived and are recorded by Eusebius, the early church historian, in his *Ecclesiastic History*. Ignatius' letter to Rome is the most famous. It gives us a glimpse of Ignatius' struggles as he faced the prospect of death in the Colosseum, and also his desire to stand for Christ until the end.

Better to Die for Christ than Reign over World.

It is probably difficult for us to understand today, but Ignatius actually pleaded with the Roman Christians to do nothing to save him from his martyrdom. He didn't want to be rescued but wanted instead to go on to his reward in heaven. Here are Ignatius' own words to the Roman church, written from Smyrna and dated August 24, AD 107 or 108.

> For if you are silent concerning me, I shall become God's; but if you show your love to my flesh [by rescuing me], I shall again have to run my race. Pray, then, do not seek to confer any greater favor upon me than that I be sacrificed to God...that, being gathered together in love, you may sing praise to the Father, through Christ Jesus, that God has deemed me, the bishop of Syria, worthy to be sent...from the world unto God, that I may rise again to Him.[34]

Ignatius knew what awaited him in Rome, but he also knew that Jesus would be on the other side of death's door to welcome him into eternal life. Although we don't have the details of his martyrdom, we do have his final word on his undivided love for Jesus Christ:

> All the pleasures of the world, and all the kingdoms of this earth, shall profit me nothing. It is better for me to die on behalf of Jesus Christ, than to reign over all the ends of the earth. For what shall a man be profited, if he gain the whole world, but lose his

34. Ibid., 148.

> own soul? Him I seek, who died for us: Him I desire, who rose again for our sake.[35]

Is It a Crime to Be a Christian?

In the sixty years since Jesus' resurrection, two Roman emperors, Nero and Domitian, had cruelly persecuted His followers. Other emperors, however, had considered the small new sect insignificant, which gave the Christian community brief times of peace. But at the beginning of the second century, the Emperor Trajan was asked a new and chilling question by one of his regional governors: *"Is it a crime to be a Christian?"*

Just after Ignatius' martyrdom, in AD 112, Pliny the Younger, the Roman governor of Bithynia (modern-day Turkey), requested counsel from the emperor on how to handle the spread of Christianity in his province. At the time there weren't any Roman laws against being a Christian, but the Roman leaders were becoming increasingly suspicious of the rapidly growing sect. Pliny's letter to Trajan became a critical turning point in the Roman Empire's policy on the early Christians. Their correspondence still exists for us to read today. In his letter, Pliny admitted to Trajan that he could not pinpoint anything specifically illegal in the Christians' lives:

> They met on a stated day before it was light, and addressed a form of prayer to Christ, as to a divinity, binding themselves by a solemn oath, not for the purposes of any wicked design, but never to commit any fraud, theft, or adultery, never to falsify their word, nor deny a trust when they should be called upon to deliver it up; after which it was their custom to separate, and then reassemble, to eat in common a harmless meal.[36]

---

35. Ibid., 152.

36. Pliny the Younger, *Letters, Harvard Classics,* vol. 9, part 4 (originally published New York: P. F. Collier and Sons, 1909–14, now released online at www.bartleby.com/9/4/2097.html), chapter 97.

Pliny described how he had arrested several Christians and conducted trials against them, giving them the opportunity to recant. Identical to Ignatius' trial, three times they were asked if they were Christians; three times they were given the chance to deny their faith. If they denied being Christians, they were required to pray and offer incense to the Roman gods and then curse Christ. Pliny remarked, "there is no forcing, it is said, those who are really Christians into [cursing Christ]."[37] Those who did offer to the gods were released. Those who refused three times to deny Christ and their Christian faith were executed or, if Roman citizens, were sent to Rome for trial and possible execution.

Pliny's opinion was that devout Christians were a threat to the Roman Empire, endangering the citizens of every age and rank within it. "This contagious superstition is not confined to the cities only," he warned, "but has spread its infection among the neighbouring villages and country."[38] Trajan's response to Pliny was the first step in making Christianity illegal in the Roman Empire. He gave the governor four official orders: 1) Do not seek the Christians out for trial (that was a waste of time); 2) If someone accuses them and the accused are guilty of being Christians, then they must be punished by death; 3) If the accused deny they are Christians and show proof by worshiping the Roman gods then they should be pardoned; 4) Pliny should not allow anyone to bring anonymous accusations against Christians.[39]

For the first time in the history of the Christian church, a Roman emperor had pronounced that Christians could be executed simply for being Christians.

Trajan's comments, although brief enough, had chilling results. For the first time in the history of the Christian church, a Roman emperor

37. Ibid.
38. Ibid.
39. Pliny the Younger, chapter 98.

had pronounced that Christians could be executed simply for being Christians. Over the next two centuries that policy sent thousands of believers on the road to martyrdom.

Jesus Changed World History Forever

Why did the Roman authorities and people consider Christianity a threat? This is something we should look at before moving on. The Romans considered themselves a very religious people, and had a fierce dedication to their gods. They believed that the deities ruled every sphere of Roman life and that they owed all of their prosperity and military success to them. Frequent, lavish celebrations were held to honor the gods in the Circus Maximus and the Colosseum in Rome and in similar arenas throughout the major cities.

In the first century BC, the Roman philosopher, Cicero, wrote about the strength of Roman piety: "If we care to compare our national characteristics with those of foreign peoples…we shall find that, while in other respects we are only the equals or even the inferiors of others, *yet in the sense of religion, that is in worship for the gods, we are far superior.*"[40]

In roughly the middle of the thousand year reign of Rome, in a small corner of the empire, the history of the world was changed forever. Jesus Christ was born in tiny Bethlehem of Judea. He came as "the way, the truth and the life;" He lived, died and was resurrected from the dead for the salvation of all mankind. Suddenly a new faith appeared in the Roman Empire, beginning slowly in Judea, Greece, and Asia Minor, and then traveling with increasing speed from city to city. It carried one message: Jesus Christ was the *only* Son of God and it was through Him *alone* the people of Rome (and beyond) could be saved.

This belief system of these "suspicious" Christians, named after the Nazarene, Jesus Christ, was completely foreign to Rome. The

40. Cicero, quoted in Robert Louis Wiken, *The Christians as the Romans Saw Them* (New Haven, CN: Yale University Press, 2003), 57, emphasis added.

Romans found reasons to mistrust and even hate them for many reasons. Christian disciples were accused of being "atheists," a word taken from the Greek word *atheos,* and translated "those without the gods" because they refused to sacrifice to the false Roman deities whom the Christians believed were actually demons. Christians were labeled "unpatriotic" because they valued their citizenship in heaven far above the privileged citizenship of Rome. In the end, the Romans viewed the followers of Christ as a superstitious, ignorant society that met in secret places and were a threat to the very fabric of Roman culture and religion.

Roman Emperors: The Good, the Bad, and the Ugly

Not every Roman emperor persecuted Christians. Some of them saw the new faith as too small to be a bother. Those emperors we would consider *the good.* Others, like Trajan and Marcus Aurelius, viewed the Christians as criminals but not much of a threat to the empire. Still, they did nothing to stop the brutal persecution by individual governors in the Roman provinces. Those were *the bad.* The cruelest of the emperors were *the ugly.* They ruled from AD 202 to 313 and launched empire-wide persecutions in an attempt to completely annihilate the body of Christ. These emperors went to great lengths to pursue and execute believers and cost thousands of Christians their lives.

Unfortunately, today secular historians are attempting to rewrite Christian church history. Many of them claim that few emperors paid attention to the Christians and that the persecution of Christ's followers has been grossly exaggerated by early Christian writers. They use words like "sporadic" and "minimal" in an effort to invalidate the foundation of church history.

While it's true that some years of peace existed for Christians in the first three centuries of the church, it was an unsettled peace. Jesus' followers were still outsiders of the earthly kingdom of Rome and knew that at any time the peace could be shattered by a new edict of terror.

Polycarp of Smyrna

"Eighty-six years I have served him, and he never did me any wrong. How can I blaspheme my King who saved me?"
—Polycarp of Smyrna, AD 155

The small, rocky island jutted out of the Aegean Sea, barely fourteen square miles in area. The desolate, windswept beaches and craggy hills were devoid of life except for the lonely prisoners in captivity. To this small island called Patmos, just sixty miles west of the prosperous city of Ephesus, the apostle John was banished by the Roman Emperor Domitian for spreading the good news of Jesus Christ throughout the Middle East during this emperor's reign. There, John received the powerful revelation from Jesus Christ, delivered by an angel of the Lord (Revelation 1:1). When Domitian died in AD 96, John was released from his exile and returned to the seaport of Ephesus with his writings, including the book of Revelation, in hand.

Church bells on the Isle of Patmos.
ivanmateev\Thinkstock

These writings would greatly affect the life of Polycarp, a young Christian man from Smyrna, a city just thirty-five miles north of Ephesus. Both cities were bustling sea harbors and both were centers of the early growth of

Christianity. When John was released from Patmos, Polycarp, in his early thirties, became one of his disciples in Ephesus. The elderly apostle was eager to share his firsthand testimony of the Savior: "*Jesus Christ the faithful witness, the first-born of the dead, and the ruler of kings on earth....* [The One] *who loves us and has freed us from our sins by his blood and made us a kingdom, priests to his God and Father*" (Revelation 1:5–6).

Polycarp became a strong and passionate Christian leader and was eventually appointed as the bishop or overseer of the church in Smyrna. Because he had studied with John, people remarked that Polycarp only "taught the things which he had learned from the apostles, and which the church had handed down, and which alone are true."[41]

A Warning to the Church at Smyrna

I am certain that Polycarp would have read John's Revelation from Patmos and was aware: persecution was prophesied for the Christians of Smyrna:

> *And to the angel of the church in Smyrna write.... "Do not fear any of those things which you are about to suffer. Indeed, the devil is about to throw some of you into prison, that you may be tested, and you will have tribulation ten days.* ***Be faithful until death, and I will give you the crown of life****. He who has an ear, let him hear what the Spirit says to the churches. He who overcomes shall not be hurt by the second death."* (Revelation 2:8, 10–11)

Fast forward to the year AD 155. The apostle John had been dead for about fifty-five years. Forty years had passed since Ignatius was thrown to the wild beasts in the Roman Colosseum. Polycarp was now eighty-six years old and had faithfully served as the leader of the Smyrna church for nearly fifty years, teaching, writing, praying, and spreading the gospel. The current Roman emperor was a man of peace and not concerned with the activities of the Christian sect. But the governors

41. Irenaus, *Against Heresies*, New Advent, http://www.newadvent.org/fathers/0103303.htm.

throughout the empire still had the freedom to abuse Christians unchecked. Smyrna became a victim of that persecution.

Christians Accused as Atheists

"Away with the atheists!" the crowds roared in the amphitheater of Smyrna. Chained together in the center of the dusty arena stood twelve Christian men. They had been captured and dragged before the Roman authorities for the crime of secretly meeting to worship the Nazarene named Jesus Christ. Just like in other Roman cities, the people of Smyrna were suspicious of Christians for their refusal to worship the pagan deities and falsely branded them as *atheists.*

Sculpture of Polycarp
by Carl Christian Peters in 1884.
Orf3us\Wikimedia Commons

Without warning, persecution broke out in Smyrna. Anger toward the "secretive" Christians had been festering among the people. During a week of festivals in the city's amphitheater, the outraged crowd declared it was time to punish the "atheists." Roman guards were commanded to round up twelve Christian men from the city and march them in chains into the arena to face trial before the governor and the incensed spectators. Refusing to renounce Jesus, the twelve men (whose names we do not know) were sentenced to death as the mob cheered. Horrifying torture and death awaited the twelve men in the arena that day, as told by Eusebius:

The account of the martyrdom of these twelve men and Polycarp a few days later has been preserved for centuries for us to read today:

We write unto you, brethren, an account of what befell those that suffered martyrdom and especially the blessed Polycarp, who stayed the persecution, having as it were set his seal upon it by his martyrdom. For nearly all the foregoing events came to pass that the Lord might show us once more an example of martyrdom which is conformable to the Gospel.... Blessed therefore and noble are all the martyrdoms [the twelve recently martyred apostles] which have taken place according to the will of God.

For who could fail to admire their nobility and patient endurance and loyalty to the Master? Seeing that when they were so torn by lashes that even as far as the veins and arteries and inward mechanism of their flesh were visible, they endured patiently, so that the very bystanders had pity and wept; while they themselves reached such a pitch of bravery that none of them uttered a cry or a groan, thus showing to us all that at that hour the martyrs of Christ being tortured were absent from the flesh, or rather that the Lord was standing by and conversing with them.

And giving heed unto the grace of Christ, they despised the tortures of this world, purchasing at the cost of one hour a release from eternal punishment. And...with the eyes of their heart they gazed upon the good things which are reserved for those that endure patiently, things which neither ear has heard nor eye has seen, neither have they entered into the heart of man, but were shown by the Lord to them.[42]

The Martyrdom of Polycarp

In the meantime, the elderly Polycarp was on his knees, praying without ceasing for the Christians in his flock. The letter continues:

42. *The Martyrdom of Polycarp*, chapter 1:1–2.3, translated by J.B. Lightfoot, 1990, http://www.earlychristianwritings.com/text/martyrdompolycarp-lightfoot.html, accessed April 20, 2016.

> So when [Polycarp] heard that they [Roman soldiers] were come, he went down and conversed with them, the bystanders marveling at his age and his constancy, and wondering why there should be so much eagerness for the apprehension of an old man like him. At that, he immediately gave orders that a table should be spread for them to eat and drink at that hour, as much as they desired. And he persuaded them to grant him an hour so he might pray.[43]

Polycarp was so filled with the grace of God that the soldiers listening to him began to regret coming against such a devout old man.

As he prayed for a full two hours, Polycarp was so filled with the grace of God that the soldiers listening to him began to regret coming against such a devout old man. After he had finished praying, however, they put him on a donkey and brought him into the city.

"Be Strong, Polycarp!"

> But as Polycarp entered into the stadium, a voice came to him from heaven; "Be strong, Polycarp, and play the man." And no one saw the speaker, but those of our people who were present heard the voice. And at length, when he was brought up, there was a great tumult, for they heard that Polycarp had been apprehended.
>
> When then he was brought before him, the proconsul [Quadratus] asked whether he were the man. And on his confessing that he was, he tried to persuade him to a denial saying, "Have respect to your age," and other things in accordance therewith, as it is their habit to say, "Swear by the genius [divine spirit] of Caesar; repent and say, 'Away with the atheists.'" Then Polycarp with solemn countenance looked upon the whole multitude of lawless heathen that were in the stadium, and waved his hand

43. Ibid., chapter 7:2.

> to them; and groaning and looking up to heaven he said, "Away with the atheists."[44]

By saying this, Polycarp was affirming that *he* was not the atheist, because he believed in the one true God—and the others were the real atheists. When pressured, he delivered this amazing testimony: "Eighty-six years I have served [Jesus], and he never did me any wrong. How can I blaspheme my King who saved me?... You vainly suppose I will swear by the divine spirit of Caesar, pretending to be ignorant of who I am. Now hear me plainly: *I am a Christian*. If you desire to learn the doctrine of Christianity, choose a day and I will tell you."

In return, the proconsul shouted to Polycarp, "I have wild beasts and I will throw you to them if you do not deny Christ." And Polycarp simply responded: "Call them."

A Miracle in the Arena

Things moved quickly in the arena after that. The frenzied spectators ran for wood for the fire. The guards prepared to nail Polycarp to the stake so that he would not flee, but he told them it wasn't necessary. Before the fire was lit, he offered a prayer that was recorded by the Christian witnesses at the scene. This is a portion of that prayer:

> O Lord God Almighty, the Father of Your beloved and blessed Son Jesus Christ…I bless You because You have granted me this day and hour, that I might receive a portion amongst the number of martyrs in the cup of Your Christ unto resurrection of eternal life, both of soul and of body, in the incorruptibility of the Holy Spirit. May I be received among these in Your presence this day…. For all things, I praise You, I bless You, I glorify You, through the eternal and heavenly High-priest, Jesus Christ, Your beloved Son, through Whom, with Him and the Holy Spirit, be glory both now and ever and for the ages to come. Amen.[45]

44. Ibid., chapter 9:1–2.
45. Ibid., 14:1–3.

The fire was lit. But instead of burning the elderly bishop, the fire rose up around him "like the sail of a vessel filled by the wind and made a wall around the body of the martyr." The flames themselves did not consume Polycarp. Realizing that something unexplainable was taking place, Quadratus ordered a Roman guard to pierce Polycarp with his sword. With Polycarp's death, the persecution of the Christians in Smyrna ended.

In spite of the fear and pain we associate with martyrdom, the faith of God's people grew stronger. The church of Christ was standing against the cruel pagan culture that surrounded them. I thank God that this report of the faithfulness of Polycarp and the other disciples has survived through nearly two thousand years of Christian history for us to be encouraged to stand strong in our godless world today. *"Be on your guard; stand firm in the faith; be courageous; be strong"* (1 Corinthians 16:13 NIV).

Justin Martyr: "A Flame was Kindled in My Soul"

"You can kill us, but you can't hurt us!"
—Justin Martyr, martyred AD 165

Walking along the sandy beaches of the Aegean Sea near the city of Ephesus, a young Greek philosopher was deep in thought, meditating on the classic writings of Plato. He looked up from his ponderings to see an old man walking toward him with a thoughtful smile. With an authority that comes from the Holy Spirit alone, the man began to share eternal truths about God the Father, God the Son, and the prophets who spoke by the divine Spirit, with wisdom beyond the wisest of the Greek philosophers.

"But," the stranger continued to the intrigued young man, "pray that, above all things, the gates of light may be opened to you; for these things cannot be perceived or understood by all, but only by the man to whom God and His Christ have imparted wisdom [by the Holy Spirit]."[46]

"Straightaway a flame was kindled in my soul," Justin explained, "and a love of the prophets, and of those men who are friends of Christ, possessed me; and while revolving his words in my mind, I found this philosophy alone [the gospel of Christ] to be safe and profitable."[47]

Justin poured over the Old Testament and the gospels and epistles circulating in the churches, soaking up God's holy Words.

A Brilliant Greek Scholar

Justin Martyr (Martyr was the surname name given to him after his death) was born in AD 100 to Greek parents in the Roman colony of *Flavia Neapolis* in ancient Judea. He was a brilliant scholar and philosopher who studied all of the Greek classics with an insatiable appetite for truth. First he was a disciple of Stoicism, then of the philosopher/mathematician Pythagoras and finally Plato, but nothing he pursued filled the void in his soul. No writings convinced him that he had found the essence of truth. Justin's journey finally took him to

Engraving of Justin Martyr by André Thévet.
Public domain.

46. Justin Martyr, "Dialogue with Trypho," *Ante-Nicene Fathers*, vol. I, chapter 7, Christian Classics Ethereal Library, http://www.ccel.org/ccel/schaff/anf01.viii.iv.vii.html.
47. Ibid., chapter 8.

the ancient shores of Ephesus in AD 132. There, on the beaches of the Mediterranean, he had his own "Damascus Road" experience and met the Lord and Savior Jesus Christ.

Justin the Greek philosopher became Justin the Christian philosopher, evangelist, and teacher. To his fellow philosophy students, to the pagans in the Roman elite, to the poor man on the street, Justin proclaimed that Jesus Christ was the entire divine *Logos*, the Word of God, and all of the truth that man needed. His message was clear. In the Greek philosophies only little traces of truth could be found, but in Jesus Christ he had found the embodiment of all truth. Christ came into the world, Justin announced, to reveal Himself as the truth and to save men and women from the power of demons and darkness.[48]

Bold as a Lion

We know that the gifts and callings of God are irrevocable. (See Romans 11:29.) Justin Martyr continued to function in his spiritual gift as a philosopher/teacher, but his philosophy had undergone a complete transformation! In spite of the accusations against Christians throughout the empire, the brilliant teacher was bold in the profession of his faith. In fact, Justin is the first great Christian *apologist*—a word taken from the Greek *apologia* which means "defender." The Holy Spirit used Justin's intellectual gifts to fearlessly defend the faith from heresies and to declare Christian truth to pagans and Christians alike. There are no coincidences or forgotten gifts in God's plan.

By AD 136, after several years of ministry in Ephesus, Justin set sail for Rome. He had a call on his life to confront the Roman Emperor with a defense of true Christianity. In Rome he established a school to teach Christian truth, he proclaimed the lordship of Jesus Christ in public without fear of the consequences, and he wrote his first defense of the Christian faith, not to his peers but to the emperor himself.

48. "Saint Justin Martyr," Encyclopedia Britannica, www.britannica.com/biography/Saint-Justin-Martyr.

Daring Letter to a Pagan Ruler

Justin Martyr's most famous letter is called the *First Apology*, written specifically to the Roman Emperor Antonius Pius and his adopted sons, Marcus Aurelius and Lucius Versus. In it, he fearlessly defended Christians from the charge of subversion against Rome. Christianity was not a threat to the empire, Justin insisted, and it should be treated as a legal religion:

> To the Emperor... and to the sacred senate, and to all the people of Rome, in the behalf of men of all ranks and nations unjustly loaded with public odium and oppression, I, Justin, son of Priscus and grandson of Bacchius.... I, who am one of this suffering multitude, humbly offer this Apology....
>
> For it is a maxim among us Christians that we cannot possibly suffer any real hurt, if we cannot be convicted of doing any real evil: "You may kill indeed, but you cannot hurt us."
>
> We pray the charge against Christians may be examined into, and if upon examination the allegations prove true, let them be punished accordingly, or rather do you who are the judges award the punishment.... But if nothing criminal can be made out against us, you cannot surely judge it reasonable to injure a harmless people barely upon an evil report.[49]

Having Church in the Second Century

Justin's letter to the emperor continues on, painting the picture of a Christian worship meeting in the second century. Does it sound familiar?

> And on the day called Sunday, all who live in cities or in the country gather together to one place, and the memoirs of the

49. Justin Martyr, *The First Apology*, edited by John Kaye (London: Griffith, Farran, Okeden, and Welsh, 1923; digitally archived at https://archive.org/stream/firstapologyofju00just#page/4/mode/2up), 1, 3.

apostles or the writings of the prophets are read, as long as time permits. Then, when the reader has ceased, the president [probably meaning "the one who is presiding," rather than being an official title] verbally instructs, and exhorts to the imitation of these good things.

Then we all rise together and pray, and, as we before said, when our prayer is ended, bread and wine and water are brought, and the president in like manner offers prayers and thanksgivings, according to his ability, and the people assent, saying, "Amen." And there is a distribution to each, and a participation of that over which thanks have been given, and to those who are absent a portion is sent by the deacons.

And they who are well-to-do and willing give what each thinks fit. What is collected is deposited with the president, who helps the orphans, widows and those who, through sickness or any other cause, are in need, and those who are in bonds and the strangers sojourning among us—in a word takes care of all who are in need.

But Sunday is the day on which we all hold our common assembly because it is the first day on which God, having wrought a change in the darkness and matter, made the world. Jesus Christ our Saviour on the same day rose from the dead. For he was crucified on the day before that of Saturn [i.e., the day before Saturday]; and on the day after that of Saturn, which is the day of the Sun, having appeared to his apostles and disciples, he taught them these things [what's contained in the rest of his defense of the faith], which we have submitted to you also for your consideration (*First Apology* 67).[50]

No Longer Living as Sinners

Justin was adamant: Christians should not be persecuted just for being Christians, and they also would not compromise their beliefs.

50. "Justin Martyr," Christian-History, http://www.christian-history.org/justin-martyr.html.

Jesus' followers, he told the emperor, had been transformed from children of darkness to children of light. Therefore, they would no longer worship pagan gods (demons in disguise) or live as sinners.

> It is certain we cannot justly be branded for atheists, we who worship the Creator of the universe, not with blood, libations, and incense...but we exalt Him to the best of our power with the rational service of prayers and praises...
>
> I could only wish you would follow our example, how by the persuasions of the Logos have revolted from these spiritual wickednesses and come over to the obedience of the only unbegotten God, though His Son Jesus Christ.[51]

Justin concluded his first apology, or defense, by eloquently and rationally requesting that the emperor no longer persecute the Christian believers living throughout his empire.

As Justin Martyr studied the Scriptures, the Holy Spirit revealed to him how Jesus Christ had fulfilled the Old Testament prophecies of the Messiah. Even today, believers still benefit from the insight the Holy Spirit revealed to him. Justin was the first Christian writer we know of to recognize a number of revelations in God's Word. He was the first to associate Satan with the serpent in the garden of Eden; the first to teach from John's Gospel that Jesus, as the Word of God, was *the only* Logos, and that everything was created through Him; the first to quote all four of the Gospels when teaching on the foundation of the Christian faith; the first to strongly defend the Holy Spirit as a full member of the Trinity; the first to proclaim that the four Gospels were an "accurate recording" of the fulfillment of Old Testament prophecy; and the first to tie the prophecy in Isaiah of a virgin giving birth to the account of Gabriel's visit with Mary in the Gospels of Matthew and Luke. Justin also recognized the connection between the prophecies in the book of Daniel and the book of Revelation concerning the appearance of the Antichrist and

---

51. Justin Martyr, *The First Apology*, edited by John Kaye, 16, 18.

the second coming of Jesus Christ. His writings brought great encouragement and strength to the body of Christ.

A Jealous Rival Brings Death

In AD 161 Antonius Pius died and Marcus Aurelius rose to the throne. Justin's *First Apology*, claiming that Christians were not a threat to the Roman Empire, had little effect on the new emperor as Christian persecution flared up in many provinces. Aurelius was a philosopher himself, and he was not impressed with the new teachings of this small sect of religious "nobodies" in his kingdom.

Bronze statue of Marcus Aurelius, Capitoline Hill, Rome.
Mari Marlcini\Thinkstock

Justin continued to boldly proclaim the truths of Christ in Rome, but he was attacked at every turn by a pagan philosopher and rival who had the emperor's ear. In AD 165, Justin was arrested and brought in chains to appear before the prefect (governor) of Rome, Junius Rusticus, along with six of Justin's Christian pupils, five men and one woman named Charito.

The Prefect Rusticus, from his lofty judgment seat, commanded, "Approach and sacrifice, all of you, to the gods." Justin standing tall before his accusers, replied, "No one in his right mind gives up piety for impiety."

"If you do not obey, you will be tortured without mercy," replied the prefect.

"Do as you wish," Justin and the martyrs standing beside him responded, "for we are Christians, and we do not sacrifice to idols."

The prefect read the sentence aloud to them: "Those who do not wish to sacrifice to the gods and to obey the emperor will be scourged and beheaded according to the laws." The seven martyrs were then taken to the Roman dungeon for scourging and afterward, still glorifying God, they were led to the Roman execution site to be beheaded.[52]

Justin Martyr was dead, but his famous writings survived for over eighteen hundred years. He was given the surname "Martyr" as an honor because his writings were such a great blessing to the infant church.

Justin Martyr was dead, but his famous writings survived for over eighteen hundred years. He was given the surname "Martyr" as an honor because his writings were such a great blessing to the infant church. God had deposited within him priceless treasures of biblical knowledge, and he sacrificed his life to share it. He had found a pearl of great price and gave all that he had to keep it: *"Again, the kingdom of heaven is like a merchant seeking beautiful pearls, who, when he had found one pearl of great price, went and sold all that he had and bought it"* (Matthew 13:45–46).

Women Face a Martyr's Death

Except for Nero's mass persecution in Rome, and an occasional woman like Charito in Justin Martyr's account, most of the first-century martyrs were men in Christian leadership. Now, in the middle of the

52. Marcus Dods, trans., *Ante-Nicene Fathers*, vol. 1, Alexander Roberts, et al., eds. (Buffalo, NY: Christian Literature Publishing Co., 1885), revised and edited for New Advent by Kevin Knight, http://www.newadvent.org/fathers/0133.htm (accessed April 25, 2016).

second century, women were singled out without receiving special consideration; they were condemned and martyred by Roman governors throughout the empire. Under the anointing of the Holy Spirit, the female confessors gave a powerful testimony of grace and strength in the face of a cruel enemy. Some of these women became well-known martyrs inspiring thousands to turn to the one true God. This was the case with Perpetua of Carthage, North Africa, and Blandina of Lyon, France, a physically handicapped servant who became the very unlikely heroine to begin our next chapter.

DEFEATING ROME'S DEATH SQUADS

4

DEFEATING ROME'S DEATH SQUADS

(AD 100–300)

Blandina and the Martyrs of Lyon

"Get away from here!" shouted the disheveled shopkeeper, viciously shoving the young mother against the wooden barricade. "You aren't permitted in my store! None of you are allowed in the marketplace!" The frightened young woman wrapped her tunic tightly around her waist, grabbed her two children by the hand and stumbled away as quickly as she could in a wild effort to escape.

"No Christians allowed!" screamed the foreboding signs on the public bath, the government buildings, the city amphitheater. "Christians forbidden!" announced the bright red banner hanging above the open marketplace. The Roman authorities, determined to put an end to the growing faith, banned Christians from all public places in the city. Any believer caught in the streets could be beaten or robbed with no recourse in court. Soon Christian homes were vandalized, and mocking crowds carried away favorite possessions.

The scene is eerily similar to the Nazi treatment of Jewish citizens in Germany and Poland in the late 1930s just before the beginning of World War II. It's similar—because the same diabolical enemy was at work twisting people's minds, unleashing a spirit of hatred and violence. In both cases, Satan did everything in his power to try to destroy God's plan for the church and for Israel.

This year of persecution was AD 177, under the reign of Marcus Aurelius. The location was Lugdunum, Gaul (modern-day Lyon), a beautiful city on the Rhone River in southeastern France. As the city prospered under Roman reign, the church of Jesus Christ grew as well. In retaliation, the fury of Satan swept through the city of Lyon and eventually the entire empire.

Accusations of Cannibalism and Incest

"The Christians are practicing cannibalism and incest in our cities!" The false rumor circulated like wildfire through the cities of Lyon and nearby Viennes. What could possibly be the reason for such a ridiculous accusation? Christians were known for sharing communion—"eating the body and drinking the blood of Jesus Christ" during their worship meetings. And married couples still addressed one another as "brother and sister," while all Christians greeted one another with a "holy kiss." These practices were twisted into a demonic lie. The pagans were enraged, because they believed the behavior of the Christians was violating the "piety" of the Roman gods!

Of course, Satan was the author of it all. As the Father of Lies (see John 8:44) and the accuser of the brethren (see Revelation 12:10), he incited the crowd against the Christians of Lyon. With vile cunning, he goaded the people into an uncontrollable frenzy until they were satisfied with nothing but the cruelest torture and execution of the Christian "atheists."

Pothinus, Bishop of Lyon

In August of AD 177, a large public festival was held in Lyon to celebrate the union of Gaul and Rome. Citizens dressed in the costumes of their favorite deities, and there was dancing and revelry. Daily they celebrated in the Amphitheater of the Three Gauls with sacrifices to the gods, gladiator combat, and wild animal games. But during the intoxicating stupor of celebration, there was an uproar in the amphitheater. A cry arose from the crowd: "The Christians have refused to join in the celebration! They dishonor the gods with their superstitious worship of Jesus the Nazarene. They must be brought to trial in the arena!"

Ruins of the Amphitheater of the Three Gauls in modern-day Lyons.
Arno\Wikimedia Commons

The first person arrested and imprisoned was the elderly Bishop Pothinus, who had steadfastly served the body of Christ in Lyon for decades. However, neither age nor frailty was pitied; the elderly Pothinus was delivered in chains to the governor while the raucous crowd shouted insults from the arena:

> The blessed Pothinus, who had been entrusted [as bishop] of Lyon, was dragged to the judgment seat. He was more than ninety years of age, and very infirm, scarcely indeed able to

> breathe because of physical weakness; but he was strengthened by spiritual zeal.... Though his body was worn out by old age and disease, his life was preserved that Christ might triumph in it....
>
> Those near him [in the arena] struck him with their hands and feet, regardless of his age; and those at a distance hurled at him whatever they could seize; all of them thinking that they would be guilty of great wickedness and impiety if any possible abuse were omitted. For thus they thought to avenge their own deities. Scarcely able to breathe, he was cast into prison and died after two days.[53]

In the end, it was the Lord's mercy that Pothinus died in prison and was spared "the fury of the heathen against the saints" that would take place in the amphitheater during the following days. The letter from Lyon contains one of the most graphic martyrdom accounts preserved from the early church. I am including excerpts from the eyewitnesses in their own words. The events are a travesty of justice beyond the understanding of most Western Christians.

Blandina, Fearless Maidservant

After Pothinus' death, the mob clamored for more of the "atheists" to be brought to the stadium. Roman guards went through the city of Lyon, seizing Christians each day until forty-eight were arrested and brutally dragged before the bloodthirsty crowd. Two servants of the Christians were also apprehended and tortured until they accused the Christians of practicing cannibalism and incest at their weekly meetings. The following is from a letter written by the church in Lyon which Eusebius recorded in his *History*:

53. Arthur Cushman McGiffert, trans., *Nicene and Post-Nicene Fathers*, Second Series, vol. 1, edited by Philip Schaff and Henry Wace (Buffalo, NY: Christian Literature Publishing Co., 1890), revised and edited for New Advent by Kevin Knight, http://www.newadvent.org/fathers/250105.htm.

When these accusations were reported, all the people raged like wild beasts against us, so that even if any had before been moderate on account of friendship, they were now exceedingly furious and gnashed their teeth against us. And that which was spoken by our Lord was fulfilled: "The time will come when whosoever kills you will think that he does God service." [See John 16:2.]...

But the whole wrath of the populace, and governor, and soldiers was aroused exceedingly against Sanctus, a deacon from Vienne, Maturus, a recent convert, and Attalus, a native of Pergamos where he was a pillar and foundation, and finally Blandina [a physically handicapped female servant], through whom Christ showed that things which appear mean and obscure and despicable to men are with God of great glory, through love toward him manifested in power, and not boasting in appearance.

Artist's rendition of Blandina.
Internet Archive\Wikimedia Commons

For while we all trembled...that on account of the weakness of her body, she would be unable to make bold confession, Blandina was filled with such power as to be delivered and raised above those who were torturing her by turns from morning till evening in every manner, so that they acknowledged that they were conquered, and could do nothing more to her. And they were astonished at her endurance, as her entire body was mangled and broken; and they testified that one of these forms of torture was sufficient to destroy life, not to speak of so many and so great sufferings.

But the blessed woman, like a noble athlete, renewed her strength in her confession; and her comfort and recreation and relief from the pain of her sufferings was in exclaiming, "I am a Christian, and there is nothing vile done by us."

...Blandina was suspended on a stake, and exposed to be devoured by the wild beasts who should attack her. And because she appeared as if hanging on a cross, and because of her earnest prayers, she inspired the combatants [the male prisoners] with great zeal. For they looked on her in her conflict, and beheld with their outward eyes, in the form of their sister, him who was crucified for them....

As none of the wild beasts at that time touched her, she was taken down from the stake, and cast again into prison. She was preserved thus for another contest....

After all these, on the last day of the contests, Blandina was again brought in, with Ponticus, a boy about fifteen years old. They had been brought every day to witness the sufferings of the others, and had been pressed to swear by the idols. But because they remained steadfast and despised them, the multitude became furious, so that they had no compassion for the youth of the boy nor respect for the sex of the woman.[54]

Even the torturers were wondering at this woman, who endured more than anyone believed possible.

Blandina and Ponticus encouraged each other to stand firm in their last hours, and when Ponticus died, Blandina even rejoiced that he was with the King. Blandina herself endured another round of torture, including being placed on a red-hot iron seat to be scorched before being tossed by a raging bull.

54. Ibid.

Surviving all of these horrors, she was finally killed with the sword by a Roman soldier. Even the torturers were wondering at this woman, who endured more than anyone believed possible. How did Blandina endure it all? Not by any strength that the world has to offer, but by the grace of God that fell upon her without measure.

Victory in Jesus!

Even after Blandina's death and the execution of all forty-eight of the Christian prisoners, the madness of the spectators continued! Desiring even further revenge, the angry citizens refused to allow the martyrs to be buried. Many corpses were thrown to the wild dogs while the people mocked, "Where is their God? What has their religion, which they have chosen rather than life, profited them?" Finally, the pagans burned all of the remaining bodies in a huge funeral pyre. Celebrating their "complete victory," they took the believers' ashes and swept them into the Rhone River, "so that no trace of them might ever appear on the earth."[55]

Why such inhumane cruelty to the very end? The crazed mob in Lyon was deceived. They thought that by burning the earthly bodies they could prevent these Christians from attaining their future hope of resurrection from the dead, because their bodies would not be buried in one place but rather reduced to ashes and scattered to the winds. How depraved and deceived the followers of Satan are. The ultimate victory always belongs to the Lord Jesus Christ and to His Word!

Consider 1 Thessalonians 4:16: "*For the Lord Himself will descend from heaven with a shout, with the voice of the archangel, and with the trumpet of God. And the dead in Christ will rise first.*" Satan just doesn't get it! Nothing can prevent the Word of God from being fulfilled or His church from being built up in the power of the Holy Spirit. As He declared in the book of Isaiah, "*So shall My word be that goes forth from My mouth; it shall not return to Me void, but it shall accomplish what I please,*

55. Ibid.

and it shall prosper in the thing for which I sent it" (Isaiah 55:11). The martyrs of Lyon *will be resurrected* at the coming of the Lord in glory, in spite of everything their persecutors had done to prevent it.

The Christians of Lyon, even after witnessing the horrors of the exhibition, believed that God and His people had gained the victory. Rather than cowering in fear to the authorities, they encouraged their fellow believers across the known world to remain strong in their faith. The account from Lyon ends: "Victorious over everything, they [the Witnesses] departed to God. Having always loved peace, and having commended peace to us they went in peace to God, leaving no sorrow to their mother, nor division or strife to the brethren, but joy and peace and concord and love."[56]

A portion of the Amphitheater of the Three Gauls still stands in Lyon today. There is a pole erected in the center of the arena as a memorial to the Christians who were martyred during this brutal persecution. It is hard to imagine, gazing at the stone ruins, that the crumbling seats once held the bloodthirsty citizens of Gaul and that the packed dirt of the arena was once covered with the blood of the saints.

The Zealous Missionaries of Gaul

After the horrifying spectacle of August AD 117 was over, persecution subsided in Gaul for a few decades. The martyrdom of these saints and the testimony of their love for God brought thousands of new believers to Christ. The Christian apologist Irenaeus of Smyrna, who heard the teachings of Polycarp as a youth, became the next bishop of Lyon. During the next twenty-five years, Irenaeus was a zealous leader of the Christian community, courageously preaching Jesus' word among the people of Gaul. He inspired countless Christian missionaries to venture out from Lyon to spread the gospel throughout the province of France, preaching eternal salvation in Christ and establishing new Christian communities.

56. Ibid.

In addition to evangelism, Irenaeus was well-known as a staunch defender against false teachings within the church. His most famous writing, *Against Heresies*, uncovered the lies of early Christian heresies, particularly Gnosticism, which Irenaeus considered the most dangerous heresy. While the Gnostics declared that they were Christians, they also denied that Jesus Christ had come to earth in the flesh, claiming He never had a material body that suffered, was crucified, and rose again. According to their heresy, Jesus had lived on the earth as a spiritual being only, not a physical one. For the Gnostics, salvation was available only for a select few who had *gnosis* or a "secret knowledge" of the spiritual world. Irenaeus staunchly repudiated this lie.

Missionary Martyrs: Irenaeus and Fabian

Unfortunately, in the year AD 202, as a result of the successful growth of the Christian message throughout Gaul, Irenaeus was also martyred in the Amphitheater of the Three Gauls in Lyon during the reign of Emperor Septimius Severus. Several decades later, Fabian, the bishop of Rome, sent "seven apostles as missionaries to the cities of Gaul," where they continued the work of the martyred bishop and established Christian communities throughout modern-day France.

In AD 240, Emperor Decius rose to the throne. Each new Roman emperor searched in vain for a successful way to stop the anointed spread of Christianity throughout the realm. Starting at the top, Decius ordered all Christian leaders to prove their loyalty to Rome by offering incense and worship to the Roman gods. Fabian, bishop of Rome, refused to submit to this idolatry. Decius was adamant and ready to make an example of Fabian to all Christians in the empire. Fabian was executed on January 20, AD 250, and buried in the catacombs of Rome. The Greek inscription on his tomb still survives today, and simply reads, "Fabian, Bishop, Martyr." The rest of his reward was given to Fabian in heaven.[57]

57. Francois P. G. Guizot, "Persecution of Christians in Gaul," *A History: Christianity*, edited by Robert A. Guisepi, http://history-world.org/persecution_of_the_christians_in.htm.

Many Christian leaders followed in Fabian's footsteps, refusing to obey Decius' edict and so signing their own death warrants. And still the church of Jesus Christ grew—for the gates of hell shall not prevail against it! (See Matthew 16:18.)

Perpetua and Felicity Face the Beasts

> *"And it shall come to pass in the last days, says God, that I will pour out of My Spirit on all flesh; your sons and your daughters shall prophesy, your young men shall see visions, your old men shall dream dreams."* (Joel 2:28; Acts 2:17)

One of the most inspiring stories of martyrdom in the early church is a firsthand account from the diary of a young Roman woman of Carthage, North Africa, who wrote from prison in the weeks before she met her death in the arena. Her name was Vibia Perpetua, and the words and visions she recorded have been read by Christians worldwide since she penned them over eighteen hundred years ago.

Her name was Vibia Perpetua, and the words and visions she recorded have been read by Christians worldwide since she penned them over eighteen hundred years ago.

At the dawn of the third century, Carthage was the second most prosperous and famed city in the Roman Empire, second only to Rome. Carthage was located at the northern tip of North Africa (modern-day Tunisia), and had been nearly leveled by Roman legions in 145 BC and then rebuilt by the Romans as a beautiful seaport entrance into Africa. By AD 203, the Roman governor, Hilarianus, in a political move to ingratiate himself with the Roman emperor, was planning a lavish birthday celebration in Carthage to honor the emperor's youngest son, Geta.

At the same time, the Christian church in Carthage was flourishing. One of the greatest early church theologians, Tertullian (AD 160–220), lived in Carthage and was an outspoken Christian teacher. He also wrote extensively on the power of the Holy Spirit and was the first Christian writer to use the Latin word *Trinity* to describe the relationship of the Father, Son, and Holy Spirit. He adamantly believed that the Holy Spirit's presence still moved among God's people in signs and wonders, in prophecies, and in visions.

Tertullian defended the Christian faith with the boldness of a lion. He wrote a daring letter to Governor Hilarianus, recorded in his *Apologeticus*, pointing out the growing presence of Christians and their importance in the productivity and growth of the Roman Empire. Even though Christianity was founded just a century earlier, he wrote that Christians "have filled every place among you—cities, islands, fortresses, towns, market places, the very camp, tribes, companies, palace, senate, forum—we have left nothing to you but the temples of your gods."[58]

Rome's Newest Attempt to "Wipe Out Christianity"

Rome, however, didn't care about the productivity of Christians. They felt that the upstart religion threatened the citizens' allegiance to Rome, and so Emperor Severus, like many before him, attempted once again to stamp it out. Rather than persecuting and making an example out of the Christians, Severus simply issued a new edict forbidding, by Roman law, anyone to become a new convert to Christianity.

In the early church, new disciples were required to become *catechumens* first—if they wanted to become Christians, they had to be instructed in the Scriptures and faith in Jesus before they could be baptized by water and added to the church. Now, under the new Roman law, anyone who was baptized as a Christian would be arrested and

58. Tertullian, quoted in Gregory P. Elder, "Evangelism in the Early Church," *Christian History* 57, 1998, https://www.christianhistoryinstitute.org/magazine/article/early-church-a-gallery-of-key-converts/.

executed. That is where our story of the brave young women, Perpetua and Felicity, begins.

Perpetua: a Powerful Roman Aristocrat

Artist's rendition of Perpetua.
Onbekende Venetiaanse Kunstenaar\Wikimedia Commons

Perpetua's testimony (also referred to as her "Passion") is an electrifying story of a young convert committed to following Jesus no matter the cost. Vibia Perpetua was a young, twenty-two-year-old Roman aristocrat and nursing mother. In Roman culture, fathers expected their daughters (even married ones) to take care of them in their old age, and the daughters were required to honor their fathers and to improve the family's social standing through marriage. In Perpetua's diary, however, no mention is made of her husband—but only her father. Perpetua bravely chose Jesus over the deepest family loyalties, over remaining alive to raise her infant son, over obeying her father, and even over retaining her noble position as a wife and mother in a wealthy Roman household. She stood upon Jesus' words to His disciples, "*Everyone who has left houses or brothers or sisters or father or mother or children or farms for My name's sake, will receive many times as much, and will inherit eternal life*" (Matthew 19:26 NASB).

Perpetua's testimony was also her slave Felicity's story. Their Christian love for one another and for Jesus became a powerful statement in Carthage that the ties of the Christian community were stronger than Roman laws regarding nobles and their slaves. Perpetua and Felicity, who was eight months pregnant at the time of her imprisonment, are presented as equals in martyrdom. In Christ, these young mothers transcended not only their maternal instincts but also the powerful Roman social structure. Just as Paul declared to the Galatian church, *"There is neither Jew nor Gentile, neither slave nor free, nor is there male and female, for you are all one in Christ Jesus"* (Galatians 3:28 NIV). This courageous noblewoman had truly become "a new creature in Christ!"

The Holy Spirit had been moving among the believers in Carthage, despite—or perhaps because of—brutal persecution at the hands of the Romans. When the group of martyrs including Perpetua and Felicity were first arrested, they were only placed under house arrest because they were still only catechumens and had not yet been baptized. If they decided not to be baptized by water and, instead, paid homage to the emperor, they would be set free.

The arrest of Perpetua.
Internet Book Image Archive\Wikimedia Commons

Just before her death, Perpetua handed over her personal writings from prison to an anonymous "editor." (Many scholars believe this editor was Tertullian.) Her writings and the eyewitness report of the executions have been saved for Christians today. The "Passion of Perpetua and Felicity" is actually the oldest writings by a Christian woman in existence. I pray you will be inspired as I was by the excerpts from the following pages.[59]

59. *Acts of the Christian Martyrs,* edited and translated by Herbert Musurillo (Oxford: Oxford University Press, 1972).

From Baptism to the Dungeon

Perpetua begins with a conversation she had with her father while she was still under house arrest:

> My father, out of love for me was trying to persuade me and shake my resolution. "Father," said I, "do you see this vase here, for example, or waterpot or whatever?" "Yes, I do," said he. And I told him: "Could it be called by any other name than what it is?" And he said: "No." "Well, so too I cannot be called anything other than what I am, a Christian." At this my father was so angered by the word "Christian" that he moved towards me as though he would pluck my eyes out. But he left it at that and departed, vanquished along with his diabolical arguments.

A few days after being put under house arrest, Perpetua and several others insisted on being baptized, even though it was only the fact that they were still catechumens that was keeping them from the dungeon. When the authorities found out, they imprisoned them:

> I was terrified, as I had never before been in such a dark hole. What a difficult time it was! With the crowd the heat was stifling; then there was the extortion of the soldiers; and to crown all, I was tortured with worry for my baby there.
>
> Then Tertius and Pomponius, those blessed deacons who tried to take care of us, bribed the soldiers to allow us to go to a better part of the prison to refresh ourselves for a few hours. Everyone then left that dungeon and shifted for himself. I nursed my baby, who was faint from hunger. In my anxiety I spoke to my mother about the child, I tried to comfort my brother, and I gave the child in their charge. I was in pain because I saw them suffering out of pity for me. These were the trials I had to endure for many days. Then I got permission for my baby to stay with me in prison. At once I recovered my health, relieved as I was of my worry and anxiety over the child. My prison had suddenly

> become a palace, so that I wanted to be there rather than anywhere else.[60]

While in the dungeon, Perpetua asked for a vision from the Lord, and He answered. "I saw a golden ladder of marvelous height, reaching up even to heaven, and very narrow, and under the ladder itself was crouching a dragon of enormous size, who lay in wait for those who ascended, and frightened them from the ascent.... And I said, 'In the name of the Lord Jesus Christ, he shall not hurt me.' And from under the ladder itself, as if in fear of me, he slowly lifted up his head; and as I trod upon the first step, I trod upon his head!"[61] After that, her vision ended with a welcome from a white-haired man into a beautiful field—it was heaven.

The interpretation of this vision was clear to Perpetua. Their imprisonment was going to result in torture and death for their faith. Yet, they would be blessed with the power to trample the head of the dragon (Satan) as true confessors of Jesus Christ—and they would be received with welcoming arms by the Great Shepherd and the saints waiting for them in heaven.

"I Am a Christian!"

A few days later, the prisoners were taken to the town hall to be interrogated. The governor asked, "Are you a Christian?" Perpetua simply replied, "I am a Christian." Each of the accused believers was thus questioned and each answer was the same. Once they finished, the disgusted governor condemned them to death by "wild beasts" at the royal celebration of Geta's birthday. The grace of Christ was resting on Perpetua because right after that she wrote: "We went down cheerfully to the dungeon!"

Even though her life ends in martyrdom, Perpetua's story reminds me of Joseph in Genesis 39–40. Like Joseph, she was arrested and

---

60. Ibid.
61. Ibid.

imprisoned for doing what was right in the sight of God. Once in prison, just like Joseph, Perpetua received favor from the overseers of the prison. She writes, "because of the great power of God among them," the guards moved the condemned Christians out of the darkest part of the dungeon into a brighter section of the prison where they could receive Christian visitors. Prison guards and pagan visitors were able to stand nearby and hear the gospel message from this new holding area as well.

Felicity and the Arena

Just days before they were to be martyred, Perpetua's slave, Felicity, was greatly distressed. Not because of the approaching martyrdom, but because she couldn't join the others. She was eight months pregnant and, by Roman law, she could not be executed until she had delivered the baby. Felicity dreaded separation from her fellow martyrs. If they went to the arena without her, she would still face the wild beasts weeks later, but this time she would have to face death with common criminals and not with her Christian friends. She asked the others to join her in fervent prayer: "Therefore, joining together their united cry, they poured forth their prayer to the Lord three days before the exhibition." Within hours, Felicity went into labor and later that day delivered a baby girl who she lovingly handed over to a sister in Christ to be raised as her own.

She was eight months pregnant and, by Roman law, she could not be executed until she had delivered the baby.

That night, the martyrs, four men along with Perpetua and Felicity, had their last meal. As the prisoners ate in the prison courtyard, they turned the meal into an agape feast, worshipping the Lord and celebrating their fellowship in Christ. Spectators who had lined up to watch the prisoners heard a final message of salvation in Christ and many walked away from the prison as believers.

The Day of Their Victory Shone Brightly

> The day of their victory dawned, and they marched from the prison to the amphitheatre joyfully as though they were going to heaven, with calm faces, trembling, if at all, with joy rather than fear. Perpetua went along with shining countenance and calm step, as the beloved of God, as a wife of Christ, putting down everyone's stare by her own intense gaze. With them also was Felicitas, glad that she had safely given birth so that now she could fight the beasts, going from one blood bath to another, from the midwife to the gladiator.[62]

A view from the chapel of Perpetua and Felicity in modern-day Carthage, Tunisia.
Verity Cridland\Flikr

The guards tried to force them to wear the robes and dresses of the Roman priests and priestesses, but Perpetua resisted so strongly that the military tribune relented. "We came to this [execution] of our own free will, that our freedom should not be violated," she said. "We agreed to pledge our lives provided that we would do no such thing [as worship an idol]." Her eloquence won the day.

62. Ibid.

As they were led out, Perpetua and Felicity, since they were women, were to be killed by a maddened female cow. Both of the women were tossed in the air by the cow, but they were only left dazed. Perpetua rose from the dusty arena floor first and offered Felicity her hand, raising her up in a gesture of sisterly love. The cow dashed away and the women were returned to the "Gate of Life" in the west entrance of the arena. Walking to the Gate, Perpetua looked at the Christian supporters standing nearby and encouraged them, "You must all stand fast in the faith and love one another, and do not be weakened by what we have gone through."

Since the beasts were no longer interested in attacking the martyrs, and it was time for the gladiator tournament to begin, Hilarianus put an end to the Christian exhibition and condemned the ones still alive to "die by the sword."

"Those who had not been killed by the beasts were called onto a scaffold to be beheaded. But they kissed one another first before ascending, that they might consummate their martyrdom with the kiss of peace." As Perpetua walked up the steps it was as though she was treading on the dragon's head one final time. Perpetua held her head high and walked in grace and peace. Unfortunately, the young gladiator who was performing the beheadings was inexperienced. His first blow to Perpetua did not kill her, and she had to guide his hand to her neck so the deed would be finished.

Perpetua and her fellow martyrs were dead. What would happen next to the church of Jesus Christ?

The Most Amazing Phenomena in History!

> It was unthinkable that a small, despised movement from a corner of [Judea] could move out to become the dominant faith of the mighty Roman Empire, an empire steeped in fiercely defended traditional pagan religions. The spread of the Christian

> church in its earliest centuries is one of the most amazing phenomena in all of human history.[63]

So how did the young faith ever make it? Bible scholars have marveled at the rapid growth of the Christian church in the first three centuries in spite of the difficult means of communication and the brutal persecution of the Roman Empire. But we have already looked at Jesus' sacred promise. *"**I will build my church** and the gates of hell shall not prevail against it"* (Matthew 16:18 ESV).

The Christian faith was born in the city of Jerusalem and spread from city to city along the Mediterranean Sea; it moved west beyond Italy to Britain, east into Greece, Syria and as far as India, south to Carthage and Alexandria in Africa, and north into the Balkan states and parts of Russia. The messengers of faith included missionary apostles, fleeing disciples, converted merchants, and common citizens of the empire. Each group had two things in common: a fervent love for Jesus Christ and the possibility of meeting persecution and martyrdom as they boldly spread their message of faith.

How the Church Grew

In his book, *The Rise of Christianity: How the Obscure, Marginal Jesus Movement Became the Dominant Religious Force in the Western World in a Few Centuries*, university professor Rodney Starkey created a model of how Christianity probably multiplied during the first three centuries of persecution. He based his model on the number of Christian believers who were added to the church as recorded in the book of Acts.

Starkey estimates that approximately 0.0126 percent (that's less than 1 percent) of the population in the Roman Empire was Christian by AD 100. This is a total of only 7,530 people out of roughly

63. Ken Curtis, Ph.D., "The Spread of the Early Church," Christianity.com, http://www.christianity.com/church/church-history/timeline/1-300/the-spread-of-the-early-church-11629561.html.

60 million in the empire! One hundred years later, by AD 200, this number would have risen to 0.36 percent (still less than 1 percent) or 217,795 people scattered throughout the Christian communities.

But their brute strength had been helpless when faced with the love of Christ in the hearts of His disciples.

But miraculously, from the time of Perpetua's death in AD 202 and through a hundred years of empire-wide persecution, by AD 300, the Christian disciples had reached double digit percentage figures. They now made up 10.5 percent of the Roman population, or 6,299,832 people! Fifty years later, following the reign of the Emperor Constantine I, Christianity was declared the official religion of the Roman Empire and the number had risen to over half of the Roman population.[64]

For nearly 1000 years (509 BC to AD 476), Rome's legions were the dominating world force, conquering every country in their path. But their brute strength had been helpless when faced with the love of Christ in the hearts of His disciples. These were men and women who fearlessly proclaimed God's offer of love, repentance and salvation in the name of Jesus Christ, His Son. And they stood on their confession of faith no matter what forces came against them! What a victory to the power of the gospel of Christ!

Unfortunately, even with over 6,000,000 Christians now living their faith throughout the empire, Christ's followers had to face one more period of Roman persecution, and it was the most severe of all. From AD 303–313, through the edicts of Emperor Diocletian, the Great Persecution was launched with one goal—to finally wipe the Christian church off the face of the earth.

64. Jonathan Hill, *The Crucible of Christianity* (Oxford, England: Lion Hudson, 2010), 82.

The Great Persecution

Now if we are children, then we are heirs—heirs of God and co-heirs with Christ, if indeed we share in his sufferings in order that we may also share in His glory. (Romans 8:17 NIV)

Galloping horses' hooves, clanking chain mail, and shouts from the Roman soldiers shattered the stillness of the night. Pounding up the hillside, the Praetorian guard came to a sudden stop outside of the Christian church of Nicomedia. Without warning, the doors of the church burst open. Emperor Diocletian's personal guards marched forcefully into the sanctuary, faces grim, helmets lowered over their foreheads as they brandished their axes high, striking everything in their path. The low benches and wooden altar were demolished in moments. "Find the writings!" the centurion shouted. "Heap them high in the center of the room!"

The angry Diocletian and his junior emperor, Galerius, sat astride their horses and watched as the church and all of its Scriptures and sacred writings were set on fire. As the golden flames rose in the night sky, Diocletian determined that this would be the first night of the annihilation of all Christian believers. It was February 23, AD 303, and the annual celebration of the god Terminalia. The cruel Roman emperors had decided that this night a new persecution would begin—one that would terminate the Christians.

The Great Persecution of AD 303–313 lasted for a brutal ten years and cost the lives of thousands of Christian disciples. Towns, churches, families fell to the sword and the flames of the ruthless Roman death squads. From one major city to the next, arrests and executions were performed in a frenzy, as though Satan was putting forth his last great effort to destroy the church.

One major reason for the madness was that the Roman Empire's golden years were passing quickly. As the fourth century progressed, Rome's enemies were growing stronger along its borders, especially the

Persians in the east and the Germanic barbarians in the west. Diocletian had ascended to the Roman throne in AD 285 and realized that one emperor could not handle all of the attacks from outside and within. He divided the empire in half—east and west—and set up a Roman Tetrarchy. A tetrarchy meant rule by four emperors, two senior emperors called *augusti* and two junior emperors called *caesars*. In the east, Domitian was the augustus and Galerius served as his caesar. In the west, Maximian was the augustus and Constantius (the father of Constantine, whom we shall meet again later) was the caesar.

Diocletian was a traditionalist who decided he would become the "restorer" of the golden days of the empire. He honored the old Olympic gods, particularly Jupiter, and adamantly believed that only the favor of the gods would bring back the glory of Rome. Seldom had a Roman emperor been more suspicious of the Christian citizens and their lack of loyalty to the throne. Diocletian was convinced that the Christian rejection of the Roman gods was the source of all Rome's troubles.

One of Diocletian's first acts as emperor was to purge the military of all believers in Jesus Christ. Perhaps Diocletian wouldn't have executed as many Christians as he did, but his caesar, Galerius, was a "passionate pagan," who continually goaded Diocletian to destroy the "superstitious Christian society" once and for all.

The Feast of Terminalia

On the eve of the Feast of Terminalia, on the last day of the Roman calendar, Diocletian and Galerius celebrated in Nicomedia (modern-day Izmit, Turkey), the capital city of the eastern empire. Finally giving in to Galerius' accusations against the Christians, Diocletian sent his pagan priests to consult the oracle of Apollos to determine the Christians' fate. When the priests returned they had no answer. "We can receive no message from the god because there is *interference* in the city," Diocletian became enraged! Galerius immediately claimed, "It is because of the Christians!" That was the night his troops rode out to destroy the church in Nicomedia and its written Scriptures.

After the Feast of Terminalia, Diocletian's first edict was published immediately: all Christian churches, Scriptures, and sacred writings were to be destroyed and all Christians were forbidden to worship together. As soon as the edict was posted in Nicomedia, a disciple by the name of Eutius tore it down in front of Roman guards and ripped it in half shouting that it was an edict from Satan! Eutius was immediately captured and executed, becoming the first martyr of the Diocletian Persecution.

After the Feast of Terminalia, Diocletian's first edict was published immediately: all Christian churches, Scriptures, and sacred writings were to be destroyed and all Christians were forbidden to worship together.

Within the next year, Diocletian issued three more edicts. The first imprisoned all church leaders, which left the prisons so full the Romans had to release the real criminals. By the second edict, some Christians were condemned to execution while others were to be maimed (losing their left foot and their right eye) and then sent off to the mines of Egypt to labor until death.[65]

Mass Executions Throughout the Eastern Empire

In the final edict, men, women, and children were gathered without mercy into public squares and forced to offer sacrifice to the gods or be executed. In one town in Phrygia, the entire town was burned to the ground and all of the Christians there perished in the flames. These edicts and mass executions were carried out in every region under Diocletian's' control. Miraculously, in the western regions under Constantius, the Christians were spared execution. After the first edict and the destruction of Christian churches, Constantius refused to carry out any of the remaining edicts.

65. "Under Diocletian," *Foxe's Book of Martyrs*, Bible Study Tools, http://www.biblestudytools.com/history/foxs-book-of-martyrs/the-tenth-persecution-under-diocletian-a-d-303.html.

Thousands died under the hands of the emperors of the east—so many that biblical scholars have never been able to confirm the total number. In addition to the innocent masses, history records that Christian officers, deacons, and leaders met their deaths at the hands of the Roman butchers. Here are but a few of the martyrs that have been named: Romanus, a Christian deacon of Nicomedia burnt alive; Sebastian of Gaul, an officer in the Roman guard beaten to death; Maximillian, a Roman officer who resigned his post and was beheaded; Vitus, a noble of Sicily, sacrificed to the gods by his own father; Victor of Marseilles, France, tortured on the rack and then crushed in a mill; Agrape, Chionia, and Irene, three sisters burnt alive in Thessalonica; Marcellinus, bishop of Rome who was tortured to death; Peter, bishop of Alexandria who was beheaded; Agnes, thirteen years of age, who was beheaded; Valentine, a priest, who was beheaded in Rome; and Erasmus, bishop of Campania, who was martyred. The list could go on and on.

Constantine Battles Under the Cross

By AD 305 Diocletian and Maximian had retired as co-emperors. The result was jealousy and years of war among the remaining caesars. In the end, Constantius' son Constantine took on the role of "rescuer" of the persecuted Christians. In AD 313 he and his legions moved against Maxentius who had proclaimed himself as emperor in Italy and was executing the Christians of Rome.

Before facing the vicious Maxentius in battle, Constantine prayed to the Christian God for help in defeating his enemy. Although Jesus may have been just another of the "many gods" to Constantine at the time, Constantine reported that the Lord answered him with a sign of a lighted cross in the sky and the message that read *In Hoc Signo Vinces*, which in Latin reads, "with this sign you will conquer." According to Eusebius' history, Constantine had a dream the next night where Jesus appeared with the same sign and directed Constantine to make the cross his battle standard.

Marching under the Christian banner, Constantine defeated Maxentius' troops at the Battle of the Milvian Bridge on the Tiber River. Maxentius fell victim to his own trap and drowned in the Tiber outside of Rome. When Constantine marched into Rome, he declared that the victory was due to help from the Christian God. Giving God the credit, Constantine refused the traditional triumphant parade up the Palatine Hill in Rome to honor Jupiter at his temple.

Constantine in battle.
Internet Book Images Archive\Wikimedia Archives

Shortly after, Constantine and his co-emperor, Licinius, signed the *Edict of Milan* which gave all Christians in the empire the freedom to worship and ordered the return of all of their church and personal property. The horror of death and dismemberment for the followers of Christ was finally over. Millions of Roman Christians were free to worship God in peace. All of the other Roman emperors in the tetrarchy who had so mercilessly executed the Christians met with a painful, fatal disease or death in battle while defending their title. By AD 324, Constantine had defeated Licinius as well and reigned as the sole emperor of Rome.

Many biblical scholars believe that, in his remaining years, Constantine became a true believer in Jesus Christ. He built huge churches or basilicas to honor Jesus' name and those who had been martyred for their faith.

We don't have the space in this book to compare the blessings and the mistakes of Constantine's rule. But we do know that in the beginning of his reign, it was a great victory and a blessed relief from centuries of brutal Roman persecution.

In the end, the church of Jesus Christ was triumphant over three hundred years of persecution and death. In spite of the evil intent of the persecutors and the number of Christians executed, Satan's tactics had failed to hold back the church of Jesus Christ.

> *For everyone who has been born of God overcomes the world. And this is the victory that has overcome the world—our faith. Who is it that overcomes the world except the one who believes that Jesus is the Son of God?* (1 John 5:4–5 ESV)

GOD NEVER PAUSES

5

GOD NEVER PAUSES

(AD 300-1300)

Despite persecution from the Roman Empire, the gospel continued to spread outward. Nothing can contain the good news! As the church grew in power, however, especially under the protective umbrella of Emperor Constantine and the Christian city of Constantinople, it gradually fell prey to Satan's more sneaky attacks in seasons of prosperity. It grew complacent, ungracious, and, as the Crusades prove, wildly misinterpreted the Bible. Many in the church had clearly lost their first love.

Yet I hold this against you: You have forsaken the love you had at first. Consider how far you have fallen! Repent and do the things you

> *did at first.... Whoever has ears, let them hear what the Spirit says to the churches. To the one who is victorious, I will give the right to eat from the tree of life, which is in the paradise of God."*
>
> (Revelation 2:4–5, 7 NIV)

These problems eventually gave rise to the Reformation in the fifteenth, sixteenth, and seventeenth centuries.

In every century before the Reformation, however, there were Christian men and women seeking truth, defying heresy, spreading the gospel to far-away lands, and cultivating the ground that would reap a rich harvest during the Reformation. And some were killed for their efforts. Here are a few of their stories beginning just before Constantine defeated Licinius and became the sole emperor of Rome.

Forty Martyrs in an Armenian Winter

Gregory of Nyssa slowly ascended the podium. It was March 10, AD 370, the Feast Day of the Forty Martyrs of Sebaste, and Gregory was standing in front of a hushed audience in the church of Caesarea that was dedicated to their memory—the Church of the Forty Martyrs. As the bishop of Nyssa, Gregory was well-known for his defense of the Nicene Creed and his theological writings on the Trinity and the infinite power of God. On this day, however, his sermon would not be scholarly; he would speak simply about the forty martyrs—and the encouragement they were to Christians everywhere.

Gregory of Nyssa, icon by Theophan the Greek in Anapausas Meteora. Public Domain.

Gregory's audience was well aware of the forty martyrs' testimonies. They were Roman soldiers in the prime of their youth who, fifty years earlier, had refused to worship pagan idols at the command of Licinus, co-ruler of Rome with Constantine I. The soldiers who defied the command "formed a battle rank because they were distinguished and fortified in the love of

Christ. These soldiers were confident in the Spirit's power and openly resisted the decree issued by such a brutal man." For that crime, they were sentenced to an exceptionally cruel death. Bishop Gregory spoke of them with reverence:

> When that cruel tyrant who issued such a harsh decree observed the saints' attitude, he cunningly matched it with passionate vengeance and planned a new, extraordinary torture for these intrepid souls. "If I menace them with the sword, they will not be disturbed and will refuse to submit. If I threaten them with other torments, they will bear them nobly. They are experienced in such things and will sustain blows and wounds because trained soldiers are accustomed to such hardships. If I devise other torments, they would bear them nobly and would remain unaffected by wounds and blows. These soldiers do not fear fire because they are constant." He was now compelled to find some torment designed to inflict sharp, prolonged pain.
>
> What did that crafty evil man devise against the saints? He carefully looked around until he found a place and time when they could be exposed to the hard climate of eastern European weather. The time was winter and the location, Armenia, a province known for its harsh climate.... In this place [Armenia], winter has not loosened the ground for sowing, and the harvest occurs when it begins to snow. Winds afflict the harvesters if they do not wear warm clothing for protection against the winds' violence. Late autumn and spring do not exist because the evil of winter sweeps it away.[66]

Gregory describes how the forty men were condemned to stand outside, on a frozen pond, without clothing, while, within easy reach, warm baths were prepared for their relief—if they would recant their Christian faith. "You must have your clothing removed and walk onto

66. Gregory of Nyssa, "The First Homily Concerning the Forty Martyrs," Documenta Catholica Omnia, http://www.documentacatholicaomnia.eu/.

the ice" the centurion commanded, "by order of the co-regent Licinius. If you will give up this Jesus Christ," the centurion sneered," and recant your faith, then you may take your place in the warm baths." Before a Roman guard could lay a hand on any of the prisoners, the men had stripped themselves and bravely marched out onto the pond, encouraging one another with stirring shouts as soldiers on the battlefield.

Suddenly, one lone man overcome by the cold raced to the warm baths to save his life. Now thirty-nine brave men stood with shoulders squared and chins held high trusting in the Holy Spirit to give them strength. One of the Roman guards, convicted on the spot by the faith of the Christian soldiers, threw off his clothes and joined them on the pond to die for Christ.

> They stood firm with trembling limbs, and their minds were constant before God in a struggle witnessed by angels, men and demons. The angels awaited the departure of their souls for the purpose of conducting them to their destiny. Men awaited their end and tested the endurance of their human nature to discover if their fear and hope for the future would triumph over pain. The demons were especially curious to see these athletes fall and come to ruin, but their expectations were dashed because God had strengthened them.[67]

One by one, the men succumbed to the cold and crumbled to the ice to die. After their death, the forty martyrs' bodies were burned, and their ashes were gathered by believers and buried in Christian love. Fortunately, as Gregory explained in his sermon, that was not the end of their influence:

> I wish to commemorate one person who spoke of their noble testimony because I am close to Ibora, the village and resting place of these forty martyrs' remains. Here the Romans keep a register of soldiers, one of whom was a guard ordered by his

67. Ibid.

> commander to protect against invasions, a practice common to soldiers in such remote areas. This man suffered from an injured foot which was later amputated. Being in the martyrs' resting place, he earnestly beseeched God [to heal him]. One night there appeared a man of venerable appearance in the company of others who said, "Oh soldier, do you want to be healed of your infirmity? Give me your foot that I may touch it." When he awoke from the dream, his foot was completely healed. He roused the other sleeping men because he was immediately cured and made whole. This man then began to proclaim the miracle performed [at the site of the martyrs' grave] and acknowledged the kindness bestowed by these fellow soldiers.[68]

Gregory was convicted and humbled by the testimony of the forty martyrs, and he wanted his audience to be, too. "I have mentioned this," he concluded his sermon, "for the purpose of strengthening our faith.... Let a Christian depend upon this hope, resist the devil's temptations, rise against evil men and the seething wrath of tyrants which resembles the sea's ferocity.... The bountiful grace of Christ is sufficient for every necessity and circumstance, to whom we should attribute all glory forever and ever. Amen."[69]

Let a Christian depend upon this hope, resist the devil's temptations, rise against evil men and the seething wrath of tyrants which resembles the sea's ferocity.

Gregory was a man of faith who strengthened the body of Christ in the early church. As the church became more prosperous, it became easier and easier to think that faith and earthly wealth go hand-in-hand. In contrast, Gregory preferred a life of quiet study, remaining a rather subdued, scholarly bishop for the rest of his life. His impassioned plea to not neglect the memory of

68. Ibid.
69. Ibid.

the martyrs is a mark of humility—surely it is a sign of a humble and thoughtful believer who seeks to learn from the suffering of believers who have come before. His actions echo Hebrews 12:1: "*Therefore we also, since we are surrounded by so great a cloud of witnesses, let us lay aside every weight, and the sin which so easily ensnares us, and let us run with endurance the race that is set before us.*"

Lives Mowed Down

Church of the Forty Martyrs in Aleppo, Syria in 2006. It is unknown whether the church still stands.
hovec\Flikr

After nearly two thousand years, this story still relates to us today. This testimony of the forty martyrs—although it has probably been elaborated upon throughout the centuries—is still treasured by Armenian Christians. Armenia officially became a Christian country in the year AD 301. Many Christians from Armenia would pilgrim to Jerusalem, and stay along the way in the city of Aleppo (modern-day Syria). In 1491, long after the church Gregory of Nyssa spoke in was gone, Armenian Christians built a new Church of the Forty Martyrs in Aleppo.

During the horrific Armenian Genocide of 1915, the Ottoman government barbarically wiped out the ethnic minority of the Armenians as well as Christian ethnic groups, and 1.5 million people were massacred. Many Armenian Christians who escaped fled to the city of Aleppo for safety. In the front of their Church of the Forty Martyrs, a monument was erected to remember the Armenian Genocide and the Christians who lost their lives.

Memorial to the martyrs inside the courtyard of the Church of the Forty Martyrs in Aleppo.
Preacherlad\Wikimedia Commons

What does this have to do with today? In the last years of the Syrian civil war, Aleppo, which was always a refuge for Arab Christians, has been ravaged by the forces fighting in Syria. As the fierce fighting continues today, it is unclear whether the Church of the Forty Martyrs still stands, but if it does, it is certainly significantly damaged.[70] Yet, even if the building has fallen, the same Holy Spirit who enabled those forty men to stand strong for Christ in the midst of persecution still enables the Christians of the Middle East today. Despite all that Satan has done to destroy it, Christianity is still alive! And not only alive—but growing. Our God is an everlasting God of promise!

And because of his glory and excellence, he has given us great and precious promises. These are the promises that enable you to share

70. "Aleppo's Forty Martyrs Church Compound Suffers Damage," *The Armenian Weekly*, April 29, 2015, http://armenianweekly.com/2015/04/29/forty-martyrs-destroyed/.

> *his divine nature and escape the world's corruption caused by human desires.* (2 Peter 1:3–4 NLT)

John Chrysostom

Constantinople was in an uproar. As the new capital of the Roman Empire, the city was a lush center of Christianity ever since Constantine the Great consecrated it in AD 330. The clergy were mostly well-fed, clever men who played in the politics and the intrigue of the church. The new bishop, however, was not an obvious choice. He had no friends in high power, and had not flattered, manipulated, or coerced his way to the top. He didn't even want the office of bishop—in fact, he had to be actually kidnapped from his post in Antioch and forcibly transferred to Constantinople to accept the post of bishop!

But Constantinople always wanted the best of the best, and John Chrysostom was famous for his bold, biblical preaching. His name, Chrysostom, meant "golden-tongue," and his sermons bore witness to his skill. As one biographer writes, "Chrysostom was a born orator, and from the very beginning conquered and charmed the people of Antioch. He is certainly one of the greatest of all the masters of rhetoric, whether sacred or profane."[71]

However, the city's religious officials soon realized that they might have gotten more than they bargained for. John Chrysostom's fame continued to spread, yes, but sometimes at the cost of the comfortable, rich church! Instead of living in opulence and throwing extravagant parties, like his predecessor, John Chrysostom sold the contents of his house, used the money for charity, and urged others to do the same.

> At the very outset of his career, when he first arrived at Constantinople, he was shocked by the laxity which had crept even into the ranks of the clergy; he wished to correct it without delay....

71. Aimé Puech, Mildred Partridge, trans., *Saint John Chrysostom* (London: Duckworth & Co., 1902, also available at https://archive.org/stream/StJohnChrysostom344-407#page/n9/mode/2up), 37.

> His predecessor Nectarius was a lordly bishop, who rivalled the civil authorities in display, kept open house, and spent enormous sums of money. Now, John's first act was to put up for sale the precious things which filled the bishop's house, to close the door against the idle and the men of the world; to make an end of the custom of those luxurious banquets.[72]

His actions were consistent with what he had preached his whole life. Raised a Christian in Antioch by a devout mother, John earnestly desired to live in seclusion in a life of prayer. But living alone in harsh conditions was too much for his health, so after a few years he returned to public life. However, he never lost the conviction that life is meant to be simple, gracious, and charitable. "Charity is the greatest of graces. Let us practice it, and we shall not be inferior to Peter and Paul despite all their miracles," he said in one message.[73]

John Chrysostom, icon by Dionisius.
Public Domain.

In Constantinople, John was unfathomably busy: in his first two years, he reformed the episcopal house and clergy, organized the church's charity, built hospitals, evangelized the areas surrounding the city, and spoke out against the Arian heresy. At the same time, he continued his weekly preaching, vehemently chastising the abuses of the rich and powerful in the city. "Amongst those who crowded to the church to hear his words, his special predilection was for the humble and simple, although he neglected no one."[74] It's no wonder that Constantinople, used to the lax leadership of the prior bishop, was in an uproar. John of

72. Ibid., 120–121.
73. John of Chrysostom, quoted in Puech, *Saint John Chrysostom*, 64.
74. Ibid., 56.

Chrysostom had become the champion of the common citizens, but he had also made many enemies.

Marched to Death

With little political tact, John easily offended rulers and governors. Over the years, the tension grew worse. Finally, "Theophilus, the archbishop of Alexandria, was able to call a council outside of Constantinople and, trumping up charges of heresy, had John deposed from office. John was sent into exile by Empress Eudoxia and Emperor Arcadius."[75] On June 20, 404, John said goodbye to the bishops and others who had been faithful to him and slipped out the door of his church, placing himself entirely into the hands of the officers. As they traveled, he was uncertain where he was to be exiled to, but finally learned it was Cucusus, in modern-day Turkey.

Painting of John Chrysostom by Pedro Orrente.
Photos.com\Thinkstock

The journey was cruel, made more so by bad health and by being poorly treated by bishops along the way. In a letter from Casaraea, he wrote, "I am quite broken down, dead a thousand times over. Those who will deliver these letters to you will be able to tell you about it better than anyone else, although they have only remained a little time with me. I could not even speak to them,

75. Mark Galli, ed., *131 Christians Everyone Should Know* (Nashville, TN: Broadman & Holman, 2000), 85.

so much exhausted was I by continual fever, despite which I had to travel day and night, tormented by the heat, worn out by sleeplessness, want of attendance, and of food. I have suffered, and still suffer worse than the criminals in the mines and prisons."[76]

At long last, he reached Cucusus, but his trials were not over. The second and third year of his exile there were worse than his first months. The climate was harsh, and his journeys were excruciating. His health continued to deteriorate. Many of the Christians of Constantinople were still devoted to him, and wrote to him frequently; this proved fatal. "He still appeared formidable to his enemies, and they decided to search for a new place of residence, where the exile, sent once more still further from home, would, perhaps, at last lose something of his indefatigable energy."[77]

In June of 407, John and two soldiers journeyed across Asia Minor once again, bound for a small town on the eastern shore of the Black Sea. In spite of his illness, the guards kept him moving under orders to wear the man down. Finally, in the little town of Comana, John's health was so depleted that they stopped and stayed overnight in a small chapel. In the morning, he was weak and begged to rest a few hours more, but the guards pressed on. Soon they realized that their captive was dying, and they retraced their steps to the chapel. Finally at the end of his journeys, John asked for a new garment, put it on, took Communion, and prayed. He died that same day at the age of sixty.

"This man was a martyr to the cause of Christian holiness, fidelity, and charity," a biographer wrote. "Not without imperfect elements, [his character] was at the same time so bathed in the spirit of Christian devotion, that the reputation of Chrysostom, placed as he was in the most difficult and trying places, and exposed to harsh and brutal criticism and opposition, has come down to us bright and spotless."[78]

---

76. John of Chrysostom, quoted in Puech, *Saint John Chrysostom, 174.*
77. Ibid., 181.
78. G. Frederick Wright, WM. G. Ballantine, and Frank H. Foster, eds. *The Bibliotheca Sacra*, vol. 47 (Oberlin, Ohio: E. J. Goodrich, 1890), 246.

Blessed is the one who perseveres under trial because, having stood the test, that person will receive the crown of life that the Lord has promised to those who love Him. (James 1:12 NIV)

Boniface

Boniface sat in the evening sunlight, reading. He was getting on in years, around seventy years old, and life as the apostle to Germany hadn't been easy. Attendants and fellow-missionaries bustled around him, preparing for a confirmation meeting, but Boniface sat, eyes glazing over, as he reflected on what he had accomplished—or rather, as he chided himself, what God had accomplished through him. The Germanic Christians organized into churches and connected to Rome. Monasteries founded where future missionaries and teachers were even now receiving instruction. Alliances formed with powerful leaders to forge peace. And, of course, the sacred oak of the Germanic god Thor at Geismar, chopped down with Boniface's own two hands when they held more strength than they did now.

Just then, a band of Frisian warriors [a violent tribe from the coastland of the Netherlands] burst into the camp waving swords and spears. The men around Boniface jumped for their weapons, but the old apostle stood up amid the clamor and yelled out to them. "Sons, cease fighting. Lay down your arms, for we are told in Scripture not to render evil for good but to overcome evil by good."[79] On that day, June 4, 754, Boniface was brutally killed by the Frisians, as were all of those with him.

Friend of Peace

Boniface was born to a noble family in Wessex, England, around AD 675, and named Wynfrid, or "friend of peace." Christianity was thriving at that time in Wessex, and Boniface received an excellent education in the Benedictine abbeys of Exeter. At age thirty, he was ordained a priest

79. C. H. Talbot, *The Anglo-Saxon Missionaries in Germany* (London and New York: Sheed and Ward, 1954), https://legacy.fordham.edu/halsall/basis/willibald-boniface.asp.

and became a missionary to the Frisian Saxons. In the early 700s, the Frisians governed much of the coastline in modern-day Netherlands and France. Radbod, the king of the Frisians, wanted nothing to do with Christianity. From 716–722, Boniface made two attempts to evangelize the Friesan Saxons but was largely unsuccessful.

Statue of Boniface in Fulda, Germany. Borisb17\Thinkstock

Realizing that he couldn't do this on his own, Boniface traveled to Rome to secure the church's support. While in Rome, his name was changed from Wynfrid to Boniface, and he was commissioned as a missionary to the Frisian lands. Radbod, in an effort to placate the nearby Franks, allowed Boniface to minister undisturbed. For the next ten years, 725–735, Boniface took advantage of the opportunity.

> Boniface was active in Thuringia, converting pagans and renewing the faith of Christians who had been converted earlier by Irish missionaries.... Boniface's handling of missionaries whose methods he deplored sheds light on his personality and temperament: he turned immediately to Rome, he expected prompt and ruthless action, and he seems at times to have been excessively severe in his judgments.[80]

80. Consuelo Maria Aherne, "Saint Boniface," *Encyclopedia Britannica*, https://www.britannica.com/biography/Saint-Boniface, accessed July 15, 2016.

Despite the fact that Boniface was too severe at times in his ministry, he undoubtedly unified the Christians in the regions where he labored and left behind many encouraging Christian writings. It is always helpful to see these men and women in light of the times they lived in. They ministered in the understanding of God that they had at the time. Boniface certainly could have been kinder and more interested in Frisian culture. However, despite his weaknesses, he was still used by God—and he possessed an energy that was amazing. I am encouraged by many of his writings, including this touching prayer attributed to him:

> Eternal God, the refuge and help of all your children,
> we praise you for all you have given us,
> for all you have done for us,
> for all that you are to us.
> In our weakness, you are strength,
> in our darkness, you are light,
> in our sorrow, you are comfort and peace.
> We cannot number your blessings,
> we cannot declare your love:
> For all your blessings we praise you.
> May we live as in your presence,
> and love the things that you love,
> and serve you in our daily lives;
> through Jesus Christ our Lord.[81]

Near the end of his life, Boniface requested to be buried at Fulda, one of the monasteries he had founded:

> There is a wooded place in the midst of a vast wilderness situated among the peoples to whom I am preaching. There I have placed a group of monks living under the rule of St. Benedict who are building a monastery. They are men of ascetic habits,

81. Ed Friedlander, "The Incident at Thor's Oak," Pathguy.com, http://www.pathguy.com/thorsoak.htm, accessed July 15, 2016.

> who abstain from meat and wine and spirits, keeping no servants, but are content with the labor of their own hands. This place I have acquired by honorable effort through the help of pious and God-fearing men, especially of Carloman, formerly King of the Franks, and have dedicated it in honor of the Holy Savior.
>
> Here I propose with your kind permission to rest my aged and worn body for a little time and after my death to be buried here. The four peoples [groups] to whom we have preached the Word of God by the grace of God dwell, as all know, round about this place, and as long as I have and retain my faculties I can with your support be useful to them.[82]

His wish was honored; after his violent martyrdom by the Frisian warriors, Boniface was laid to rest at the monastery in Fulda. And Christianity in Germany continued to grow.

First Missionary to the Muslims: Ramon Llull

One night Ramon Llull, a wealthy man who infamously loved wine, women, and song, was sitting in his opulent home on the island of Majorca, off the coast of modern Spain. Wasting his life in frivolity and pleasure, he was composing a new tune on his lute. His quick fingers couldn't keep up with his even quicker mind as he spun new poetry on the spot, intent on winning the heart of his latest lover in a long string of ladies at court. But then a vision came to him that changed his life forever. His biographer records:

> Suddenly, in the midst of the erotic song, he saw on his right hand the Savior hanging on His cross, the blood trickling from His hands and feet and brow, look reproachfully at him. Ray[mon], conscience-struck, started up; he could sing no more.... Eight

82. Boniface, "Letter to the Pope, 751," quoted in C. H. Talbot, *The Anglo-Saxon Missionaries in Germany* (London and New York: Sheed and Ward, 1954), 136, available at https://legacy.fordham.edu/halsall/basis/boniface-letters.asp.

> days after, he again attempted to finish the song and again took up the plea of an unrequited lover. But now again, as before, the image of Divine Love incarnate appeared—the agonized form of the Man of Sorrows. The dying eyes of the Savior were fixed on him mournfully, pleadingly.... Lull cast his lute aside, and threw himself on his bed, a prey to remorse.... He felt engraved on his heart, as it were, the great spectacle of divine Self-sacrifice.[83]

Ramon would later call this moment "his conversion to penitence." His focus was now on the painful acknowledgment of the wrong he had done to Christ. Thirty years old, with a wife and two children, a great deal of money, and a prestigious position as administrative head of the royal household of Aragon, Ramon realized with remorse that he had accomplished nothing—and worse, that he had hurt people he loved, as he explained in his prayer of confession:

> Trees bring forth every year flowers and fruit, each after their kind, whence mankind derive pleasure and profit. But thus it was not with me, sinful man that I am; for thirty years I brought forth no fruit in this world, I cumbered [made worse] the ground, nay, was noxious and hurtful to my friends and neighbors. Therefore, since a mere tree, which has neither intellect nor reason, is more fruitful than I have been, I am exceedingly ashamed and count myself worthy of great blame.

Ramon was distraught over his thirty wasted years, and didn't know where to turn or what to do.

A New Calling

At this point, at the end of the thirteenth century, the Crusades had been going on for two hundred years (1095–1291), had taken tens of thousands of lives, and created animosity between Christians and Muslims. (Western Christianity may feel distant from the act of

83. Samuel Zwemer, *Raymond Llull: First Missionary to the Moslems* (New York: Funk and Wagnalls, 1902), 34–36.

the Crusades, but to radical Islam, it is still a recent memory.)

On this map of Spain, you can see the island of Majorca (Mallorca) on the far right.
pavalena\Thinkstock

Ramon Llull lived on the Spanish island of Majorca, which, only three years before he was born, was taken by the Christians from the Muslims. By the time of his conversion, however, the crusading fervor was dying down. One-half of Spain was under Muslim rule. Northern Africa was quickly embracing it. The Christian Copts in Egypt were leaving their faith to join the Muslim conquerors.

One day after his conversion, during the festival of St. Francis of Assisi, Llull went to church and heard a Franciscan friar preach on the lifestyle and love of St. Francis. Like Llull, in his early years, Francis lived like the prodigal son, but, also like Llull, he received a vision of Christ and became a bearer of mercy in Jesus' name, tending the sick and preaching the gospel, eventually even to the Muslims.

Llull was set on fire. He now knew his life's purpose: to evangelize the Muslims of the Middle East, but not in the way of the Crusades. As he wrote,

> I see many knights going to the Holy Land beyond the seas… thinking…they can acquire it by force of arms; but in the end all are destroyed…. It seems to me that the conquest of the Holy Land ought not to he attempted except in the way in which Thou and Thine apostles acquired it, namely, by love and prayers, and the pouring out of tears and of blood.

To this end, Llull devised a three-part plan. First, learn Arabic, the language of the Muslims. Second, study Islamic literature and doctrine in order to defend the Christian faith with understanding and reason, instead of by force. And third, to be willing to die as a martyr to bring the Muslims to Christ. He gave away everything except what his family needed and withdrew from the world back to the island of Majorca, along with a slave who taught him Arabic. For nine years, Llull did nothing but study to prepare for his task. He studied Arabic, Hebrew, Latin, and his native Catalan. In that day, Islam was the religion of the learned, the scholars, and the scientists. He planned to be just as prepared as the scholars he would encounter.

> Llull knew that the presentation of the simple Gospel to scholars like these would not be enough to convince them. He set himself to read and understand their writings, and develop a detailed apologetic. He devised a complex philosophical system for persuading non-Christians of the truth of Christianity. He wanted to be able to answer convincingly any question or objection which could be put by Muslim or pagan."[84]

Llull Builds a Prototype of the First "Computer"

Llull's system, known as the *Ars magna,* used logic and complex mechanical techniques to connect and relate all forms of knowledge. Out of paper, he created a logical machine that could combine elements of thinking, represented by the twenty-eight letters of the Arabic alphabet, in order to reach answers to his questions. Scholars have recognized his invention as a computer prototype! "Llull is one of the first people who tried to make logical deductions in a mechanical rather than a mental way."[85] Today, Llull is remembered in history books for his contributions to logic, his scholarly use of the common Catalan language, and

84. Jack Voelkel, "Ramon Llull: From Profligate to Prophet," Urbana.org, July 16, 2014, https://urbana.org/go-and-do/missionary-biographies/profligate-prophet.
85. "Ramon Llull," history-computers.com, http://history-computer.com/Dreamers/Llull.html.

his prolific writing—over his lifetime, he wrote more than two hundred and fifty books! As Christians, however, we can remember him for his extraordinary love for the Muslim people.

First Trip: Debating the Muslims in Tunis

Ramon Llull was unusual for his high regard for Muslim nations at this time in history:

> The Christian world did not love Moslems in the thirteenth century, nor did they understand their religion. Marco Polo, a contemporary of Llull, wrote: "Marvel not that the Saracens [Muslims] hate the Christians; for the accursed law which Mohammed gave them commands them to do all the mischief in their power to all other descriptions of people, and especially to Christians."

In spite of the harsh feelings of others toward the Muslims, Llull knew he was following God's will; he took the time and interest to study their works, literature, and science, in order to be a more effective missionary. Not only that, but he also traveled all over Europe to promote his plan of converting the Muslims, not by Crusades, but through the work of missionaries. He received little support, but a great deal of attention.

In 1292, already sixty years old, Llull set out on his first missionary journey, and left Paris for Genoa—but there he encountered a true Jonah experience.

Overwhelmed with Terror

> At Genoa the story of Lull's life was not unknown. Men had heard with wonder of the miraculous conversion...and now it was whispered that he had devised a new and certain method for converting the "infidel" and was setting out all alone for the shores of Africa. The expectations of the people were raised to

> a high pitch. A vessel was found ready to sail for Africa.... The ship was lying in the harbor.... But at this juncture a change came over him. Lull says that he was "overwhelmed with terror at the thought of what might befall him."[86]

Llull hurried back to shore with his books and his trunks, too frightened to continue. But no sooner had the ship sailed than he was thrown into terrible remorse that quickly led to a fever.

Llull hurried back to shore with his books and his trunks, too frightened to continue. But no sooner had the ship sailed than he was thrown into terrible remorse that quickly led to a fever. Experiencing a "Jonah change of heart," as soon as he booked another passage, and stayed on board, his health once again improved and his peace of mind returned. Once he arrived in Tunis, the western center of the Muslim world, Llull got busy. He invited all the Muslim scholars to a conference and announced that he was willing to submit Christianity and Islam to a fair comparison. He even promised that if he was convinced, he would embrace Islam! The scholars were happy to agree. Remember, Llull was able to speak to them fluently in their own language because of his years of study. After a long, fruitless discussion, Llull stuck with two weak points of Islam: the lack of love in the being of Allah, and the lack of harmony in his attributes. Christianity, on the contrary, has both a loving God and the revelation of that love and goodness in the Person and sacrifice of Jesus Christ.

> This style of argument, whatever else may be thought of it, is orthodox and evangelical to the core.... The office of the cross is met everywhere in Llull's argument with the Moslems. He never built a rickety bridge out of planks of compromise.... The result

86. Zwemer, 82–83.

> proved it when persecution followed. There were some who accepted the truth and others who turned fanatics.[87]

Llull was thrown into prison, and one imam (religious leader) pointed out to the sultan of Tunis that it was dangerous to allow such a teacher to claim that there were errors in Islam. Another imam, however, argued that Llull's devotion was commendable, and recommended a release. Eventually, Llull was banished and a Muslim mob tried to stone him on his way to the boat! Contrast his courage here with his earlier fear in Genoa. Llull did not heed the conditions of his banishment right away; he returned to strengthen the faith of his converts before finally sailing to Europe. Over the next fifteen years, he tried to drum up likeminded followers for his cause in Naples, Rome, Paris, and Barcelona, all the while writing prolifically. His constant movement despite the harsh conditions of medieval life is proof of his tenacity and courage.

Statue of Ramon Llull on the island of Majorca, Spain.
Sebastian Hamm\Thinkstock

Second Trip: Bejaia in 1307

As Llull traveled throughout Europe, he also showed love to and labored on behalf of the despised Jews. In 1253, Jews were expelled from France. In 1290, they were expelled from England. Many were put to

87. Zwemer, 90–91.

death by the Spanish Inquisition, and few Christians dared to defend Jews in politics, even if they aided them in private.

> This despised race, however, was not outside the circle of Llull's love and interest. He wrote many books to prove to them their expected Messiah was none other than the Jesus of Nazareth. His great mission to the Saracens [Muslims] in Africa did not blind him to the needs of missions at home.[88]

Now in his mid-seventies, Llull traveled again to Bejaia, North Africa, a fortified seaport in modern-day Algeria. He immediately went to the public square and preached Christianity over Islam.

> Instantly, a mob gathered and attacked him. The authorities rescued him but then threw him into a dungeon, where he remained imprisoned for six months. While there he was bribed and tortured to entice him to recant his faith, but he steadfastly refused to deny Christ and continued to preach the Gospel even in prison. The Muslim authorities feared to bring him to court lest his arguments prove unanswerable, yet they hesitated to execute him because of his intellect and his favor with European kings. So they once again put him aboard a ship, this time well-guarded, and expelled him. Although shipwrecked on this journey, Llull survived and arrived in Pisa, Italy, a hero of the church.[89]

As a direct result of Llull's determination to reach the Muslims for Christ, in 1311, the Council of Vienne decreed that the universities of Paris, Salamanca, and Oxford should all teach Islamic languages and literature so that Christians could have a positive effect when sharing Christianity with Muslims. This was quite a victory for Llull who

---

88. Zwemer, 103.
89. Dr. Rex Butler, "Raymond Lull-Missionary to the Muslims," September 24, 2015, Gatekeeper Blog, New Orleans Baptist Theological Seminary, https://nobtsgatekeeper.wordpress.com/2015/09/24/raymond-lull-missionary-to-the-muslims-2/.

desperately desired a greater understanding among Christians of Islamic thought.

Third Trip: Again to Bejaia in 1314

Raymon Llull was now an old man, seventy-nine years old. His friends anticipated that after his victory in Viennes, he would surely rest on his laurels and live the rest of his days in peace and scholarship. But Llull had different ideas. He had no intention of dying as a philosopher: he wanted to die as a missionary.

> [Llull] longed not only for the martyr's crown, but also once more to see his little band of believers. Animated by these sentiments, he crossed over to [Bejaia] on August 14, and for nearly a whole year labored secretly among a little circle of converts, whom on his previous visits he had won over to the Christian faith.[90]

He ministered for over ten months, hiding, talking, and praying with Christians in Bejaia; urging them and others to remember God's unsurpassable love in Christ—the depth, breadth, and height of this love. Finally, tired of hiding, Llull made the move that he knew would bring his death.

On June 30, 1315, he walked into the open market, as he had done before, and proclaimed himself to be the Christian whom the city had banished. He preached Christ—not Mohammed—as the one and only way to heaven. The result is no surprise. An enraged mob grabbed him and dragged him out of the city. There, either by the command or the implicit agreement of the sultan, they stoned him.

Whether he died that day or was rescued, put on a ship, and died later on board from his wounds, is debated by biographers. One thing, however, is certain: Llull devoted his entire life from conversion on to the study and persuasion of God's salvation through Jesus Christ, and in the end, he gave his dying breath to proclaim that eternal truth.

90. Zwemer, 138–139.

To be stoned to death while preaching the love of Christ to Moslems—that was the fitting end for such a life. "Llull," says Noble, "was the greatest of medieval missionaries, perhaps the grandest of all missionaries from Paul to Carey and Livingstone. His career suggests those of Jonah the prophet, Paul the missionary, and Stephen the martyr."[91]

God's Work Never Pauses

Sometimes it's easy to ignore the Middle Ages. They're called the "Dark Ages" for a reason—it's a perception that not much good happened during those centuries until the light of the Renaissance and the Reformation. But it's important for Christians to realize that God's work is never put on "pause." He never takes a nap and lets the world spin out of control. For every minute since Christ walked here on earth, Christians have been diligently praying, studying, preaching, loving, working, and living. This chapter has highlighted a few lesser-known martyrs, but rest assured that there are many more that I could have written about! Despite the increasing corruption of the Roman church at that time, there were believers inside and outside the church doing the Lord's work with pure hearts. What a testament to God's faithfulness!

For every minute since Christ walked here on earth, Christians have been diligently praying, studying, preaching, loving, working, and living.

As the psalmist praised in Psalm 121, "*My help comes from the Lord, who made heaven and earth. He will not allow your foot to be moved; He who keeps you will not slumber. Behold, He who keeps Israel shall neither slumber nor sleep*" (verses 2–4).

This was true for the church in the Middle Ages, true for the Reformation church we will look at next, and true for the church today!

91. Zwemer, 146.

ONE THOUSAND YEARS TO FREEDOM

6

ONE THOUSAND YEARS TO FREEDOM

(AD 1300–1500)

John Wycliffe: "Ambassador of Light"

"The Gospel alone is sufficient to rule the lives of Christians everywhere...any additional rules made to govern men's conduct add nothing to the perfection already found in the Gospel of Jesus Christ."
—John Wycliffe, 1358

Manuscript scrolls filled with words that had been carefully translated from the sacred Scriptures lay on the carved wooden desk. Two men stood above the pages with eyes

A page from the manuscript of the John Wycliffe Bible translation. Notice the intricate detail!
Photos.com\Thinkstock

raised to heaven as tears of joy—and exhaustion—wound in slow rivers down their etched faces. "It is finished!" they breathed exultantly in the quiet sanctuary.

After years of labor, their dream was fulfilled. The Bible, both Old and New Testaments, had been translated into English, "the mother tongue" of the British islands. Soon English men and women would be pouring over the pages of the Holy Scripture, reading the words of Christ for themselves after centuries of spiritual darkness. No longer would the words of God's prophets and His Son be hidden from the body of Christ; no longer would they be available only in Latin and only to the clergy of the Catholic Church.

More than two centuries before the King James Version of the Bible was begun and one hundred years before Johannes Gutenberg invented the printing press, Oxford professor and Christian teacher John Wycliffe completed the first English translation of the Bible. Nicholas of Hereford, a fellow professor and friend, helped with the translation from the Latin into English. When they were finished, Wycliffe declared, "Englishmen will learn Christ's law best in English! Moses heard God's law in his own tongue and so did Christ's apostles!"

I have to admit that today we wouldn't recognize much of that early translation! It was written in the Middle English language of 1382, over six hundred years ago. Look at a comparison between Wycliffe's translation and the King James Version:[92]

92. Taken from "The Lord's Prayer in Middle English" http://www.ruf.rice.edu/~kemmer/Words04/ history/paternoster.html, accessed April 25, 2016.

Wycliffe:	King James Version:
Oure fadir that art in heuenes,	Our Father that art in heaven,
halewid be thi name;	hallowed be thy name;
thi kingdoom come to;	thy kingdom come;
be thi will don in erthe	thy will be done on earth
as it is in heuene…	as it is in heaven…

Still, history had been made. The first English Bible was complete. A vision had been fulfilled, but a war had also begun. A war that pitted not country against country, but spiritual kingdom against spiritual kingdom. A war that would engulf Europe in the flames of the Reformation for the next two hundred years. A war that would reveal the courage of Christ's true disciples who fearlessly faced martyrdom rather than deny the truth of biblical salvation in Jesus Christ.

A Holy Spirit Revelation

John Wycliffe spent years reading the Word of God, first the Latin Vulgate translation at the university and then his English translation. As he studied, the Holy Spirit opened his eyes to the apostasy and sin of the Roman Church. One hundred and fifty years before Martin Luther challenged the Catholic Church with his Ninety-Five Theses, the Holy Spirit revealed the depth of their hypocrisy and sin to John Wycliffe.

How had the church fallen into such darkness? It had been one thousand years since the last Christian martyr died in the Colosseum of Rome. After Constantine became the Roman emperor, Christian persecution ended and Christianity became the state religion of Rome. People became "Christians" to please the government or to be successful in business. Slowly, the church began its slide into complacency and then spiritual darkness. During these years, the Holy Spirit and the Word of God were so often hidden from the light.

During these dark years, church leadership became mired in a swamp of greed and sexual immorality. Murder, sexual promiscuity, robbery—the church hierarchy was full of sinful men who were enslaved by *"the lust of the flesh, the lust of the eyes, and the pride of life"* (1 John 2:16). Popes, cardinals, bishops, priests—many of them purchased their way into "spiritual leadership" just like Simon the sorcerer tried to do in the book of Acts:

> *And when Simon saw that through the laying on of the apostles' hands the Holy Spirit was given, he offered them money, saying, "Give me this power also, that anyone on whom I lay hands may receive the Holy Spirit." But Peter said to him, "Your money perish with you, because you thought that the gift of God could be purchased with money!"* (Acts 8:18–22)

Of course we saw in the last chapter that there were people who loved Jesus living among the wicked; the Holy Spirit has never left the world and a remnant of Christ's church has existed ever since the church was born on the day of Pentecost. But like a black tunnel which appears to have no end, the church had entered a deep well of spiritual darkness. Into this blackness the Holy Spirit sent John Wycliffe, God's ambassador of light.

The Truth of the Word

Through the revealing light of the Holy Spirit, Wycliffe understood that it was the Bible and not church law that was the sole foundation for Christian living. And he refused to be silent! Protesting the sin that engulfed the church, Wycliffe challenged teaching that wasn't supported by the Word of God. "All Christian life is to be measured by Scripture; by every word contained there!" Wycliffe declared. "No man is to be given credit just because of his authority [not even a bishop or a pope], unless he can show Scripture for the foundation of his opinion."[93]

93. Quotations in this section taken from chapter three of John Foxe, *Foxe's Book of Martyrs* (New Kensington, PA: Whitaker House, 1981), 50–67.

Portrait of John Wycliffe.
Photos.com\Thinkstock

Wycliffe wrote three booklets on the errors of the Catholic Church. The first was entitled "On the Truth of Holy Scripture" where he declared that any church doctrine or tradition not based on the Word of God was in error. "The New Testament is our full authority," he wrote, "and is open to the understanding of simple men concerning the points most needed for salvation."

In his works *On the Eucharist* and *On Apostasy,* Wycliffe declared in particular that transubstantiation, purgatory, and selling indulgences, were beliefs and practices in direct opposition to the Bible. Wycliffe's teachings caused a huge uproar among the Catholic leaders. They railed at him with threatening accusations, but he continued to spread God's truth throughout the universities and churches of London. Because of his bold witness, he was dismissed from his position at Oxford and threats were made on his life. Wycliffe fled England for Europe to continue to work on his Bible translation into English, secluded with just a few friends. He returned to England after the translation was complete.

The Truth Could No Longer Be Hidden!

As his writings increased in popularity, Wycliffe's followers increased, too—as did the anger of the Catholic hierarchy. Fortunately, John Wycliffe escaped martyrdom. But, the same thing can't be said for his followers, referred to as *Lollards,* which comes from an Old Dutch word meaning "mumbler" and was meant as a derogatory comment directed at Wycliffe's "uneducated" followers. For two centuries after his death in 1384, the Lollards faced persecution and death.

Fortunately, no matter how hard the Catholic clergy tried to force the people back into spiritual darkness, it was too late. The truths revealed to Wycliffe by the Holy Spirit could no longer be hidden. They spread like wildfire throughout all of Europe and became the rich soil for the growth of the Protestant Reformation.

Although Wycliffe was not martyred, I have included him as one of God's Generals here because all of the Reformers of the next two centuries built upon Wycliffe's teachings as they confronted the errors of the Roman Church. The Holy Spirit used this courageous and determined man of God to light a candle of "faith in Christ alone" that *did not go out* through two hundred years of persecution and death and *will not go out* until the Lord returns for His bride, the true church of Jesus Christ.

> "I am ready to defend my convictions even unto death. I have followed the sacred scriptures and the holy prophets."
>
> —John Wycliffe

William Sawtrey: First to Burn for Heresy

A solitary figure shuffled through the prison gates to a dark freedom, his shoulders slumped, his head hanging low. "I've denied the Lord's Word," he could be heard whispering over and over as he walked dejectedly through the town of Lynn in Norfolk, England. After four weeks of imprisonment, days of relentless examination by Bishop le Despenser, and cries of "heresy" from his fellow priests, William Sawtrey had broken down in exhaustion and denounced his Lollard beliefs.

To seal his rejection of Wycliffe's teachings, Sawtrey appeared in public before Bishop le Despenser and swore on the Gospels of Christ that he would never preach against the doctrines of the Catholic Church again. Fear had overwhelmed Sawtrey's heart, and the bitter taste of Satan's victory filled his mouth. As a young pastor, he had freely preached about Jesus' sacrifice on the cross as man's only means for salvation. But now, in fear, he had denied the gospel message and the writings of John Wycliffe, even though he knew they were God's truth.

A Dangerous Decision

The year was 1399, fifteen years after Wycliffe's death; Sawtrey had served as a Catholic priest in St. Margaret's Church in the town of Lynn, England. Soon after he denied the biblical teachings on salvation, a heartsick Sawtrey moved to London and was reassigned as the pastor at St. Osyth's Church. Preaching from the pulpit for two years, Sawtrey read and reread Wycliffe's English Bible and was convicted once again. He repented and began to preach again on salvation *in Christ alone,* this time without fear of the consequences.[94]

Heroes of the Reformation.
Internet Book Images Archive

This was a dangerous decision! In 1400, in response to the growing influence of Wycliffe and the Lollard uprising, King Henry IV and

94. "William Sawtrey," The Reformation, http://www.thereformation.info/sawtrey.htm, accessed August 8, 2016 .

the British Parliament passed a new law: The Statutes of Heresy. In them, Wycliffe's writings and the Lollard movement were denounced as heresy. The penalty for heresy was excommunication from the church (which was considered eternal damnation) and death by burning at the stake. Why such a horrific method for punishing those who disagreed with the church? Parliament's answer was clear: they wanted to strike fear in the hearts and minds of everyone else. This would be their position for the next one hundred and fifty years.

On February 12, 1401, William Sawtrey was ordered to appear before Archbishop Thomas Arundel of London. This time, under hours of cross-examination, Sawtrey stood firm in his faith, proclaiming that the Scriptures were the sole basis of Christian life and doctrine. Without fear, he denounced the sale of indulgences and the transformation of the communion bread into Christ's literal physical body. In response to worshiping statues, Sawtrey declared, "Instead of adoring the cross on which Christ suffered, *I adore Christ* who suffered on it."[95]

The First Lollard to be Executed

After a hasty trial and an unsuccessful appeal to Parliament for his freedom, on February 26, 1401, William Sawtrey was convicted of heresy and sentenced to die at the stake. Before his execution, he was put through a "degrading ceremony," a seven step process where the condemned was dressed in all of his priestly vestments and then stripped of them one by one as an act of dishonor. Remember, the earliest reformers were not planning to start a new denomination. They were Catholics, many of them priests, who wanted to change the church from within; their desire was to see the clergy repent of their error and embrace the Bible as the only foundation to life in Jesus Christ.

In March of 1401, a faithful William Sawtrey was taken to the Smithfield area of London as the first reformer to be burned alive for heresy. A large crowd of supporters walked solemnly behind him,

95. Ibid.

grieving for his death but encouraging him that he would join his Savior in heaven that very day. Remaining strong in Christ, Sawtrey was the first Lollard to be executed for his beliefs, but he would certainly not be the last.

The cruel death of William Sawtrey caused an uproar among his followers and a new wave of Lollard support swept through the cities and the villages of England. Students at Oxford took Wycliffe's teachings more seriously and many joined the Lollard ranks. John Oldcastle, a loyal knight and captain of the guard for the Prince of Wales, became a famous Lollard sympathizer who hid preachers from punishment and pleaded with King Henry IV to retract the laws against the Bible teachings. In spite of his friendship with the king, in 1417 a condemned John Oldcastle was hanged and then burned at the stake "gallows and all."[96]

The persecution continued, but in spite of the church's power, it could never overcome the power of the Holy Spirit alive in the hearts of men and women who were unbreakably committed to Christ.

John Hus: Courageous Warrior of the Word

"For whoever dies for Christ, he is a conqueror and is delivered from all misery and attains the eternal joy which it pleases our Savior to bring us."
—John Hus, 1415

Their embossed satin robes, high collared and adorned with large gold chains, were a stark contrast to the emaciated prisoner clothed in rags. The gold chains clanked as two bishops strode toward the man

96. "Sawtrey, William," *Dictionary of National Biography*, vol. 50 (London: Smith, Elder & Co. 1880), 381.

they held in such contempt. Shoving him backward, they jerked his chin up and jammed a paper cap on his head in disgust. Painted on the rounded hat were the fiery red words "This is a heretic" along with a picture of three fearsome devils, leering victoriously as if they had just received a condemned soul to hell.[97]

Thankfully, Satan had not really gained a victory that dark day in July of 1415. Although condemned by the Catholic cardinals and bishops surrounding him, the prisoner, John Hus, was not facing eternal damnation for his confession of salvation in Jesus Christ alone. Instead, he was about to receive his heavenly reward for fighting the good fight of faith and proclaiming truth in Jesus' name.

Mighty as a Two-Edged Sword

John Hus wanted to confess his faith before his accusers. Even though he was condemned by his confession, just like the early church martyrs, he was eager to testify, eager to share the life-transforming truth of God's Word. Hus knew that the Scriptures were alive and could be wielded like a *"two-edged sword"* (Hebrews 4:12) to convict his merciless captors of their errors.

Sadly, John Hus was denied the freedom to speak at his trial. Instead, he was convicted on his writings against the errant practices of the Catholic Church. John Hus' voice was silenced because of fear—fear that the people's hearts would turn from the corrupt traditions of men to the infallible freedom of God's Word.

Hus Sets Europe Ablaze

John Hus was born to a peasant family in a small village in southern Bohemia (modern-day Czech Republic), in 1372. Due to his mother's diligence and prayer, he received a valuable education and eventually went to the University of Prague where he studied and received his bachelor and master's degrees in theology by 1396. While reading the

97. John Foxe, *Foxe's Book of Martyrs*, 131.

Bible in Latin, Hus discovered the grace and salvation of faith in Jesus Christ.[98]

Bethlehem Church, where John Hus preached, still stands today in Prague.
Murmakova\Thinkstock

In the meantime, the writings of John Wycliffe had spread rapidly from England to central Europe, and, by God's grace, they came across Hus' desk. His spirit was renewed by the truth of Wycliffe's teachings. He spent many evenings discussing the stark contrasts between the Scriptures and the church's practices with a small group of university friends, including Stephen Palec and an instructor named Stanislav. Years later, these same "kindred brothers" would betray John Hus before the cardinals of Europe.

In the first years of his ministry, Hus was an up-and-coming clergyman, assigned as the parish priest in Bethlehem Church, which had

98. You can read about Hus' life in greater detail in my book *God's Generals: The Reformers* (New Kensington, PA: Whitaker House, 2003).

a three-thousand-seat sanctuary in the center of Prague. He was commended by the Catholic bishops as a strong theologian and preacher. But that changed quickly when he was introduced to the truths in God's Word. From 1403 to 1409, Hus' reputation as a reformer grew. Every day, he preached a message either from his pulpit or the university classroom, exposing the error of the church's practices of prohibiting lay people from reading the Bible, selling indulgences to gain "salvation," and insisting that Jesus' life was sacrificed again in every celebration of Communion.

Forbidden to Preach

Believe it or not, in the Middle Ages, many parish priests had never even read the Bible. Instead they stood in their pulpits preaching "fables and fanciful stories." Determined to preach only the truth, Hus taught directly from the Czech Bible and trained his university students to do the same. "Preach the Bible," he would exhort them, "not some entertainment or fables or plundering lies."[99]

In 1410, alarmed by the spread of Wycliffe's messages throughout Europe, Pope John XXIII (not the modern pope by the same name) issued a papal order banning all of Wycliffe's books and teachings and forbidding the free preaching of God's Word by men like Hus and his students.[100] The city of Prague, from the wealthiest leaders to the poorest shopkeepers, was in turmoil. The country of Bohemia was full of Wycliffe and Hus supporters.

With Christian support rallied around him, Hus ignored the ban and preached on salvation in Christ with an even greater boldness. He renounced the excesses of the Catholic clergy and their sins of sexual immorality and greed, and he encouraged the people to love God with their whole heart.

Hus insisted on preaching in the Czech language, instead of holding mass in Latin, so that even the least educated could understand the

99. See *God's Generals: The Reformers*.
100. John Foxe, *Foxe's Book of Martyrs*, 91.

gospel message. The Bethlehem Church, which had become the center of the Czech reform movement, was filled to capacity and beyond in every service.

Excommunicated but Still Preaching

Soon after the ban, the pope declared war on a prince in Italy. Because wars are costly, the pope needed to raise some quick funds, so he started selling more indulgences—church assurances of eternal salvation. Hus and his followers began to protest and threatened a rebellion. It was the last straw for the church leaders; John Hus was excommunicated from the Catholic Church. He was considered an outcast and his parishioners were forbidden to even speak to him under threat of excommunication.

Hus went into hiding to protect his followers. During his seclusion, he wrote a book entitled *On the Church*, a compilation of his teachings on the true church under the headship of Jesus Christ and the critical need for repentance by the Catholic clergy.[101]

The Betrayal of a Friend

While Hus believed his seclusion was a safe haven, the Catholic archbishops and King Sigismund of Germany were secretly plotting to eliminate him once and for all, and invited him to the Council of Constance in Germany. Hus was assured the king's promise of safe passage to present his case before the pope, cardinals, and archbishops that were gathered for the conference. In October of 1414, full of hope in Christ, Hus left for Constance under the protection of the king's knights. In the weeks it took to make the trip, Hus' supporters greeted him with enthusiasm in towns all along the way.

Meanwhile, behind the scenes, his old university friends, Palec and Stanislav, had betrayed Hus, writing accusations of heresy to the pope against him. Not long after Hus arrived in Constance, the trickery of

101. Ibid., 94–95.

For four months with little food or care, Hus waited for the promised opportunity to present his defense before the council—but it never came.

the council was revealed. Hus was deceived into accompanying one cardinal to a special church meeting but instead was captured by Sigismund's guards and imprisoned in a dungeon in the local abbey. For four months with little food or care, Hus waited for the promised opportunity to present his defense before the council—but it never came.[102]

By God's Grace I am Truly a Christian

Six months after his capture, in June of 1415, an emaciated Hus was transported from the dank dungeon to the council hall. There, resplendent in their robes and crowns, sat the pompous charlatans. Instead of being able to defend himself before his accusers with God's Word, however, Hus was only permitted to answer yes or no to their questions. Day after day he was dragged from the dungeon to the council and forced to answer the same accusations over again. The bishops badgered Hus to recant, to save his life and his eternal soul; but even in his sickly state, Hus had the strength in Christ to stand his ground.

The last day of Hus' trial was on June 8, 1415. The cardinals sat in full regalia on seats like thrones, with an army of bishops surrounding them, and read Hus' statements from his book *On the Church*. To his persecutors, Hus' writings against the church's false practices were enough to condemn him to death. When accused of not being a true Christian, Hus responded, "I hope by God's grace that I am truly a Christian, not deviating from the faith. I would rather suffer the penalty of a terrible death than wish to affirm anything outside of the faith or transgress the commandments of our Lord Jesus Christ."[103] Despite his

102. Ibid., 105.
103. Ibid., 121–122.

humble attitude and contrite heart, John Hus was condemned to burn at the stake.

"I Will Die This Day with Gladness"

After being disrobed of everything but his tunic, and with the devilish paper hat planted firmly on his bleeding head, that same day, June 8, 1415, Hus was led to the stake under armed guard for fear that his followers would stage an uprising. Seeing the stake with the wood and straw piled high around it, Hus dropped to his knees to pray and commit himself once more to the living God. His hands were tied behind his back with ropes and his neck was attached to the stake with a chain.

Monument dedicated to John Hus in Prague, Czech Republic.
Kaetana_istock\Thinkstock

Hus was given a final moment to recant, but he firmly declined. His reply was heard clearly by the large crowd of supporters that came to offer him strength, "God is my witness that I have never taught that of which I have been accused by false witnesses. In the truth of the

Gospel which I have written, taught and preached, I will die today with gladness."[104]

In a final blow of vindictiveness, the kindling used for the fire was John Wycliffe's manuscripts. With the straw and wood piled all the way to Hus' neck, he greeted the flames by singing, "Christ, thou Son of the living God, have mercy upon me." Once he was dead, they burned the rest of his body to ashes, and, just like the early Christian martyrs, his ashes were scattered into the Rhine River. Satan's tactics had not changed in one thousand years. He was still trying to wipe every trace of the saints of God from the face of the earth, but he *could not* win the victory.

> *For we do not wrestle against flesh and blood, but against the rulers, against the authorities, against the cosmic powers over this present darkness, against the spiritual forces of evil in the heavenly places. Therefore take up the whole armor of God, that you may be able to withstand in the evil day, and having done all, to stand firm.*
>
> (Ephesians 6:12–13 ESV)

Some sources record that just before he died Hus uttered a prophetic word: "In one hundred years, God will raise up a man whose calls for reform cannot be suppressed." One hundred years later, in October of 1517, John Hus' prophecy was fulfilled. Martin Luther nailed his Ninety-Five Theses to the door of the Wittenberg Church and Jesus Christ's church has never been the same.

To the very end, Hus was burdened for the spiritual condition of his fellow priests. His last prayer was for their eternal salvation. What a lesson in forgiveness for all of us!

> *O Lord, Jesus Christ, into thine hands I deliver my soul, which Thou hast redeemed with Thy blood. Father in heaven, do not hold against them the sins which my enemies commit against me, and let my eyes see them blissfully with Thee, when their souls fly to Thy throne after*

104. Ibid.

an easy death. Oh Holy Spirit, enlighten their deceived hearts, so that the truth of the holy Gospel may open their eyes and its praise be spread everywhere, forever and ever, Amen.[105]

Portrait of William Tyndale.
Public domain.

William Tyndale: God's Anointed Translator

"Christ is with us until the world's end. Let His little flock be bold therefore. For if God be on our side, what does it matter who is against us, be they bishops, cardinals, popes or whatsoever names they will."
—William Tyndale, 1535

105. Ibid., 128.

William Tyndale stood at the bow of the ship as she raised her sails and gained wind in the English Channel. Behind him lay the rocky shores of his beloved England, a land that had become increasingly hostile to him in recent years. There was no room for him anywhere in England to fulfill the passion of his heart—to place an English New Testament into the hands of every person in the land, from the wealthy merchant to the poor ploughboy.

Landing on the shores of the continent, Tyndale traveled into central Europe until he reached Hamburg and then on to Wittenberg, Germany. With great anticipation, he met Martin Luther for the first time. Safely hidden among the Lutheran supporters of Europe, Tyndale traveled to Antwerp, Holland, where he could complete his lifelong dream, the translation of the Bible from the original Greek and Hebrew into the English language.

God Prepares a Scholar

There are amazingly gifted Bible translators who are blessed with the ability to write and speak in multiple languages. William Tyndale was one of those men. He was born in 1494, just south of Gloucestershire, England, and became a student at Oxford University as a young man, receiving his master's degree in 1517 at the early age of twenty-one. He attended Cambridge University as well, studying for the priesthood with the great scholars of England. Even as a young man, Tyndale was fluent in eight languages: Hebrew, Latin, Greek, Italian, Spanish, French, English and German.

Since he was so gifted academically, Tyndale could have risen to a high rank within the Catholic hierarchy except for one thing. As he read the Latin Scriptures at Oxford, he was awakened by the Holy Spirit to the true gospel message—Christ's gift of eternal salvation was not earned by anything that the church offered or any indulgence a man purchased. *"For by grace you have been saved through faith, and that not of yourselves; it is the gift of God, not of works, lest anyone should boast"*

(Ephesians 2:8–9). Tyndale had a new focus for life—getting this message into the hands of the common people through an English translation of the Bible directly from the original Hebrew and Greek.

Tyndale recognized his important calling: "He perceived that it was not possible to establish the lay people in any truth, [unless] the Scriptures were so plainly laid before their eyes in their mother tongue, that they might see the meaning of the text."[106]

"We Would Be Better Without God's Laws"

In 1523, Tyndale traveled to London, naively believing that the bishop of London, Cuthbert Tunstall, would give his blessing for an English Bible translation. As early as 1297, a French translation of the Bible was written, followed by a Czech Bible in 1360, and a German Bible in 1466. At that moment in Wittenberg, Germany, Martin Luther was working on his new German translation called the *Luther Bible*. The *Luther New Testament* had already been printed by Gutenberg's press and widely distributed just a year earlier. Surely, thought Tyndale, England's leaders with their strong support of academics and the church would want a Bible in the English language. But he was greatly mistaken; Tunstall soundly rejected the idea.

Shortly after, Tyndale was talking to a priest who gruffly scolded Tyndale for his pursuit of the Bible. "We would be better without God's laws than the Pope's!" Tyndale responded defiantly: "I defy the Pope, and all his laws, and, if God spares my life, before many years, I will cause the boy that drives the plow to know more of the scriptures that thou dost!"[107]

Tyndale had no choice. After this outspoken remark, he fled England for Germany for his personal safety and to fulfill God's call. Just like Abraham left his homeland thousands of years ago, Christians are often called by the Lord to leave familiar places and people to embark

106. Ibid., 129.
107. Ibid., 138–139.

on a new journey for Christ. God plants His plans and purposes in our hearts and then works out the details so that we can fulfill them. *"For it is God who works in you, both to will and to do for His good pleasure"* (Philippians 2:13). This was God's plan for Wycliffe and his Bible translation.

Smuggling Bibles into England

There were several cities in Europe where Martin Luther's teachings had been accepted and Tyndale could work in relative safety, although his exact lodgings were always kept a secret. In Antwerp he worked day and night on the Bible translation. Two years later, six thousand copies of the English New Testament were produced by printer Peter Schoeffer in Worms, Germany, and smuggled into England and Scotland. What a time of rejoicing for the people who could read English! This translation was even clearer than Wycliffe's had been. I believe that they wept as they read the Word of God in their own language!

In Antwerp he worked day and night on the Bible translation. Two years later, six thousand copies of the English New Testament were produced.

Obviously, the New Testaments were not well-received in Tyndale's home country. Both the king and the church leaders were furious! Palace and church guards were sent out into the cities and villages to confiscate the new Bibles wherever they could find them. Tyndale was openly condemned in London as a heretic.

In a somewhat humorous turn of events, a secret supporter of Tyndale, Augustine Packington, overheard Tunstall threatening to buy all of the English Testaments to burn them. Packington offered to find and buy the New Testaments and deliver them directly to Tunstall's doorstep. When the Testaments arrived, the bishop paid Packington a high selling price and then threw the books into a raging bonfire. Packington immediately sent all of the money to Tyndale who then printed thousands of copies of a newly revised edition and smuggled those New Testaments back into England![108] Before long, Tunstall was confronted with his embarrassing mistake. Satan's fury raged, but Christ's work continued to move on!

For nine years, Tyndale was safely hidden in Antwerp working on the Old Testament translation with the help of a university friend, Myles Coverdale. Tyndale's translations also included his personal commentaries that pointed out the specific errors of the church doctrines. Those commentaries angered the Catholic Church even more than the event of the translation. In 1530 Tyndale wrote a pamphlet soundly denouncing King Henry VIII's divorce from Catherine of Aragon to marry Anne Boleyn. Now, Tyndale was accused as a heretic by both the Catholic Church and King Henry the VIII and his newly established Church of England.

The Wiles of the Betrayer

Tyndale was so focused on the Word of God that he was naive to the wickedness of the world. In spite of his gifted intellect, he was a humble and trusting man who had few suspicions about the ongoing plot to destroy him. Tyndale couldn't comprehend the desperation of church leaders to protect their man-made kingdom and to keep people in the dark with "vain superstitions and false doctrine." Tyndale's supporters understood the wickedness of the Lord's enemies who were combing Europe for Tyndale, and they kept him hidden in safe houses throughout Germany and Belgium. He was completing his translation work at the home of Thomas Pointz, a Christian merchant in Antwerp.

Occasionally, Tyndale left his lodgings for a quiet dinner with Pointz and fellow merchants of the city. One evening a man named Henry Phillips joined their group and appeared to share Tyndale's excitement for the Word of God. Within days, Tyndale had taken Phillips into his

108. Ibid., 142–144.

confidence, showing him his current work on the Old Testament and his commentaries on salvation in Christ. Pointz was suspicious of the quickly formed friendship and questioned Phillips closely on his next visit. Still uneasy, Pointz left Antwerp for a month-long business trip.

Emperor Charles V (considered the Holy Roman Emperor of most of central Europe) held his royal court in the city of Brussels just twenty-four miles away from Antwerp. Phillips secretly traveled to the emperor's court with the victorious news that he had discovered the hiding place of the heretic William Tyndale. To this day, no one knows who Phillips was actually spying for—the pope, the emperor, or King Henry VIII. What is certain is that Phillips returned triumphantly to Antwerp with the emperor's High Counselor and a detail of palace guards.

The next day, Phillips paid a visit to Tyndale allegedly to talk to him about his work before inviting him to dinner. As Phillips and Tyndale left Pointz' home, they walked through a long narrow entryway out to the street. Phillips walked behind the kindly Bible translator until they neared the roadway, and then he stealthily pointed Tyndale out to the guards standing in wait. As soon as Tyndale stepped foot on the public street, the soldiers seized him roughly and placed him under arrest.[109]

A Black Dungeon and Death

Tyndale was escorted to the castle of Filford outside of Brussels and thrown into the dungeon. He had no idea it was his last day of freedom. Merchants and friends throughout Europe wrote letters of protest to the Brussels' court requesting his release. Pointz delivered all of the letters personally and pleaded for the judges to reconsider the arrest, but all of the pleading fell on deaf ears. Tyndale was kept locked up in the dank dungeon for a year and a half while the emperor's courts discussed the matter of his guilt. Finally, Emperor Charles V sent a royal edict from his palace in Augsburg that Tyndale was to be burned as a heretic.

109. Ibid., 148–149.

On October 6, 1536, Tyndale was taken to the place of execution and chained by the neck to the stake. The executioner stood behind Tyndale waiting to twist the chain to end his life. John Foxe records that Tyndale's final words were "O Lord, open the King of England's eyes."[110] The executioner pulled roughly on the chain and strangled Tyndale to death. At least he was spared the horrific pain of being burned alive. His body was still engulfed in the flames and burned to ashes along with copies of his Bibles.

Five Hundred Years Later!

Tyndale's friends, Myles Coverdale and John Rogers, stayed hidden and evaded arrest so that they could complete Tyndale's Old Testament work. Within one year, they published the entire Bible translated from the original languages into English—the fulfillment of William Tyndale's calling.

In 1539, King Henry VIII's eyes *were* opened and he ordered that an English Bible be placed in every church in England for the common people to read. Nearly one hundred years after that, when James II of England authorized the translation of the King James Version of the Bible, over 83 percent of the New Testament and 76 percent of the Old Testament were taken directly from Tyndale's translations.[111] That means that today—500 years after Tyndale's death—when we read the King James Bible, we are still reaping the blessings of William Tyndale's work and his unflinching determination to complete God's call on his life.

That means that today—500 years after Tyndale's death—when we read the King James Bible, we are still reaping the blessings of William Tyndale's work.

110. Ibid., 152.

111. David Daniell, *The Bible in English* (New Haven, CT: Yale University Press, 2003), 448.

Will you do the same? Will you complete the call, large or small, that God has given you?

> *To this end also we pray for you always, that our God will count you worthy of your calling, and fulfill every desire for goodness and the work of faith with power; so that the name of our Lord Jesus may be glorified in you, and you in Him, according to the grace of our God and the Lord Jesus Christ.* (2 Thessalonians 1:11–12 NASB)

The only known portrait of Patrick Hamilton, by artist John Scougal.
Public domain.

Patrick Hamilton: Scotland's Noble Martyr

> *"For I consider that the sufferings of this present time are not worth comparing with the glory that is to be revealed to us."*
>
> (Romans 8:18 NASB)

The most famous name associated with the Scottish Reformation is John Knox, fearless, bold preacher of God's Word and founder of Scottish Presbyterianism. However, few people know of the Scottish martyrs who came before Knox. Their valiant courage in the face of gruesome Reformation fires stirred Knox to become a stalwart preacher of the gospel and brought about a powerful revival in Scotland, England, and Ireland. Three of these Scottish heroes, Patrick Hamilton, Dean Thomas Forret and George Wishart, have brave stories to tell.

Patrick Hamilton was born of noble birth in 1504, in the city of Glasgow, Scotland. As the grandson of the Duke of Albany and the great-grandson of James II of Scotland, he could have spent a life of leisure in the courts of Scotland and England. Instead, Patrick felt the love of God stirring in his heart and chose to dedicate his life to studying theology. By the age of thirteen, he was studying at the University of Paris and at sixteen he received his Master of Arts. Immediately afterward, he was ordained as a young priest in the Catholic Church.

While studying in Paris, Hamilton was introduced to the transforming teachings of Martin Luther, and his heart was won over by the truth of justification by faith in Christ alone. After studying at several European universities, Hamilton returned to St. Andrews, Scotland, in 1527, eager to share the powerful truths of God's Word with the Scottish people.

As the twenty-three-year-old Hamilton traveled through St. Andrews and the nearby towns preaching in the power of the Holy Spirit, large crowds were drawn to the young priest's liberating Sunday messages. No longer did the Scots need to live in fear of the priests and their legalistic rules as they heard the Bible's assurance, *"If the Son makes you free, you will be free indeed!"* (John 8:36 NASB).

It wasn't long before James Beaton, the archbishop of St. Andrews, heard of Hamilton's "heretical preaching" and ordered his arrest for trial, so Hamilton fled Scotland for protection in Germany and enrolled in the University of Marburg, meeting with Reformation leaders, including William Tyndale. Lutheranism was widely accepted in Germany, and Hamilton could freely study and preach God's truth there. He was tempted to stay, but his conscience weighed heavily on him. His was the only voice preaching biblical truth in Scotland at the time. By 1527, Hamilton returned home to the sea coast of St. Andrews, and began to preach once again throughout the countryside.[112]

Beaton's Wicked Plot

Archbishop Beaton was a clever and wicked man. He was well aware that Patrick Hamilton was of noble rank and well-loved by the Scottish people. Instead of sending guards to arrest Hamilton, Beaton extended an invitation for the young priest to attend a month-long church conference. Patrick accepted willingly.

A tourist stands in front of the initials "PH" for Patrick Hamilton in St. Andrews, Scotland.
DonFord1\Thinkstock

For the entire month of the conference, Hamilton was given the freedom to preach the gospel message. However, on February 29, 1528, as soon as the conference ended, Beaton sprang into action. Church

112. Foxe, *Book of Martyrs,* 236–238.

guards seized the young Hamilton and brought him before a council of Catholic bishops in St. Andrews Church. In a hasty trial, and without any testimony on Hamilton's behalf, Patrick was condemned as a heretic, dragged in chains before the front entrance of St. Salvador's Chapel in St. Andrews, and burned alive at the stake, all in one day! Beaton made certain that none of Hamilton's powerful friends in the courts of Edinburgh would have the opportunity to rescue him. The church was determined to maintain its fearsome control over the country.

It was a gruesome death—according to records, Hamilton burned at the stake from noon until 6 pm. His last words were, "Lord Jesus, receive my spirit." The effects of his death were felt far and wide—as one Scottish leader exclaimed, "The smoke of Patrick Hamilton has infected as many as it did blow upon."

From that day forward, the voices of Christian freedom rang louder and stronger throughout the cities and highlands of the rugged Scottish countryside. Hamilton's courage in the face of such cruelty and deception won over more hearts than his words had accomplished.

> *Those who are wise will shine like the brightness of the heavens, and those who lead many to righteousness, like the stars for ever and ever."* (Daniel 12:3 NIV)

Dean Thomas Forret: "Not Ordained to Preach!"

> "*He* [Jesus] *commanded us to preach to the people and to testify that he is the one whom God appointed as judge of the living and the dead.*" (Acts 10:42 NIV)

Approximately two years after Patrick Hamilton's death, in the Scottish capital of Edinburgh, a young priest named Dean Thomas Forret embraced the truth that it was the Bible and not the church which was the foundation for life in Christ. Excited by his newfound freedom in Christ, Forret began teaching the gospel directly from the Word of God every Sunday morning. He preached boldly without fear of the consequences of sharing Bible truth directly with the "common people." Forret knew that his preaching was a violation of church law and considered by the bishops as throwing pearls before swine. (See Matthew 7:6.)

Forret's actions were investigated by a panel of priests, and he was arrested and accused of heresy for revealing the "mysteries of the Scriptures to the vulgar (common) people of Scotland," a practice that the priests believed would weaken their power and superiority over their congregations.

As someone who has preached the Word of God for years, it is hard for me to fathom that the following conversation could have ever happened! But it did!

According to *Foxe's Book of Martyrs*, the Bishop of Dunkfeld met with Forret to persuade him to recant from his "heresies." It went like this:

> Bishop: "My friend, Dean Thomas! I've been informed that you preach the Epistle or Gospel every Sunday to your parishioners.... In doing this you may make the people think that the rest of us should preach likewise! It is good enough for you to find a good Gospel that sets forth the liberty of the holy Church, to preach that alone, and let all the rest be."
>
> Forret: Your lordship, although you think it is too much to preach every Sunday, I think that it is too little, and I wish that your lordship would do the same thing."
>
> Bishop: "No, never, Dean Thomas! Let that preaching alone! *For we are not ordained to preach!*"
>
> Forret: "You have asked me to only preach a good Gospel. I have read the New Testament and the Old, all the Epistles and the Gospels, and I could never find anything evil among them.... If

> your lordship will show me the good epistles and the good Gospels, then I shall preach the good ones only and omit the evil."
>
> Bishop, responding angrily: "*I thank God that I never knew what the Old and New Testament was!* [He had never read the Bible!] I will know nothing but my *portese* and my *pontifical* [church warnings and papal orders]. Be on your way, Forret, and let go of all these fantasies! For if you persevere in these erroneous opinions, you will desire to repent when it is too late to save yourself!"
>
> Forret: "I trust that my cause is just in the presence of God, and therefore I will not worry about what will happen after this."[113]

Within days, Forret was called before the archbishop of St. Andrews and immediately pronounced guilty of heresy. He was condemned to death as a "chief heretic" because he had also attended the marriage of a former priest. Forret, along with a small group of his followers, was chained to the stake and burned on the Castle Hill in Edinburgh in 1530. In spite of the furor caused by the burnings, the believers in Christ's truth in Scotland continued to grow.

George Wishart: John Knox's Mentor and Friend

The captain of the castle guard stepped in front of one hundred men, dressed for war, standing at military attention. The cardinal of St. Andrews had commanded the captain and all of the available men, soldiers and servants alike, to dress themselves in their most warlike uniform with *knapskal* (metal skull-cap), *splent* (metal armor for arms and legs), spear, and axe. On the cold Scotland morning of March 1, 1554, the men marched in formation as one.

Why were they dressed for a mighty battle? Were they about to defend the castle from a foreign enemy? No! They were preparing to accompany one lone man, disheveled and dressed in dungeon rags, to a

113. Ibid., 240–243, emphasis added.

trial for his life, who was accused of nothing more treacherous than preaching directly from the Bible. Who was this man that required the captain of the guard and one hundred armed soldiers to convey him to the Abbey Church and the council of bishops?

But who did the cardinal really fear? He feared the fiery Scottish reformers who were pledged to protect George Wishart from the evil cunning of church villains—and he feared the resounding drum roll of God's eternal truth.

The accused was George Wishart, a godly man, a humble and yet powerful preacher of God's Word to the people of Scotland. But who did the cardinal really fear? He feared the fiery Scottish reformers who were pledged to protect George Wishart from the evil cunning of church villains—and he feared the resounding drum roll of God's eternal truth.

Escaping the Black Death

George Wishart was born in Scotland in 1513. Like many of the Reformation preachers, he was well-educated and had studied at the University of Leuven in Belgium as well as at the University of Cambridge, London. He was a tall man with black hair and a long beard, but his overbearing appearance was deceiving. In spite of his stature and education, Wishart was a humble Jesus-follower anointed by the Holy Spirit to passionately preach the liberating truth of Christ's redemption on the cross.[114]

Wishart loved his fellow Scotsmen, and he was eager to share the truths that would set them free—free from the overlords of a corrupt "church" hierarchy that was focused solely on maintaining their "kingdom" status in this world. After completing his education in Europe,

114. Ibid., 247–248.

he returned to Scotland and began teaching young scholars from the Greek New Testament. Soon after, Wishart was accused of heresy for teaching from the Bible; he fled first to England and then to Germany to escape his accusers.

In 1543, the thirty-year-old Wishart was drawn back home to Scotland, where he knew his countrymen were hungry for God's Word. While preaching in Dundee, the plague, otherwise known as the Black Death, broke out. Most of the citizens fled the city in terror, but Wishart remained and spent weeks caring for the desperately sick and preaching the saving grace of Jesus Christ to those who remained. Many people came to Christ from his messages of life in Christ during such dark times. No sooner had the plague lifted than Wishart thwarted a premeditated attempt on his life. In a scheme devised by Cardinal Beaton, Wishart was attacked from behind by a dagger-wielding priest. Wishart wrestled his assailant to the ground—and then protected the frightened priest from the angry citizens of Dundee. From that time on, the young and fiery preacher John Knox traveled with Wishart as his bodyguard and protector from future attacks.[115]

"One is Sufficient for Sacrifice!"

When the plague was over, Wishart and Knox traveled together throughout Scotland. The men were as opposite as possible in temperament; Wishart with his calm and loving presentation of the gospel truth and Knox with his bold, battle-like cry for repentance and reformation. But the men were kindred spirits in their conviction to preach God's Word without compromise, and John Knox's faith was greatly increased by George Wishart's Christ-like life.

For a few months, Wishart filled Scotland's cities and towns with the powerful preaching of biblical salvation—*"Jesus Christ is the same yesterday, today, and forever"* (Hebrews 13:8). Large crowds, thirsty for the living water of God's Word written in their native tongue, surged

115. "George Wishart Evangelical Tracts," Tracts.ukgo.com, http://www.tracts.ukgo.com/george_wishart.html.

around the young Scotsman. Wishart avoided the Catholic authorities as long as he could, but he preached like a man on a serious mission who knew his time was short.

The ruins of St. Andrews today.
Personal photo.

In 1545, Wishart traveled to St. Andrews on Scotland's rugged eastern seacoast because it was the center of Christianity in the country. St. Andrews was also the most dangerous place in Scotland to preach on justification by faith in Jesus Christ. Knox wanted to remain at Wishart's side as his bodyguard as they entered the historic city, but the preacher was adamant: Knox must stay away from St. Andrews! "One is sufficient for one sacrifice," Wishart exhorted Knox.

"Like a Lamb to the Slaughter"

In December of 1545, Cardinal David Beaton (the nephew of James Beaton who had burned Patrick Hamilton at the stake) sent his palace guards to arrest Wishart for heresy and throw him into the dungeon of St. Andrews Castle. Beaton was an evil leader, more brutal than his uncle, but still a favorite of King James V of Scotland. Several years earlier, Beaton was appointed as a cardinal by the church in Rome, and then, in 1539, he succeeded his uncle as the archbishop of St. Andrews, the highest position in the Catholic Church of Scotland. All of this privilege and authority had made Beaton a cruel man who basked in the honor and admiration he received from other men; he was not at all concerned with honoring God or His Word.

George Wishart before Cardinal Beaton.
Photos.com\Thinkstock

"Like a lamb being led to the slaughter," on the day of his trial, Wishart was taken in chains by the captain of the castle and one hundred armed soldiers to the Abbey Church of St. Andrews to face his accusers.[116]

116. Foxe, *Book of Martyrs*, 248.

Shouting from the pulpit, John Lauder, a Scottish archbishop, railed against Wishart, brashly accusing him of false statements. Lauder called down curses from heaven and hurled them at the quiet and resolute Wishart. Finally, he lashed out "How do you answer these accusations, you renegade! Traitor! Thief! We have many witnesses against you!"[117]

George Wishart quietly knelt down in the pulpit to pray and then requested the opportunity to share his true beliefs with his accusers. Surprisingly, they agreed, but first they ordered all of the common people to leave the Abbey immediately. Fear had gripped the leaders; they knew that Wishart's words could persuade the people against them. These false "kingdom" leaders didn't realize that they could never defeat the power of the Holy Spirit flowing through the anointed man of God.

Wishart spoke passionately:

> It is found plainly and certain in Scripture that we should worship and honor one God.... Therefore I exhorted all men equally in my doctrine that they should leave the uncertain way and follow that way which was taught us by our Master, Jesus Christ. He is the only Mediator and He alone makes intercession for us to God His Father; He is the door by which we must enter in. He that does not enter by this door but climbs in another way is a thief and a murderer. Jesus is the Way, the Truth and the Life. Everyone who goes out of this Way, there is no doubt that he will fall into the mire of sin, that he is already in sin.... Truly that which I have heard and read in the word of God I taught openly.... And now you shall hear the same...unless something agrees with the Word of God, I dare not be bold to affirm it as truth.[118]

117. Ibid., 249.
118. Ibid.

Pronouncing the Death Sentence

The arrogant bishops turned their heads in disdain, their hearts hardened against God's truth. Without hesitation, Beaton pronounced the death sentence against Wishart. English and Scottish law declared that the church could condemn a man to death but only the secular authorities could carry out the death sentence. But Cardinal Beaton ignored the law and rushed Wishart to his death both out of cruelty and out of fear that Wishart's brazen supporters would arrive armed and ready to fight to the death to free Wishart before the flames could engulf him.

Before the horrified citizens of St. Andrews who loved George Wishart, the royal guards immediately prepared a fire for his death on March 1, 1546. To flaunt his power, Beaton had all of the castle guns turned to face the stake; the guns would stand prepared for attack until the grisly execution was completed.

All was ready. Wishart's hands were bound behind his back with chains and he was led to the pyre with a rope around his neck and an iron chain around his waist. When he came to the place where the logs were piled high, the thirty-three-year-old Wishart dropped to his knees and prayed, "O thou Savior of this world! Have mercy upon me. Father of heaven! I commend my spirit into your holy hands."

When Wishart turned to face the mourning people, his final words were for their souls: "Christian brothers and sisters, do not be offended with the Word of God because of the torments you see prepared for me; I exhort you to love the Word of God.... For the Word's sake and true preaching, which was given to me by the grace of God, I suffer this day by men, not sorrowfully, but with a glad heart and mind. For this cause I was sent to the people of Scotland, that I should suffer this fire for Christ's sake. Behold my face; you shall not see me change color from fear. This grim fire I do not fear. I know surely that my soul shall sup with my Savior Jesus Christ this very night."[119]

119. Ibid.

As Wishart finished speaking, the hangman dropped to his knees beside him in tears, "Sir, I pray you will forgive me, for I am not guilty of your death." Wishart answered him, "Come to me." When the hangman stepped solemnly to stand beside the chained prisoner; Wishart kissed his roughened cheek and spoke, "Here is a token that I forgive you. My dear man, do your job."

Shortly after, Wishart was hung from the wooden gibbet and burned alive until there was nothing left but his ashes. The people's mourning quickly turned to anger at the barbarous death of an innocent man.

Reformation Rebellion Breaks Out

Portrait of George Wishart.
Pictore\Thinkstock

In the early morning of March 29, 1546, just twenty-eight days after Wishart's murder, a muffled cry broke the silence of St. Andrews Castle. The guard at the front gate had been stabbed to death, a hand held over his mouth to silence his cry. Twelve black-clothed men, led by Norman and John Leslie and William Kirkcaldy, made their way stealthily to the bedchamber of Cardinal Beaton. Daggers were raised high in vengeance; Beacon woke up just before the first dagger fell, "Alas! Alas! Don't kill me! I am a priest!" he cried. But the men who had come to repay Beaton for the death of George Wishart and the stealing of their lands by the church ignored his pitiful cries. John Foxe's comment on the death of this cruel clergyman was, "Like a butcher he lived and like a butcher he died."[120]

The murderers mutilated Beaton's corpse and hung it from the cardinal's window, the same window where he had watched Wishart burn to death. Foxe wrote that the cardinal's body lay unburied for more than seven months near the walls of the castle and then was buried without honors "like carrion in a dunghill."

Because he was a humble and forgiving man, I don't believe George Wishart would have approved of the vengeful murder of his enemy. He would have fervently prayed for Beaton's salvation instead. But the rugged men of Scotland decided that they had enough of Catholic tyranny. For them the Reformation was freedom from the pope as well as freedom from the control of any other country. Beaton had ties with France as an ambassador and with Italy as an emissary of the pope. The Scots wanted the freedom to self-govern and to follow the Lordship of Jesus Christ without the interference of a foreign leader. They saw Beaton as an enemy to both of those causes.

Raising Wishart's Banner High

Nothing had touched John Knox's heart more than the humble and scriptural preaching of George Wishart. After the martyrdom of his close friend, Knox was determined that Wishart's message would not be silenced. Knox had nothing to do with Beaton's murder, but when the assassins seized St. Andrews Castle and moved in along with their families to create a Reformation stronghold, Knox joined them. He preached as their pastor until the Scottish nobility retook the castle and the Reformers escaped.

For the next twenty-four years, Knox preached his fiery message of justification by faith throughout Germany, Switzerland, England, and Scotland. Thousands of men and women responded to his message and

120. Ibid., 253.

accepted Jesus as Lord. Eventually, Knox became known as the father of Scottish Presbyterianism. His ministry was a testimony that none of the early martyrs of Scotland's reformation had died in vain.

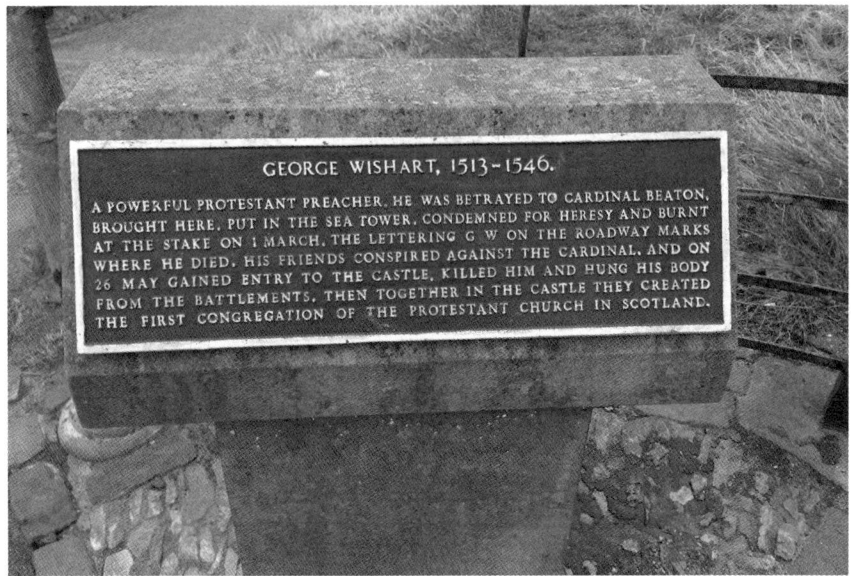

Plaque remembering Wishart at St. Andrews.
Personal photo.

Today in St. Andrews, not far from the rugged Scottish seacoast, stands a white monument commemorating George Wishart and Patrick Hamilton and other Scottish martyrs who gave the ultimate sacrifice so that the message of Jesus Christ would sweep through the cities and highlands of Scotland. They were Christians who had taken up the cross of Christ to follow Him to the very end.

> *If anyone desires to come after Me, let him deny himself, and take up his cross, and follow Me. For whoever desires to save his life will lose it, but whoever loses his life for My sake will find it.*
>
> (Matthew 16:24–25)

✯✯✯✯✯

FLAMES OVERCOME THE DARKNESS

7

FLAMES OVERCOME THE DARKNESS

(AD 1500–1600)

Anne Askew: Tortured in the Tower of London

"They took me to the bottom room in the White Tower and put me on the rack because I would not confess of any ladies or gentlewomen who share my [Christian] *beliefs. Because I lay still and did not cry, my Lord Chancellor and Master Rich took pain to rack me with their own hands until I was nearly dead."*
—Anne Askew, 1546

Many of the early martyrs of the Reformation were men—former Catholic priests who found a powerful faith in Jesus by reading the Bible and who tried to change the church's errors from within. However, it wasn't long before women also took up the cry for freedom in Christ. One of the most famous was Anne Askew of Lincolnshire, England, the first woman to be tortured in the Tower of London and the only one (to this day) to be tortured there *and* burned at the stake. Anne was a courageous, intelligent, and strong-willed woman who refused to bow to the rule of false church authority. She deserves to be celebrated for her bravery as a martyr for Christ.

Anne was born in 1521, in Lincolnshire, England, to William and Elizabeth Askew. Her father was a wealthy landowner and a counselor in King Henry VIII's court. After Elizabeth's death, William paid a rich dowry for his oldest daughter, Martha, to marry Thomas Kyme, a wealthy Catholic landowner. Unfortunately, Martha died before the wedding took place and, to protect the dowry, William forced fifteen-year-old Anne to marry Kyme in Martha's place.[121]

Young ladies didn't usually receive an extensive education in sixteenth-century England, but William had given Anne a rare opportunity; she could read and was a student of the Bible and English law. She was also a committed and outspoken Protestant before she even entered her marriage—a marriage to a Catholic that was doomed to failure.

King Henry VIII's Egotistical World

Anne Askew lived in the middle of King Henry VIII's reign when the battle between the Catholic Church and the English Reformation was growing fierce. Under the self-centered and erratic King Henry, it was dangerous to have strong religious views as a Catholic or a Reformer. The king was such a shrewd egotist that in 1531 he renounced all association with the pope and the Catholic Church and founded his own Christian domination. It was not for righteous reasons or to support

121. James Gairdner, "Askew, Anne" *Dictionary of National Biography*, vol. 2 (London: Smith, Elder & Company, 1885).

the truth of God's Word. Henry claimed his "lawful" position as the sovereign head of the Church of England just so he could interpret the Bible to satisfy his own ends.

Henry had been crowned King of England in 1509 and immediately married Catherine of Aragon, a Spanish princess and his older brother's widow. After twenty-seven years of marriage to Catherine (she gave birth six times but only one daughter, the future Queen Mary, lived beyond childhood), Henry was searching for a "scriptural reason" to have his marriage annulled. He was captivated by the young and beautiful Anne Boleyn and wanted another chance to produce a male heir. His reason for the annulment was an intentional misuse of the Scriptures based on Leviticus 20:21: *"If a man marries his brother's wife, it is an act of impurity; he has dishonored his brother. They will be childless"* (NIV). Henry petitioned the pope for an immediate annulment claiming that, according to Leviticus 20, his marriage was "a sin before God."[122]

Portrait of Anne Askew by Hans Eworth.
Public domain.

Pope Clement VII, who was not a favorite of Henry's, saw through the king's manipulation of the Bible verse and refused to grant the annulment. Henry VIII was furious—like a child throwing a temper tantrum to get his own way! Theologians in London and Rome wrote heated letters back and forth defending both sides of the argument. In the end the pope was adamant. There would be no annulment.

122. "Henry VIII, King of England 1491–1547," Biography.com, http://www.biography.com/people/henry-viii-9335322.

In a rage, Henry broke off all ties with the Roman Church. In 1531, he rejected the pope's authority throughout England and demanded that all of England's Catholic clergy take the Oath of Supremacy which recognized Henry as the sovereign leader of the new Church of England. Catherine was stripped of her title as queen and given a lesser role as the Princess Dowager of Wales; heartbroken, she was exiled from court and sent to live the rest of her life in Kimbolton Castle.

One year later, when Sir Thomas More, the king's close friend and the Lord High Chancellor of England, refused to take the Oath of Supremacy or recognize the annulment, More was accused of treason, thrown into the Tower of London, and then beheaded. Later that year, Parliament granted Henry's annulment and he happily married an already-pregnant Anne Boleyn.

England's ties with the pope were severed, but the bishops and priests still considered themselves Catholics and retained all of the traditional Catholic doctrine as the basis of faith for the English church, including celebrating the Mass.

In 1539, at the insistence of his cardinals, Henry signed a new edict, the Act of the Six Articles, which made it heresy to deny the physical presence of Christ's body and blood in the Eucharist, to reject the necessity for priests to celebrate the Mass, or to refute the doctrine that all sins must be confessed to a priest to receive forgiveness. This Six Articles would cost hundreds of English Christians their lives in the decades to come. One of the only positive results of Henry's reign was that—just to spite the pope—the king allowed one copy of the English Bible to be placed in every church in England for the common people to read.

Preaching on the Streets of London

In this tumultuous spiritual environment, Anne Askew accepted the message of salvation in Jesus Christ alone. Studying the English

Bible became the focus of her life. She announced to anyone who would listen, "I would rather read five lines of the Bible than to hear five masses in the temple."[123] Since the Bible could always be stripped from the people again, Anne made it her mission to memorize as much of the New Testament as possible. She remained with Thomas Kyme for nearly ten years and bore him two children, even though he treated her cruelly. But as her outspokenness for Jesus Christ grew, their marriage became unbearable. Finally, Kyme "violently drove her out of his house," and Anne set off for London. She never referred to herself by the name Anne Kyme again.

As a woman, Anne wasn't allowed to preach from the pulpits of London, but she boldly shared the gospel on the busy city streets. She became known as a "gospeller," a lay person who could preach for hours from memorized Scriptures. London was full of Bible studies attended by both nobles and common people, and Anne soaked it up. Because of her father's role in King Henry's court, Anne was given a position in the court of Henry's sixth wife, Catherine Parr, who was secretly a Protestant supporter.

Outsmarting the Court's Attorneys

On March 10, 1545, Anne was arrested in violation of the Six Articles Act and accused of "heresy and acts against the Catholic Church." Twelve days of imprisonment and interrogation by the bishop and the lord mayor followed. Anne kept a personal journal of her trial with an account of the interrogators' questions and her responses at the end of each day. Some scholars have called her *brilliant* for the way she countered each accusation from the court's counselors with wisdom and the Word of God. She understood her rights in an English court of law and maintained control over the conversations, avoiding her accusers' traps. Here are some of her personal accounts from *The First Examination of*

123. Foxe, *Book of Martyrs*, 329.

Anne Askew as she was questioned first by the Lord Mayor Christopher Dare.[124]

Dare began: "Do you believe that the sacrament hanging over the altar is the actual body of Christ? (The priests kept a piece of the Eucharistic bread in an ornate container hanging above the altar.) Just as Jesus often answered the Pharisees, Anne answered him with another question: "Answer this first, Sir, was St. Stephen stoned to death?" "I cannot say," Dare replied. He was completely unfamiliar with the Bible. "Then I won't answer your question, either," Anne concluded.

Later she added, "I do know this; God does not dwell in temples made with human hands. Neither does He dwell in a box. '*Heaven* is my footstool' says the Lord in Psalm 113: Christ taught us when we pray, 'Our Father, *which art in heaven*' and not 'Our Father which art in the box.' Now you discern and judge!"

Realizing he had been outwitted, Dare chose a priest to continue the questioning. Anne's journal records that conversation as well: "The priest asked if I thought that private masses for the dead helped the departed souls reach heaven sooner. I answered, 'It is great idolatry to believe more in these masses than in the death that Christ died for us!'" The priest questioned next, "Mistress, why are you accused?" Anne's quick reply, "Ask my accusers, for I do not know yet."

After twelve days of victory in the interrogations, Anne was released into her cousin's custody. For the next year, she continued to preach on the freeing power of God's Word and the sacrifice of Jesus Christ for eternal salvation.

Tortured on the Rack

Anne's freedom to preach wouldn't last long. On June 16, 1546, just a few short months after George Wishart burned at the stake in St.

124. The following dialogue is taken from the *Select Works of John Bale, First Examination of Anne Askew*, Henry Christmas, ed., (Cambridge, MA: University Press, 1851), 149–155. Digitized by the Internet Archive, 2014. https://archive.org/stream/selectworksofjoh00bale/selectworksofjoh00bale_djvu.txt.

Andrews, Anne Askew was summoned to the King's council in Greenwich, London, and accused of preaching in public, rejecting the Catholic mass, and, most importantly, denying that the bread and wine was completely transformed into the physical body and blood of Christ. It was for that last doctrine, and her refusal to reveal the identity of Protestant believers at court, that she was viciously tortured and burned at the stake.

A replica of the rack in the Tower of London.
Personal photo.

Shortly after her arrest, Anne was cross-examined for five hours. For the first time, Anne was threatened with burning for heresy. But she replied to her accusers, "I have searched all the Scriptures, yet I could never find that either Christ or His apostles put any creature to death."[125]

When her accusers demanded that she confess that the Eucharist was "flesh, blood and bone," she responded in the wisdom of the Holy Spirit:

> Jesus spoke to His disciples, "Take, eat; this is my body which shall be broken for you" (1 Corinthians 11:24). Christ's meaning there was the same as in four other scriptures: "I am the door" (John 10:9); "Behold the Lamb of God" (John 1:29); "I am the vine" (John 15:5); "The rock was Christ" (1 Corinthians 10:4). If you take Christ for each of these things that He is signified by,"

125. Ibid., 201.

> Anne replied. "then you would make him a door, a vine, a lamb, a stone, contrary to the Holy Ghost's meaning... The sacramental bread was left to us to be received with thanksgiving in remembrance of Christ's death....And though Jesus did say 'Take, eat this in remembrance of Me,' yet He did not bid them hang up that bread in a box and make it a God or bow to it. 'God is a spirit and must be worshipped in spirit and in truth.'"[126]

Unmoved by her responses, Anne's prosecutors demanded that she recant her beliefs and reveal the names of other female Protestants, especially Queen Catherine and her ladies-in-waiting. Anne's answer was adamant; she knew of no one who shared her beliefs or opinions. At the end of the day, she was taken back to her cell while the enraged counselors plotted how to force Anne's submission; they would use the rack on a woman for the first time in English history. Their plan was from Satan himself.

"Her Body Was Drawn Apart"

Anne was taken from her cell, at about ten o'clock the next morning, to the lower room of the White Tower. She was brought straight to the rack and was demanded to name those who believed as she did. Anne declined to name anyone at all, so she was asked to remove all of her clothing except her nightgown. She was then made to climb onto the rack, and her examiners tied her wrists and ankles to the wood. Again, she was asked for names, but again, she refused. The wheel of the rack was turned, pulling Anne and lifting her so that she was held taut about five inches above its bed and slowly stretched.[127]

When the Constable of the Tower refused to continue torturing Anne, the Lord Chancellor Thomas Wriothesley and Sir Richard Rich, determined to hear the guilt of the queen or her ladies, continued the heinous torture. Standing on either side of the rack, they cranked the

126. Ibid., 204–205.
127. See Elaine V. Beilin, *The Examinations of Anne Askew: Women Writers in English 1350–1850* (Oxford: Oxford University Press, 1996), 130.

handles so hard that Anne was pulled apart, her shoulders and hips were yanked from their sockets, and her elbows and knees were popped out of place. Her cries could be heard throughout the Tower gardens, but, by God's grace, Anne never betrayed one of her sisters in Christ.

The Tower of London.
Personal photo.

Anne recorded in her journal later that she fainted twice from the excruciating pain and was lowered from the rack just long enough to be revived before the torturous stretching continued. Still she remained silent.

Anne was taken from the rack and laid on the bare floor where her torturers spent two hours trying to convince her that he would set her free if she would just confess. But she didn't!

She recorded a prayer in her prison journal, "Lord, I have more enemies now than hairs on my head. Yet, Lord, don't let them ever overcome me with their vain words. Fight, O Lord, in my stead; for on Thee I cast my care. With all the spite they can imagine they fall upon me, yet Lord let me not take the side of those who are against Thee. For You are my whole delight."[128]

Condemned for Heresy

On June 18, 1546, twenty-six-year-old Anne Askew was condemned for heresy and sentenced to be burned at the stake. After nearly a month of lying in prison suffering from her injuries, on July 16, Anne was martyred in Smithfield market square, just outside the London Wall. She had endured so much torture that she had to be carried to the stake on a chair. A huge crowd of supporters followed her to the execution, crying out words of encouragement, pressing the guards on every side. The soldiers forcibly pushed the crowd back to have enough room for the execution. Anne was chained to the stake by her waist to support her body. Three other Reformers, John Lassells, John Hemley (a priest) and John Hadlam (a tailor) were condemned to die with her that day. Gunpowder was sprinkled on their bodies so that they would die more quickly in the flames.

The Lord Chancellor, the Lord Mayor, and several other court persecutors sat on their official bench at St. Bartholomew Church to watch the execution. The Lord Mayor cried out *"Fiat justitia!"* which in Latin means, "Let justice be done!" and the fire was laid to the wood. The men sat and watched as Anne died a brutal death, her body consumed by the fire until it was ashes. They celebrated their victory.

But it was short-lived. The next year Henry VIII died from illness, and the majority of Anne's accusers fell out of power under the Protestant King Edward VI. Just four years later, the wicked Lord Wriothesley, rejected by the king's court, died alone from illness.

128. *Select Works of Bale*, 238.

The order and maner of the burning of Anne Askew, Iohn Lacels, Iohn Adams, Nicholas Belenian, with certayne of the Councell sitting in Smithfield.

Woodcut of the burning of Anne Askew.
Public domain.

In the months following her execution, Anne's prison journal was smuggled out of England and into the hands of John Bale, a staunch Protestant supporter. Bale published copies of it under the titles *First and Latter Examinations of Anne Askew* and distributed her courageous testimony throughout Europe. In his own commentary, Bale recognized the startling similarities between Anne's sufferings and Blandina's martyrdom in the Colosseum of Lyon in AD 177. (See chapter 4).

Both were indomitable Christian women chained to the rack and tortured until their bodies were broken apart, yet neither grew fainthearted nor gave up their testimony for Christ. Both women were brave in the face of their captors even while experiencing the searing pain of fire. Both women were an encouragement to their fellow male prisoners, and in each case three men were martyred beside them. Finally, both women were recorded as Christian heroines in church history for their irrepressible faith in Jesus Christ as Lord and Savior.[129]

In spite of the court prosecutors attempt to destroy her, Anne Askew gained the final victory; as her testimony was read throughout Europe, the Reformation truths spread far and wide in response to her fearless courage. Anne's final prayer from prison is a reflection of her heart before God:

> Lord, I heartily desire of thee that thou wilt, out of thy most merciful goodness, forgive them that violence which they do and have done to me. Open their blind hearts, that they may hereafter do that thing in thy sight which is only acceptable before thee and to set forth thy truth aright, without all of the vain fantasies of evil men. So be it. O Lord, so be it. By me, Anne Askew.[130]

Who Was John Foxe?
Proclaimer of Christ Before Kings

"Princes, kings, and other rulers of the world have used all their strength and cunning against the Church, yet it continues to endure and hold its own."
—John Foxe, 1558

John Foxe was not martyred at the stake. In fact, he was not martyred at all. Just the same, he deserves a place among our Generals because the church owes its history of so many Christian heroes to his writings.

Born in Boston, Lincolnshire, England, in 1516, John attended Oxford University at age sixteen and there became close friends with

129. Ibid., 142–144.
130. Ibid., 239.

Reformation giants William Tyndale and Hugh Latimer. While at Oxford, all three embraced the Protestant faith. Foxe stood out, however, then and for the rest of his life in one particular area: he was adamantly opposed to the execution of *anyone* for religious reasons, particularly the horrific death by burning at the stake. Foxe agreed with Anne Askew: there is no biblical support for a Christian executing another human being over the differences in their beliefs. Jesus faced great opposition and so did His apostles, yet none of them even hinted at taking a life because of heretical beliefs.[131] Foxe believed that it is the Lord's job to convict, His job to judge, His job to exact vengeance if necessary. It is the Christian's role to preach the gospel and pray that those who are in error will repent and accept the truth of God's Word. Throughout his lifetime, John Foxe protested to royals and church leaders alike begging them to overturn the death sentences for Protestants, Anabaptists, and Catholics.

Throughout his lifetime, John Foxe protested to royals and church leaders alike begging them to overturn the death sentences for Protestants, Anabaptists, and Catholics.

A Protestant King at Last

John Foxe was an important leader in the Reformation movement from Henry VIII's reign through the reign of Edward VI, Mary I and the early years of Elizabeth I. During that time, he preached and wrote of God's availing grace to save everyone who comes to Him with an open heart.

King Henry VIII died on January 28, 1547, and, his only son, nine-year-old Edward VI, ascended to the throne with a Protestant Regency

131. S. L. Lee, "Foxe, John," *The Dictionary of National Biography*, vol. 20 (London: Elder, 1885).

Council to help him rule. For the next six years, the Protestant faith in England gained great freedoms. The archbishop of Canterbury, Thomas Cranmer, the bishop of London, Nicholas Ridley, and the bishop of Worcester, Hugh Latimer, were all dedicated Protestants. They appointed men in church leadership who would lead the people to God's throne of grace. The stone altars were torn down and replaced with wooden communion tables. The statues that remained in England were set aside. Most importantly, the English people heard true and powerful preaching each week directly from the Holy Scriptures.

Portrait of John Foxe.
GeorgiosKollidas\Thinkstock

Tragically, in July of 1553, England's court physician left the royal bedchambers with a creased brow and a forlorn expression to share the news that shattered the peace of England. Young Edward Tudor's cough was considerably worse; blood covered the royal handkerchief held up to his mouth. At just fifteen years of age, the young king's battle with tuberculosis was nearly at an end. And with his death would come the death of all that the Protestant reformers had accomplished in the six years of his reign. What would this mean for the Church of England? What would it mean for John Foxe, Thomas Cranmer, Nicholas Ridley and the church leaders who had successfully converted all of the country's churches to houses of prayer? What would happen next?

"Bloody Mary" Claims the Throne

Edward VI died on July 6, 1553; by the middle of July, Lady Mary, Henry VIII's oldest daughter, had declared her right to her father's throne in a letter to the Privy Council. She quickly gathered men of power around her and formed a small army. In an act of artful deception, Mary promised the Protestants who supported her ascension to the throne that she would not force the country to return to the pope's authority. It was a promise that she had no intention of keeping.

The Protestant leaders were afraid of the rule of a foreign king in England. And this is exactly what happened. During the first year of her reign, Mary married Catholic Prince Philip II of Spain and established her foreign husband as her co-regent over all of England. The Privy Council and the church leadership were replaced by men loyal to the pope and the queen. Mary's earlier Protestant supporters were incensed by her deception, but they were helpless to overcome the queen's self-focused decisions.

In an era of constant religious volatility both in England and in continental Europe, Mary I distinguished herself for her particularly relentless pursuit of Protestants. Her nickname, Bloody Mary, fit her well as she ordered the heartless burning at the stake of nearly three hundred Bible-believing Christians in her five-year reign.

God's Call to Write

Once Queen Mary seized the throne, England's Protestant leaders faced an agonizing decision. They could flee England for the religious haven of Germany or Switzerland and wait for the end of Mary's reign, or they could remain in England to defend their faith in Christ.

I believe that all those who sought the Lord in prayer were given personal direction by the Holy Spirit, whether to stay *or* to leave. When we reach a crisis situation and are faced with difficult decisions that will impact our lives and others, it is prayer and the leading of the Holy Spirit that will set us on a straight course. The rest of this chapter will contain the stories of many heroes who followed God's leading to remain in England.

With the inevitable persecution and martyrdom of his friends weighing heavily on his heart, Foxe packed his meager belongings and sailed from the English seacoast.

John Foxe, however, had a different calling from the Lord. His role was to flee to the continent and to use his writing gift to record one of the most important historical events of the Christian church. With the inevitable persecution and martyrdom of his friends weighing heavily on his heart, Foxe packed his meager belongings and sailed from the English seacoast with his wife and five children. They settled first in Frankfurt, Germany, and then in Basel, Switzerland. In Basel, he began writing the first pages of his life's work, *The Acts and Monuments,* which later became known as *Foxe's Book of Martyrs.*

Foxe began his book with the testimonies of the first-century martyrs and early Reformers like John Wycliffe and John Hus, and what they had sacrificed to preach the gospel of Jesus Christ. At the start, he had no way of knowing that Mary's death squads in England would soon swell the pages of his history book and make it one of the most famous Christian journals ever published.

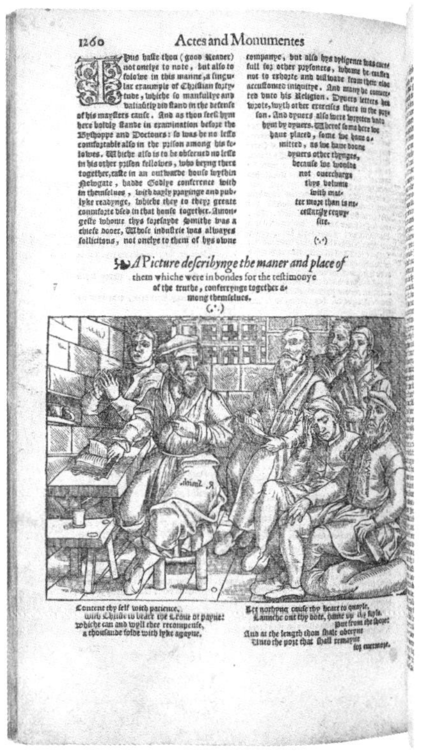
1260 Actes and Monumentes

Thus haste thou (good Reader) not onelye to note, but also to folowe in this manne, a singular example of Christian fortytude, whiche so manfullye and valiantly did stand in the defense of his maysters cause. And as thou seest hym here boldly stande in examination before the Byshoppe and Doctours: so was he no lesse comfortable also in the prison among his felowes. Whiche also is to be obserued no lesse in his other prison fellowes, who beyng there together, caste in an outwarde house wythin Newgate, hadde Godlye conference with in themselues, with dayly prayinge and publyke readynge, whiche they to theyr greate comforte used in that house together. Amongeste whome thys forsayde Smithe was a chiefe doer, Whose industrie was alwayes sollicitous, not onelye to them of hys owne companye, but also hys dyligence was carefull for other prysoners, whome he ceased not to exhorte and dissuade from their olde accustomed iniquitye. And many he conuerted unto his Religion. Dyuers letters hee wrote, wyth other exercises there in the prison. And dyuers also were wrytten unto hym by dyuers. Whereof some here we haue placed, some we haue omitted, as we haue doone dyuers other thynges, because we woulde not ouercharge thys volume with matter more than is necessarilye requysite.

A Picture describynge the maner and place of them whiche were in bondes for the testimonye of the truthe, conferrynge together among themselues.

Content thy self with patience,
With Christe to beare the crosse of payne:
Whiche can and wyll thee recompense,
A thousande folde with lyke agayne.

Let nothyng cause thy heart to quayle,
Launche out thy bote, hale up thy sayle,
Put from the shore:
And at the length thou shalt obteyne
Unto the port that shall remayne
for euermore.

A page from the first edition of Foxe's Book of Martyrs, published in 1563.
Wikimedia Commons.

In Frankfurt, John Knox told him about the fiery deaths of the Scottish martyrs, Hamilton, Forret, and Wishart. A copy of *Anne Askew's First and Second Examinations* reached him soon after, and suddenly his book on God's martyrs became much more personal. Queen Mary's reign raged on and gruesome accounts of Christians burning at the stake were sent to him in Europe. Grieving for his university friends, as well as hundreds of other brothers and sisters in Christ, Foxe was determined to honor the courageous martyrs of England. He worked feverishly to weave their testimonies into his manuscript.

The Acts and the Monuments

On November 15, 1558, five years after gaining the throne, the forty-two-year-old Queen Mary died. Her half-sister, Princess Elizabeth, daughter of King Henry VIII and Anne Boleyn, was crowned the new Queen of England. One year later, Foxe and his family eagerly returned to a Protestant England, and on September 1 of the same year, the first edition of *The Acts and Monuments* was published. Once in England,

Foxe uncovered additional journals and letters written by "Marian" martyrs near the time of their deaths. With this new information in hand, *Foxe's Book of Martyrs* expanded to over 2300 pages.

John Foxe reminded his readers, "For hundreds of years, the Holy Spirit was withheld and the Bible was hidden. Hence the monstrous errors that deformed the church and created all the frightful evils that afflicted the world!"

Under the freedom of Queen Elizabeth, Foxe was ordained by the Church of England and began his ministry as a powerful preacher of God's Word. He lived most of his life with little in earthly riches, but he was well-known for his compassion and aide to the needy around him. Since the first edition of the book in 1559, *Foxe's Book of Martyrs* has never been out of print.

Foxe lived a long life, dying in April 1587 at the age of seventy-one. He had been spared the searing flames of Reformation martyrdom so that he could fulfill his calling to record the testimonies of the following heroes of faith which include nobles and church leaders, laborers and housewives. We are grateful to John Foxe for remaining faithful to his call from God.

> *But when they arrest you and deliver you up, do not worry beforehand, or premeditate what you will speak. But whatever is given you in that hour, speak that; for it is not you who speak, but the Holy Spirit.*
>
> (Mark 13:11; see also Matthew 10:18–19; Luke 21:12)

John Rogers: "Bloody Mary's First Victim"

"That which I preach, I will seal with my blood."
—John Rogers, 1555

John Rogers was born around 1505 in Birmingham, England. As a young man he attended Cambridge University and was ordained a priest just before King Henry VIII broke with the Roman Catholic Church. In 1534, Rogers was sent by his bishop to Antwerp, Germany, to serve as the chaplain of a company of English merchants. By God's grace, he met William Tyndale who was still secretly working with Myles Coverdale on the translation of the Old Testament into English. After hearing the truth of salvation through Christ, Rogers embraced his newfound freedom in Christ. He rejected his priestly vows and married Adriana de Weyden, a native of Antwerp.

After Tyndale's betrayal, arrest and execution, Rogers worked with Myles Coverdale to finish the Old Testament translation. Most of the actual translation work was Tyndale's, but Rogers and his wife were instrumental in bringing the entire Bible to publication. Her uncle owned a printing press in Antwerp and worked in secret to publish Tyndale's entire translation. This English Bible was referred to by a code name, "The Translation of Thomas Matthew" because Tyndale's name was still a powder-keg all over Europe. Hundreds of copies were then smuggled into England.

Rogers spent fourteen productive years in Germany, attending the University of Wittenberg and serving as the pastor in a Lutheran church in Meldorf, in the north. But when Henry VIII died and Edward VI was crowned the English king, Rogers, his wife, and their ten children returned to England to further the gospel in his own country.

Nicholas Ridley, now the bishop of London, appointed Rogers as the pastor of St. Paul's Cathedral. After years of freedom in Germany, Rogers preached with a bold confidence seldom heard by the English reformers. He denounced the greed of many church leaders who were hoarding the money gained from the closing of Catholic monasteries, and he refused to wear the ornate vestments of the Church of England. A simple robe and round cap was all that John Rogers needed to stand before his congregation and preach in the power of the Holy Spirit.

The Reformers Were Not Perfect

Unfortunately, although the reformers had discovered many of God's biblical truths, they were not perfect; they had their sins and faults. One of the ugliest was their willingness to condemn other Protestant believers who they considered "radical Protestants." These believers, such as the Anabaptists, went further than the Protestants in their rejection of the Catholic Church and all worldliness; they believed it was wrong to hold a position in a secular government or have a role in the military. For this reason they were labeled radicals. The Anabaptists (forerunners of the Mennonites and Amish) were the first to insist on a "believers' baptism" for adults and a call to holiness.

In 1550, when an Anabaptist woman, Joan of Kent, was sentenced to the stake for heresy, John Foxe begged Rogers to intervene and save her. Rogers refused. His misguided declaration was that "burning was 'sufficiently mild' for a crime as grave as heresy." I imagine that Rogers remembered his statement just five years later when he faced the same martyr's fire.

A Fiery Voice for Jesus

The Sunday after Edward VI died and Lady Mary was crowned Queen of England, Rogers preached a fiery sermon at St. Paul's Cathedral on the biblical doctrine of faith in Jesus for the justification of sin; he did not mince words as he warned his congregation to beware of the idolatry of Catholicism. This sermon would be his last.

Queen Mary hastily issued an edict against "true preaching" of the Bible and, on August 16, 1553, Rogers was called to stand before the Privy Council and then placed under house arrest. John Rogers had a perfect opportunity to save himself. His friends pleaded with him to escape with his family to the peace of Germany. But he would not be persuaded. Instead, Rogers insisted, "I will stand my ground to answer for Christ's cause among the people of England."

The following January, Rogers was sent to Newgate Prison and locked in the dungeon with fellow reformers John Hooper and John Bradford. They spent a year discussing the Scriptures and praying for God's salvation for the people of England. Mary denied all of their requests to present the scriptural reasons for their beliefs. Yet, she still kept them in prison. What was the queen waiting for?

Mary could have executed the prisoners at her will, but she was waiting for Parliament to reinstate the heretical laws established under Henry VIII. It happened in December of 1554, and within two days, John Rogers and the other prisoners were brought up before Lord Chancellor Stephen Gardiner and the council to hear further allegations. At the end of January, Rogers was brought in chains to the council one last time and condemned as a heretic for "denying the church of Rome and the presence of Christ in the sacrament of communion."

Confident in God's sovereignty, John Rogers "went cheerfully" to the stake at Smithfield on February 4, 1555. Rogers was denied a private meeting with his wife on the day of his death, but she and their ten children accompanied him to Smithfield, singing praises and offering words of encouragement and love. They blessed the Lord with him until he slipped away into eternity.

John Rogers was officially the first of nearly three hundred "Marian" martyrs to be burned for heresy under Queen Mary's reign. Just a few days later, John Hooper and John Bradford became the second and third martyrs to face death at the same execution site for the cause of Jesus Christ.

Fixing our eyes on Jesus, the author and perfecter of faith, who for the joy set before Him endured the cross, despising the shame, and has sat down at the right hand of the throne of God.

(Hebrews 12:2 NASB)

Portrait of Hugh Latimer.
GeorgiosKollidas\Thinkstock

Hugh Latimer: Unflinching Herald of Christ

"Be of good comfort, Mr. Ridley, and play the man!
We shall this day light such a candle by God's grace, in England,
as I trust shall never be put out."
—Hugh Latimer, 1555

Soon after Queen Mary's coronation, a messenger on horseback arrived from London to a quaint country cottage. Breathless from his hasty ride, he jumped from the weary horse and ran to the front door. Knocking feverishly, he cried out, "Master Latimer! Master Latimer! Please open at once! The queen's guards are following close behind. They will arrive within the hour. You must get away at once. Master Latimer, please open!"

Opening the door wide to his young messenger, Hugh Latimer smiled and welcomed his guest inside. The man of God, now seventy years old, knew that with the help of friends he had the time to escape England and flee to Switzerland's comforts. But he had served Jesus Christ for nearly thirty years in England, and he would make a stand in the name of His Lord and Savior in the country that he loved.

Hours later, the palace guards arrived and were surprised when Master Latimer greeted them at the door. "Why didn't you escape while you had the chance?" one guard asked. Latimer cheerfully replied, "My friend, you are a welcome messenger to me! Let it be known to you and to all of the world that I go as willing to London—in order to give a reason for my doctrine—as I have ever gone to any place in the world. I do not doubt that God, who has made me worthy to preach His Word before two excellent princes, will also enable me to witness the same to a third, either for her comfort, or for her discomfort *for all of eternity.*"[132]

Zeal Without Knowledge

Hugh Latimer was born in 1487 in Leicestershire, England; as a young teenager he excelled at Cambridge University and was ordained a priest on September 15, 1515. In the beginning of his ministry, Latimer was a zealous priest, with a desire to please God in everything he did. But as we know from the apostle Paul's letters, it is possible to have religious zeal without knowledge, to strive to establish our own righteousness instead of surrendering to the righteousness of God in Christ Jesus:

> *Brethren, my heart's desire and prayer to God for* [them] *is that they may be saved. For I bear them witness that* ***they have a zeal for***

132. Foxe, *Book of Martyrs*, 275–276.

> ***God, but not according to knowledge.** For they, being ignorant of God's righteousness, and seeking to establish their own righteousness, have not submitted to the righteousness of God.* (Romans 10:1–3)

The Power of God's Word

Thomas Bilney, a friend and fellow priest, saw Latimer's enthusiastic faith was misdirected. Bilney, already a Protestant, wondered how he could "win his zealous yet ignorant brother to the true knowledge of Christ."[133] Bilney came up with a plan to "innocently" share God's Word with his friend.

One afternoon, Bilney approached Latimer and asked him if he would "hear his confession." Naturally, Latimer said yes and then listened attentively while Bilney shared the spiritual freedom he found in the Scriptures and how Christ's gift of salvation had completely changed his life. By the end of his testimony, Latimer was weeping. From that day to the end of his life, Hugh Latimer preached the irrefutable power and truth of God's Word. (Thomas Bilney became a martyr for Christ just a few years later, burned at the stake in 1531 under Henry VIII's reign.)

During the Christmas of 1529, Latimer handed out Scripture cards to his congregation of the Sermon on the Mount. These were the only verses of the Bible that the people had read for themselves. In his weekly sermons, Latimer invited everyone to serve the Lord from their heart, to worship Him in spirit and in truth and not in outward ceremonies and vestments.

Hugh Latimer understood that Satan's plan was always to discourage and defeat God's people. He warned him that "the true servants and preachers of God in this world are commonly scorned and reviled by the proud enemies of God's Word." His next words could be today's headlines. "The world considers Christian believers as madmen, fools, brainless, and even drunkards!"[134]

---

133. Ibid., 263.
134. Ibid., 267.

Latimer Escapes the Trap!

Latimer's preaching was so full of the Holy Spirit and power that King Henry VIII invited him to Windsor Castle to preach to the entire court. Although Henry was a fickle ruler, he admired Latimer's integrity and pure preaching of God's Word. When the Catholic bishops of London began to harass Latimer, pulling him into their chambers three times a week to question him about his beliefs, King Henry ordered the religious persecutors away. Once Henry broke ties with the pope and proclaimed himself the supreme head of the Church of England, he rewarded Latimer by appointing him as the bishop of Worcester.

Latimer's fellow ministers followed the Catholic traditions closely and were always looking for ways to trap him. At one informal meeting, they encouraged Latimer to speak to them from his heart. He was thrilled, certain that the priests were ready to hear the truth of God's grace from the Scriptures.

As Latimer spoke, he heard a strange scratching noise in the nearby chimney. He ignored it at first until it dawned on him—someone was hiding in the chimney and writing his words with quill and paper. It was a trap! His fellow ministers wanted to catch him with his own confession of faith. Subtly, Latimer changed the direction of his message to something less controversial and then left the men with a polite "Good evening" and an innocent smile. That night he recorded, "God was with me and gave me the right answers to say; there is no other way that I could have escaped their trap!"[135]

From Prison to a King's Garden

For years Latimer walked this spiritual tightrope until Henry VIII passed away and Edward VI ascended the throne. Then, he was given a place of honor as one of Edward's favorite preachers at court. In the same royal gardens where Henry had celebrated with lavish, worldly parties, Edward set up a courtyard for Christian prayer and

135. Ibid., 271.

worship, and there Latimer preached the Word of God with freedom and power.

One of the greatest blessings for a Christian is when the Holy Spirit speaks to us in the depths of our own spirit:

> *When the Spirit of truth comes, he will guide you into all the truth, for he will not speak on his own authority, but whatever he hears he will speak, and he will declare to you the things that are to come.*
> (John 16:13 ESV)

Prison Prayers Are Answered!

When King Edward succumbed to tuberculosis and Mary I gained the throne, Latimer, with little surprise, was imprisoned in the Tower of London alongside two other Reformation leaders, the archbishop of Canterbury, Thomas Cranmer, and the bishop of London, Nicholas Ridley. The three men were transported together to Oxford University reportedly to defend their faith before the school's "theological giants." Unfortunately, once they stood in the prisoners' docket, they had no opportunity to share God's Word over the shouting accusations of their prosecutors. Back to the Tower they went and spent five more months together sharing the Word, praying for hours on their knees, and writings letters of encouragement to thousands of believers throughout England.

Latimer had three specific prayers, first, since God had called him to preach the Word, he prayed that God would give him the divine grace to stand upon that Word until the very end; second, that God, in His mercy, would restore the true gospel of Jesus Christ to his beloved England; and third, that God would supernaturally protect and preserve Princess Elizabeth from Mary's bloody executions so that she would sit on the throne of England one day soon. By the grace of almighty God, all three of Latimer's prayers were answered.[136]

136. Ibid., 277–278.

During his trials, Latimer's accusers reminded him of his age and pleaded with him to recant, reminding him of their belief that if he dies a heretic, he is denied eternal life as well as physical life. But Latimer denied their fears, confident of his life in Christ.

Hugh Latimer and Nicholas Ridley were condemned for heresy and sentenced to burn together outside of the Bocardo Gate at Oxford University in the sight of the same theologians who had condemned them. Who was this Nicholas Ridley? Let's see.

Nicholas Ridley: "I Cannot Burn!"

"As long as God gives me life, He shall have not only my heart, but my mouth and my pen to defend His truth."
—Nicholas Ridley, 1555

Under the reign of Edward VI, Nicholas Ridley, the bishop of London, spent an afternoon with Lady Mary Tudor (the future Queen Mary), speaking to her about the freedom found in God's Word and offering to preach for her on the following Sunday. Ridley ended with, "Madam, I trust you will not refuse God's Word."

Mary answered him in anger, wanting nothing to do with the man or his message. "You wouldn't have dared to preach from the Bible in this same way in my father's day!" she retorted. "As for your new books, I thank God that I never read any of them. I never did, nor ever will do!"[137]

Rising Through the Ranks

Nicholas Ridley had the opportunity to talk with a member of the royal family because he was an excellent theologian and preacher who

137. Ibid., 284–285.

rose up in the ranks of the Catholic Church and was appointed as a chaplain to Thomas Cranmer, the archbishop of Canterbury. When King Henry VIII renounced the authority of the pope, Ridley was promoted again and became the bishop of Rochester in the new Church of England. Soon after, he came to a saving knowledge of Jesus Christ and began to preach the truth of God's Word. Together, he and Cranmer wrote the first *Common Book of Prayer,* parts of which are still used by the Anglican Church today.

Finally, under Edward VI's Protestant reign, Ridley became the bishop of London where he used his influence to preach the love of God revealed to us in Christ's sacrifice on the cross. To every person in his congregation who could read, Ridley gave an English New Testament and encouraged them to memorize as many verses of the Scriptures as possible.

In the spring of 1553, when England's leaders realized that young King Edward was dying, Ridley made a very risky choice—politically and spiritually. He was one of the counselors who convinced Edward to denounce his father's Third Succession Act and bypass Lady Mary to hand over the throne to his cousin the Protestant Lady Jane Grey. It was a desperate attempt to save the country from returning to Catholicism. Ridley personally signed the legal documents declaring Lady Jane as the new heir. With that signature, he also signed his own death warrant.

The Oxford Martyrs

As soon as Mary gained power, she renounced Nicholas Ridley as the bishop of London and imprisoned him in the Tower of London, along with Hugh Latimer and Thomas Cranmer. There, as I wrote earlier, they spent months in prayer and studying God's Word. It was on March 10, 1555, that the three men were escorted from the Tower of London to Oxford University to answer the accusations of the leading theologians of both Oxford and Cambridge. The theologians had three questions for the prisoners: 1) was the natural body of Christ really in the sacrament after the priest prayed and consecrated it?; 2) after the prayer of consecration of the Eucharist, did any substance of the bread and wine remain?; and 3) during each mass, was there a renewed sacrifice for the sins of the living and the dead?

Painting of Nicholas Ridley writing in his prison cell.
Photos.com\Thinkstock

Dr. Ridley answered immediately; communion was a spiritual commemoration of Christ's death; the bread and wine were still present in the Eucharist, and Jesus' sacrifice for sins did not have to be renewed in every mass—His death on the cross was "once for all." When Ridley tried to explain the biblical truth behind his answers, the theologians refused to listen. The room erupted into tumultuous confusion with cries of "Blasphemy! "Blasphemy!" echoing off of the walls. The reformers' trial ended in chaos, and the men were returned to prison. From that point on they were referred to as the *Oxford Martyrs*.

Kissing the Stakes

On September 28, Latimer and Ridley were brought to trial again; when the priests demanded that Ridley recant, he answered without hesitation, "I utterly refuse and renounce the usurped supremacy and abused authority of the bishop of Rome. I do not in any way give my obedience or honor to him lest by doing that I might dishonor the truth of God's Word."[138]

Latimer and Ridley were scheduled for execution on October 16, 1555. The last night of Ridley's life, his brother offered to stay up with him throughout the night to comfort him in his sorrow. But Ridley's answer was full of faith in the God that awaited him in heaven. "No, no, that you shall not do. For I plan, God willing, to go to bed and to sleep as quietly tonight as I ever have in my life."[139]

The next morning, the men were paraded slowly down the streets of London to a location outside the Bocardo Gate of Oxford University. Thomas Cranmer hadn't been sentenced yet, but he was taken under guard to a nearby tower and forced to watch his friends cruelly burn. As the godly men were brought to the stake in their tattered prison clothes, they embraced one another with the confidence of Christ, looking up to the tower where they thought Cranmer might be stationed. Then both men knelt down and kissed the stakes.

As one long metal chain was wrapped around both men's waists to secure them to the stake. Hugh Latimer turned to Nicholas Ridley and made the statement that is still so well-known today: "Be of good comfort and play the man, Master Ridley; we shall this day light such a candle, by God's grace, in England, as I trust shall never be put out."[140] And the fires were lit.

With eyes uplifted, Master Latimer gave a cry, "O Father of heaven, receive my soul;" he reached out his arms as though he was embracing the flame and died soon after.

Tragically, Nicholas Ridley's execution was particularly horrific. It was common practice to allow the condemned to place pouches of gunpowder under their arms to hasten their deaths. Once the fire touched the gunpowder it would bring a quick end. Latimer and

138. Ibid., 296.
139. Ibid., 305.
140. Ibid., 309.

Ridley both had pouches placed under their arms, and once the fire reached Latimer's chest his pain was over. For Ridley it was not so easy. Not enough logs had been placed under him causing a small but intense fire; his lower body nearly burned away while he remained alive. As he cried out, "Let the fire come unto me! I cannot burn!" his brother-in-law foolishly threw more kindling on the pyre which smothered the fire but kept it burning from underneath. When Ridley cried out again, a Christian bystander reached into the flames and pulled the planks off of the top. The fire shot up to Ridley's chest and the gunpowder exploded. Finally, the man of God could join his Savior in heaven.

Today, there is a small cross on Broad Street, Oxford, which marks the spot of Nicholas Ridley's death. Ridley Hall at the University of Cambridge, Ridley College in Ontario, Canada, and Ridley Melbourne, a theological college in Australia, are all named after the faithful martyr. Ridley had "played the man" well for the sake of the gospel and his Master, Jesus Christ.

> *For I am already being poured out as a drink offering, and the time of my departure has come. I have fought the good fight, I have finished the course, I have kept the faith; in the future there is laid up for me the crown of righteousness, which the Lord, the righteous Judge, will award to me on that day; and not only to me, but also to all who have loved His appearing.* (2 Timothy 4:6–8 NASB)

Thomas Cranmer: Forgiveness at the Flames

"In the midst of life we are in death, earth to earth, ashes to ashes, dust to dust, in sure and certain hope of the Resurrection!"
—Thomas Cranmer, 1555

The learned Thomas Cranmer.
GeorgiosKollidas\Thinkstock

Thomas Cranmer was born on July 2, 1489, in Nottinghamshire, England. At the very young age of fourteen he was sent to Jesus College at Cambridge University to train for a career in the church. Unlike other priests who cared little about the Bible, Cranmer spent three years of his education studying the Scriptures in detail, laying a strong foundation for his life's work.

Cranmer was so well-read in the Bible that when King Henry VIII was looking for a "scriptural" reason to divorce Catherine, two of his counselors recommended Thomas Cranmer as the man for the job. Cranmer was reluctant to get involved; he hated controversy all of his life and wanted to remain on good terms with both the king and queen. He was angry with the king's advisors for putting him on the spot. However, the king commanded and Cranmer obeyed.[141]

Remember the Scripture from Leviticus 20:21 that the king used for his annulment concerning not marrying your brother's wife? Well, Cranmer was the one who came up with the idea of applying that Scripture to the king's situation and helped write the king's official annulment request to the pope. In these early days, Cranmer was a man who

141. Ibid., 354.

had some knowledge of God's Word, but he didn't have the Holy Spirit's indwelling to help him understand it.

We know that Henry's attempt to receive an annulment from the pope failed, but the king never forgot Cranmer's attempt to help. This launched an unusual fifteen-year friendship between Cranmer and the irascible king. Although Thomas had little church leadership experience, King Henry rewarded him for his help by appointing him the archbishop of Canterbury, the highest spiritual position in England. Bishops throughout the country were shocked, and, in their jealousy, they spent the next decade looking for ways to destroy Cranmer's reputation.

In the midst of this political controversy, Cranmer spent several months in Germany on business for the king. With his own eyes he saw how the power of God's Word was transforming lives in Germany and Switzerland. For the first time, Cranmer looked at the Word of God as it related to his personal salvation. With a full heart, he accepted Jesus Christ's sacrifice on the cross for his sins, and a whole new world opened up to him. Now when he read the Scriptures, he saw clearly how church doctrine was in direct opposition to God's Word. Cranmer returned from Germany a changed man, but still with a very cautious personality. Instead of making open statements about his new faith, he continued to support Henry and to gradually begin replacing older bishops and priests in England with ones who were born again into new life in Christ.

Freedom for Change

Thomas Cranmer was with Henry VIII on the evening of his death, January 28, 1547. He prayed for the king while gripping the ruler's hand tightly. Instead of performing the last rites of the Catholic Church, Cranmer read the Reformed statement of faith to his king, praying that he would accept Christ's full salvation for his soul.

With young King Edward on the throne, Cranmer was finally free to makes changes to the Church of England. He had originally written most of *The Common Book of Prayer* and now he added corrections including a strong statement on the doctrine of justification by faith. Cranmer condemned the adoration of the bread and wine in the Eucharist and rejected all prayers for the dead. In 1549, he petitioned Parliament to legalize marriage for Anglican priests.

"I Thank God That I Am My Own Man!"

In May of 1553, Cranmer also joined the king's Privy Council in convincing the dying Edward to name a Protestant successor to the throne. As dangerous as the decision was, he felt it was worth the risk. Queen Mary did not agree!

Edward died on July 6, 1553, and one month later, on August 8, Cranmer directed the young king's funeral out of the *Common Prayer Book* without any interference from Queen Mary. Secretly, the archbishop was advising all Protestant leaders to flee the country, but he was convinced through prayer that God wanted him to remain.

After the funeral, Cranmer requested an audience with the queen but she refused to see him. On September 14, 1553, Cranmer was called before the council and then sent straight to the Tower to join Latimer and Ridley. With a plan to break Cranmer's will, the queen had him separated from the other two men and he spent the next seventeen months isolated in prison. Cranmer faced a third trial on September 12, 1555, but still no sentence was set.

As I wrote earlier, Ridley and Latimer were burned at the stake on October 16, 1555, and the former archbishop was forced to be a spectator from a nearby tower. Horrified, Cranmer stood beside the queen's counselors and watched the barbaric execution. Cranmer was shaken to the core. How could he face the same fate; could he still stand strong in his testimony? It is hard to blame Cranmer for what happened next.

Stumbling Near the Finish Line

Reading Cranmer's story, we need to each examine our own hearts closely—how would we react to the horrifying sights, sounds and smells of close friends burning at the stake? Each one of us has to consider how we would handle the threat of barbarous execution for the cause of Christ. Many martyrs have given their lives for Jesus, but none of them were perfect. Only Jesus Christ's sacrifice was a perfect one. This is the story of a saint who stumbled but still found the grace to return to his testimony of faith before it was too late.

This is the story of a saint who stumbled but still found the grace to return to his testimony of faith before it was too late.

In December, Cranmer was suddenly released from prison, given a comfortable room in a noble's home and treated like a visiting guest. Queen Mary was using a new tactic. It would be excellent PR if a man who had been the archbishop of Canterbury for two decades would recant and return to the Catholic faith. While Cranmer was in the sudden comfort and friendliness of his enemies, he was invited one last time to recant. This time he succumbed. Cranmer began a series of recantations, submitting to the authority of Queen Mary, her husband, Prince Philip, and the pope as head of the church. He rejected all Protestant faith and doctrines, confessed his sins to a priest, and participated once again in the Catholic Mass. For the next three months, he submitted to the will of the Catholic bishops and broke down weeping in a confession of his errors.[142]

The queen and her advisors had defeated the enemy. They decided to celebrate their complete victory by still requiring his death at the stake. Although he had recanted, the queen refused to grant the

142. Ibid., 380.

sixty-six-year-old Cranmer a pardon. She would not forgive the man who had been instrumental in the destruction of her mother's marriage and her position as the queen. The day of Cranmer's execution was set.

I believe that Satan over-played his hand in dealing with Thomas Cranmer. Having his recantation wasn't good enough for the devil; he wanted Cranmer to die, and so he pressed the queen to send him to the stake. If Satan hadn't pushed so hard, the queen may have had a great victory. Cranmer might have remained a mouthpiece for Mary I and broken down the resolve of the English people. Instead, the victory went to Cranmer and to the true church of Jesus Christ.

Vanquishing the Enemy

Before the execution, a priest entered Cranmer's prison cell and ordered him to write a letter denouncing his former beliefs to be read to the people in the public square. Cranmer agreed, but secretly he wrote a second letter denouncing the pope and begging forgiveness of Jesus and the English people. He tucked the secret letter into the folds of his robe.

As the new archbishop of Canterbury, Reginald Cole, read the recantation letter that Cranmer had originally written, the prisoner hung his head in sorrow and tears of shame slipped from his eyes "dropping down his fatherly face." Then Cole turned to the forlorn Cranmer and announced, "Brethren, lest any of you have a doubt about this man's earnest conversion, you shall hear him speak before you. Please Master Cranmer, express the true profession of your faith that all men may understand that you are a Catholic indeed."[143]

"Lord Jesus, Receive My Spirit"

"I will do it," replied Cranmer. "For I have come to the end of my life, and here hangs all my life to come, whether I will live with Christ forever in joy or else be in pain forever with wicked devils in hell.... I shall therefore declare to you my true faith.... I believe in God the Father

143. Ibid., 384.

Almighty, the Maker of heaven and earth. And I believe every word and sentence taught by our Savior Jesus Christ, His apostles and prophets in the Old and New Testaments." The queen's counselors began to shift uneasily.

"*And now I renounce and refuse those things written by my hand that are contrary to the truth that I believe in my heart.* They were written in fear of death and to save my life.... I have written many things untrue, and my hand which has offended shall be punished first, for when I come to the fire, it shall first be burned. As for the Pope, I refuse him as Christ's enemy and antichrist with all his false doctrine."[144]

Thomas Cranmer burned at the stake.
Photos.com\Thinkstock

The university theologians jumped to their feet shouting, "Liar! This is not your true confession!" The entire execution site was in an uproar. The accusers had "looked for a glorious victory and a perpetual triumph but instead they had been defeated." There was nothing they could do because Cranmer was no longer under their control. He was already facing the ultimate punishment.

"Stop the heretic's mouth and take him away!" shouted Cole. Cranmer was pulled from the pulpit and dragged to the site where Latimer and Ridley's ashes had settled just six months earlier. Cranmer fell to his knees and prayed to God, stood to remove his outer gown down

144. Ibid., 384–385, emphasis added.

to his shift, and turned to shake hands with several old friends. The iron chain was fastened around his waist and the fire was kindled. As the flames rose, Cranmer stuck his right hand into the fire fulfilling his promise that his hand would suffer the fire first. His last words were, "Lord Jesus, receive my spirit.... I see the heaven open and Jesus standing at the right hand of God."[145] He stood perfectly still as the flames shot up around him and he slipped into eternity.

"Thomas Cranmer renounces the pope!" It took only a day or two before the glad news spread throughout London: Thomas Cranmer had denied the pope, renounced his recantations, and thrown himself on the mercy of Jesus Christ, the King of Kings and Lord of Lords. Like the thief at the cross, when Cranmer had one last chance to repent and make things right in the Lord's sight, he took it.

> *In the same way, I tell you, there is joy in the presence of the angels of God over one sinner who repents.* (Luke 15:10 NASB)

The Stratford Martyrs

As Queen Mary's persecution grew more intense, she became obsessed with finding anyone who rebelled against the Catholic doctrines. Although the academics and Protestants in prominent positions were targeted first, soon the common people were in danger. The queen's palace guards went through the cities and villages of England, looking for people who refused to attend Mass or were guilty simply of reading their English Bibles. The church persecutors began to condemn groups of people for execution, tying them to the stakes and burning them in one fiery holocaust.

In 1556, in the town of Stratford-le-Bow just outside of London, eleven men and two women were arrested for heresy, denying one or more of the Catholic doctrines. John Foxe has recorded their names and I want to name them as well for their sacrifice for the name of Jesus

145. Ibid., 386–387.

Christ. They were: Henry Aldington, Laurence Parnam, Henry Wye, William Hallywel, Thomas Bowyer, George Searles, Edmund Hurst, Lyon Cawch, Ralph Jackson, John Derifall, John Routh, Elizabeth Pepper, and Agnes George.

After the thirteen were condemned, the sheriff separated them into two separate rooms and attempted to trick some of them into recanting. On the morning of June 27, 1556, as they were about to face the fires of death, the sheriff walked briskly through the door of one prison cell and announced, "Your friends in the other cell have recanted. They do not wish to see their flesh burn on this sorry day. Their lives will be saved, and they will be released. You must make the same choice! Do not cast your lives away for nothing!"

Answering with one voice, the first group responded, "Our faith is not built on man, but on Jesus Christ crucified. We will not recant."

There was no way that the sheriff could persuade them to change their minds, so he left them in disgust and walked into the second cell to try again. "Be just as wise," he counseled them, "Don't kill yourselves today." Praise God, this group of believers were also grounded on the rock of Jesus Christ and answered willingly, "Our faith is not built upon man but on Christ and His sure Word."

The sheriff and his guards led the thirteen men and women to the execution site walking through a loving and supportive crowd of families and friends. When they arrived, the sheriff was astonished at the joy with which the prisoners knelt before the stakes and kissed them. The eleven men were herded around three stakes and fastened to them with a chain while the women stood loose in the middle of the fire circle. With love in their hearts for one another and a constant faith in Jesus Christ, they were burned together in one huge funeral pyre. The spectators, both Protestant and Catholic, marveled at the strength and fervency of their faith in the Lord Jesus Christ.[146]

146. Ibid., 399–400.

Appointed and Anointed

During the five years of Mary I's reign, the records show 287 people by name who were martyred by burning at the stake. The final testimony, as Queen Mary I lay on her deathbed, was November 15, 1558 when three men and two women were burned for heresy in Canterbury. Remember, the first name of Queen Mary's martyrs was John Rogers; the last name was an elderly woman named Katherine Knight who laid down her frail life on November 15 for Jesus' sake. Two days later, November 17, 1558, Bloody Mary was dead. The newly crowned Queen Elizabeth called all heretical burnings to an immediate halt.

During the five years of Mary I's reign, the records show 287 people by name who were martyred by burning at the stake.

A jubilant John Foxe wrote, "Suddenly, the Lord called to remembrance His mercy and, forgetting our former iniquity, made an end of all these miseries. Queen Elizabeth was appointed and anointed...through whose true and natural crown, the brightness of God's Word was set up again to confound the dark kingdom of the Antichrist."

In the beginning of Elizabeth's forty-five year reign, she was openly tolerant of Catholic citizens as long as they remained loyal to her as queen. However, thirty years later, in 1558, her throne was seriously threatened by Catholic revolts. On one side by Mary Stuart, Queen of Scots and her attempt to take over the English throne. On the other side, by Philip II, King of Spain and his attack on England's navy with the Spanish Armada. Both of these threats were defeated, but to protect her throne, Elizabeth authorized the execution of rebellious Catholic priests over the next fifteen years. She did not condemn them for heresy by burning at the stake, but for treason against the crown, by hanging.

It's Hard to Wrap Your Head Around It

So, how do we, as twenty-first century Christians, process the heroic accounts of these English Reformers and the horrifying deaths that they faced? Hundreds of men and women who trusted Jesus enough to die in gruesome ways rather than deny the Bible as the true Word of God. They died to affirm the truths of "justification by faith" in Christ, the priesthood of the believer, and the forgiveness of our sins without the mediation of an earthly priest. They kissed the fiery stakes so that the false adoration of bread and wine and the worshiping of statues would come to an end. Finally, they perished so that they could own and preach from the same English Bibles that we might be guilty of tossing on a table and leaving unopened for days.

They stood strong for righteousness' sake, and I believe that the grace of God will be sufficient to give the same strength to all of His children who may face persecution in the days and years ahead. The victory will always lie in Jesus Christ and the power of His death and resurrection.

I am the resurrection and the life. He who believes in Me, though he may die, he shall live. And whoever lives and believes in Me shall never die. Do you believe this? (John 11:25–26)

MISSIONARIES GO INTO ALL THE WORLD

8

MISSIONARIES GO INTO ALL THE WORLD

(AD 1600–1800)

> [Jesus] *said to them, "Go into all the world and preach the gospel to all creation."* (Mark 16:15 NIV)

A chilling scream broke the silence. Chinese warriors led by their fearsome leader, Koxinga, had swept over the walls of Fort Provintia on the island of Formosa. As the sword-wielding Chinese forces raced through the compound, Dutch soldiers lay slain on the ground overcome by the fearless raiders. Arriving at the door of the pastor's home, the warriors burst in to find the Reverend Antonius

Hambroek hiding along with his wife and two of his teen-aged daughters. The four were immediately bound and taken as prisoners of war to face Koxinga at his new headquarters inside the fort. The year was 1661. What were these Dutch soldiers and missionaries doing so far from the northern shores of Europe?

Caught in the Middle

As the Reformation ended, a new obsession hit the European continent. Instead of in-fighting over Catholic and Protestant beliefs, European countries began to look for quick wealth outside of their borders, sending newly-designed ships all over the world. Their goal was to colonize native countries and bring their wealth back to Europe. Before long, faithful Christians with a desire to spread the gospel to the nations began to travel along to these newly colonized lands.

Christian missionaries of the 1600s, 1700s, and 1800s circled the globe bringing the message of Jesus Christ to native people who had never heard His name. This was their fulfillment of the Great Commission: *"Go into all the world and preach the gospel to all creation"* (Mark 16:15 NIV). But it was much more complicated than it seemed. Christian missionaries were often caught in the middle: between their missionary zeal to make disciples, the European scramble to claim new lands and riches, and the native peoples' desire to be self-governing. The unfortunate result was often confusion, mistrust, and death. To many of the native inhabitants, the foreigners who brought the gospel of peace and salvation through Jesus Christ were the same ones who brought military domination and colonialism to their land.

It was a turbulent period of contrasts with phenomenal church growth led by faithful Christian disciples versus political oppression and death caused by mercenary greed. At times, the Christian missionaries flourished; other times it resulted in their martyrdom. Here are some of their stories.

The Dutch in Formosa, Early 1600s

Colonialism began very early in the 1600s, and one small country that made its presence known throughout much of the world was the Netherlands. The Dutch East India Trading Company owned more territory and was considered more powerful than most nations. In 1623, it expanded to the island of Formosa (modern Taiwan). Being under the rule of white foreigners was naturally resented by the island natives as well as mainland China. To make matters worse, while establishing their colony, the Dutch committed many atrocities, including setting fire to villages and killing any protesting natives. Into this environment of conflict, Christian missionaries began to arrive, eager to share the gospel message.

The first came in 1627—the first Protestant international missionary.[147] By 1643, there were several flourishing mission works in Formosa, including schools, Sunday Schools, and churches. Most of these missionaries truly longed to spread the Christian gospel, to carry the message of salvation in Christ. They were not looking for riches or to take advantage of the indigent people. Unfortunately, those missionaries had to work in an environment of hostile resentment toward colonialism, and they got caught in the crossfires.

An Early Missionary Massacre

In 1661, Koxinga, a fearsome Chinese leader of the Manchu-Tartar dynasty on mainland China, swooped in to oust the Dutch from the rich island of Formosa. While the Dutch troops holed themselves up in forts in an unsuccessful attempt to ward off the invasion, Koxinga's warriors terrorized the island. As an experienced general, Koxinga centered his attack on what he considered the greatest weakness of the Dutch, the Christian missionaries:

147. See James Croil, *The Noble Army of Martyrs* (Philadelphia: Presbyterian Board of Publication, 1894), 76, also available at babel.hathitrust.org/cgi/pt?id=nnc1.cr59898534;view=2up;seq=108.

> Especially were the ministers and schoolmasters singled out for every form of cruel indignity and even death itself. Koxinga issuing orders for their arrest, and causing some of them to be crucified in those very villages where they had been [performing] their gracious and self-denying work."[148]

Once his soldiers captured the missionary Antonius Hambroek, (as we saw in the chapter opening), Koxinga planned to use him as an important pawn in the surrender of the larger Dutch stronghold, Fort Zeelandia.

Large modern-day statue commemorating the achievements of Koxinga.
SvetlanaSF\Thinkstock

Koxinga held Fort Zeelandia under siege, prepared to do whatever was necessary to force the Dutch from the island. The Chinese leader sent Reverend Hambroek to the fort with the demand that the Dutch

148. Rev. W. Campbell, *Sketches from Formosa* (London, Edinburgh, New York: Marshall Brothers, Ltd., 1915), 346.

forces surrender. If they didn't agree, the missionary would be executed when he returned to his family. Once Hambroek entered the blockade at Fort Zeelandia, he urged the fort's commander not to surrender. The missionary must have decided that he would be denying his Christian faith if he gave into Koxinga's threats. When he returned to Koxinga at Fort Provintia, the enraged Chinese chief was true to his word. Hambroek was beheaded along with missionaries Arnold Winsheim, Petrus Mus, and Jacobus Ampzingius. Hombroek's oldest daughter became Koxinga's concubine and was added to his harem that very day.

While most of the Dutch men were executed, the women and children were sold into slavery. The daily journal of the Dutch fort included a sad report concerning the captured women: "the best were preserved for the use of the [Chinese] commanders, and the remainder sold to the common soldiers."

More than five hundred Dutch men, women, and children were killed during the weeks of conflict and the Dutch were driven from Formosa. The villagers, it is recorded, gleefully threw away their Christian textbooks and joined in the headhunts. However, these people were the ancestors of those who, two centuries later, would once again open their arms to Christianity and its missionaries as the church in Asia grew.

First Missionary to Labrador, Canada, 1752

"A wind West South West brought a ship called the *Hope* into a secluded harbour on the Labrador coast on Monday, the 31st of July, 1752. On board were four Moravian missionaries and the man who had inspired the voyage: Johann Christian Erhardt, a thirty-three-year-old mariner from the Baltic port of Wismar."[149]

Johann Christian Erhardt was born in 1720 in a seacoast town of northern Germany with an early love for sailing the high seas. Long before he turned twenty-one, he became a sailor and sailed across the

149. "First Moravian Exploration of Labrador in 1752," Memorial University, http://www.mun.ca/rels/makkovik/nisbet.htm.

Atlantic to the West Indies. By God's grace, in 1741, while in port at St. Eustatius in the Caribbean, he met Moravian missionaries whose Christian message transformed his life. Erhardt immediately resigned his commission and signed on with the Moravian vessel, the *Irene*. He was determined to spread the gospel message by sailing the Moravian missionaries to their new locations on the North American continent.

The Moravian Missionary Vision

The Moravian Church, which has its roots in the Hussite movement started by Jan Hus, was officially founded in 1722, when a group of Christians sought out protection from Nikolaus Ludwig von Zinzendorf, a nobleman in the eastern part of modern-day Germany. The Moravian refugees established a village called Herrnhut, which grew rapidly and became the center for Christian missions during the eighteenth century. (See my book *God's Generals: The Missionaries* for details on the Moravian missionary movement.) Within years of settling in Herrnhut, the Moravians were sending missionaries to Greenland, to South Africa, and to the Native Americans of the New World. This is where Johann Erhardt saw his call in Christ.

In the late 1740s, Erhardt sailed several times to Labrador (northeastern Canada), with supplies for the settlers there. As he roamed the beautiful wilds of the coastland, he dreamed of a mission in Labrador to the Inuit natives. His dream became a reality when Claude Nisbit, a Moravian businessman, offered Johann a joint missionary and trade journey to Labrador.[150] Erhardt had already picked up some of the Inuit language when he visited Greenland, so he believed the Labrador outreach would be a blessing. He wrote to a Moravian bishop, "It would be a source of the greatest joy if the Saviour would discover to me that he had chosen me and would make me fit for this service."[151]

---

150. Ibid.

151. William H. Whiteley, "Erhardt, John Christian," *Dictionary of Canadian Biography*, vol. 3, University of Toronto/Université Laval, http://www.biographi.ca/en/bio/erhardt_john_christian_3E.html, accessed April 14, 2016.

A short time later, Erhardt, second-in-command of the *Hope*, set sail from England with four Moravian missionaries on board. After landing in Labrador, Erhardt bartered with a group of cautious Inuit while the crew "labored to set up a prefabricated house brought from Europe, in case the missionaries should decide to winter in Labrador." They named the new little settlement Hopedale.

Before returning to mainland Europe, the *Hope* sailed farther north with plans to trade with another Inuit tribe. Erhardt, the captain, and five crew members rowed ashore with their last small boat. They were never seen alive again. Two days later, in great discouragement, the *Hope* sailed back to Hopedale, picked up the four missionaries and returned to England. The following summer, the ship's crew returned and found the bodies of the missing men as well as the destroyed mission house. "There can be little doubt that they were killed by [Inuit]: some of the murderers were actually pointed out to later missionaries."[152]

Today, the majority of the people of Labrador are still Moravians. Christianity has remained constant there for nearly two hundred and fifty years.

Thankfully, that was not the end of the Moravian outreach in Labrador. Erhardt's vision inspired a young Danish man to keep the dream alive. "A Moravian carpenter, Jens Haven, was stirred by a strong desire to carry the Gospel to Erhardt's murderers. He took a leading part in the Moravian expeditions of the 1760s which led to the establishment of the first mission post in 1771."[153] Today, the majority of the people of Labrador are still Moravians. Christianity has remained constant there for nearly two hundred and fifty years.

152. Ibid.
153. Ibid.

For all the promises of God find their Yes in him. That is why it is through him that we utter our Amen to God for his glory.
(2 Corinthians 1:20)

The Gnadenhutten Massacre, 1782

A young Christian Lenape male, scalped but still alive, slipped into the cellar of a one-room cabin in the Ohio valley. Above, his family, friends, and entire community lay sprawled on top of each other—martyred. As he crouched below, their blood dripped through the ceiling. He quietly made his way to a window, waited for dark, then escaped into the woods. His name was Jacob, and he was one of two survivors of the Gnadenhutten Massacre during America's Revolutionary War. Ninety-six Lenape men, women, and children were slaughtered that day by Revolutionary militia.[154]

Sign at the site of the Gnadenhutten Massacre proclaims it a "Day of Shame."
Michael\Flikr

154. See Croil, *The Noble Army of Martyrs*, 78.

As we know from Johann Erhardt's story, Moravian missionaries had sailed to North America where they established flourishing Christian communities in New York, North Carolina, Pennsylvania, and among the Lenape Indians in eastern Ohio where their mission was "not merely to preach to a few, but to convert a whole nation."[155] They came astonishingly close to reaching that goal, establishing large Lenape settlements with natives who had committed their lives to Jesus Christ.

Site of the Gnadenhutten Massacre in Ohio.
Bwsmith84\Wikimedia Commons.

Everything abruptly changed in 1776 when the chaos of the American Revolutionary War erupted. In the early war years, both the British and the American military leaders solicited the help of the Lenape, but the Moravians—whose tenets include non-violence—stoutly refused. The missionary leader David Zeisberger wrote:

> "We will not go to war, and will not buy anything of warriors taken in war;" and not knowing or caring much about the points at issue, both he and his colleagues endeavored to preserve an

155. J. E. Hutton, *A History of Moravian Missions* (London: Moravian Publication Office, 1922), 102, also available at babel.hathitrust.org/cgi/pt?id=nyp.33433068281066;view=1up;seq=116.

> attitude of strict neutrality. "If the Delawares [Lenape] go to war," he said, "we are lost." To that policy Zeisberger held firm.[156]

Unfortunately, because he refused to become an ally of either side, both the British and the Americans regarded Zeisberger and the Lenape as the enemy. Eventually, in March of 1782, it led to the tragic massacre of Lenape Christians in Gnadenhutten, Ohio.

> Just when they [the Lenape] had completed their labors, an American Colonel, David Williamson, arrived, with a few troops, upon the scene. For reasons which have never been fully explained, but which, to him, must have seemed satisfactory, Colonel Williamson was convinced that all those converts were British spies, and after dividing them into two lots, placing the men in one barn and the women and children in another…the soldiers flung open the barn-doors, and asked the prisoners if they were prepared to die.
>
> "We have committed our souls to God," was the answer, "and trust to Him to give us the needful courage."

The soldiers fell upon them, killed them, and hurried off with their scalps on their belts. This was one of the most vivid atrocities of military aggression against a peaceful Native American tribe on record. The tragedy is increased by the fact that the Christian Lenape were probably killed by men who considered themselves Christians as well. These are the times when martyrdom in Jesus is very hard to explain. May the Lord forgive us for the sins of ignorance and hatred.

Scotland's First Modern Missionary: Peter Greig, 1797

In the late eighteenth century, Christians in England and Scotland were alive with a new fervor for foreign missions, following the

156. Ibid, 110.

leading of William Carey, the British "father of modern missions."[157] The Edinburgh Missionary Society of Scotland chose two young men to send to the Susoo people living near the Rio Pongas River of western Africa. Peter Greig, a former gardener, and Henry Brunton both petitioned the Edinburgh Missionary Society to send them as lay missionaries to West Africa. They left Scotland for what is modern-day Sierra Leone, eager to introduce the Susoo natives to the Savior Jesus Christ.

The following year brought fruitful ministry for the young men. After arriving on Africa's west coast, Greig and Brunton traveled one hundred miles into the interior to work among the Susoos in a region that is now modern Burkina Faso. They were eager to learn the language and to reach out to the violent Foulah tribe in the area. They each moved to different tribes where they were welcomed by the local chiefs.

He welcomed them wholeheartedly, giving them a place to stay for the night and befriending them by showing them some of his Scottish possessions.

Peter established a friendly relationship with Chief Fantimanra who gave the missionary a portion of tribal land and a home so that he could become a part of the village. Each night Peter sat around the village fires with the Susoo people learning their native language and customs. When he left the tribe to visit other villages, he was welcomed back enthusiastically at his return. Some of the adult natives may have hesitated to accept the gospel, but they eagerly sent their young boys to live with and be trained by Greig in his home.[158] Peter's work was prospering.

157. See my book, *God's Generals: the Missionaries* (New Kensington, PA: Whitaker House, 2014) for more details.
158. Thomas Smith, *The Origin and History of Missions* (Boston: S. Walker, Lincoln and Edmands, 1834), 213–216.

One day, in late January 1800, seven men from a nearby Foulah tribe visited Greig, pretending to be curious about salvation in Christ. He welcomed them wholeheartedly, giving them a place to stay for the night and befriending them by showing them some of his Scottish possessions from home. He even presented them with an unusual gift, a small metal razor.

> With true missionary hospitality he took them into his own house, already somewhat full with Susoo boys, and he sought to attach all the seven to himself by showing them the various European articles which he had. The evening of the 31st January passed pleasantly, and Peter Greig retired to rest with the hope that he had thus secured entrance into Foulah-land which he had persistently sought. But…their leader, to whom Mr. Greig had presented a razor, rose at midnight, and with it…cut [Grieg's] throat from ear to ear. Joined by his six companions, the assassin plundered the house and fled.[159]

While the murder was taking place, one of the young boys awakened and, trembling with fear, pretended to be asleep. After the murderers fled, the native boys cried in anguish and rushed out to alert the tribal leaders. Chief Fantimanra and his warriors pursued and captured the murdering band and retrieved most of Greig's stolen goods, but nothing could make up for the loss of the village friend who was so loved.[160]

Peter Greig was only twenty-five years old.

Mission work in the Foulah tribe slowed down for a time, but the gospel work that was closer to the African coast in present-day Sierra Leone prospered.

> In 1822, nearly two thousand of the freed slaves, adults and children, were in the mission schools, several thousands were attending public worship, and some hundreds had become sincere

159. George Smith, *Twelve Pioneer Missionaries* (London, Edinburgh, New York: Thomas Nelson and Sons, 1900), 133.
160. Thomas Smith, *The Origin and History*, 213–216.

> Christians.... In 1862 the Sierra Leone Church was organized on an independent basis, and undertook the support of its own pastors, churches, and schools, aided by a small grant from the society.[161]

Today, twenty percent of the population of Sierra Leone is Christian, predominately Protestant evangelicals.

Revolution in India: 1857

"I was at one time blind, but now I see. God mercifully opened my eyes, and I have found a refuge in Christ. Yes, I am a Christian, and am resolved to live and die a Christian."
—Wilayat Ali, 1857

Martyrs for Jesus have never been limited to foreign missionaries. In fact, today, the majority of Christian martyrs are native to their homelands. By the mid-1800s, Christian communities were alive and prospering throughout the world. Unfortunately, there was growing resentment in colonies because of European rule. This was a major problem in India, where the British ruled the nation for nearly 200 years and tensions were often high. The result, at times, was the martyrdom of faithful Christian converts.

The Indian Mutiny of 1857, as it was called by the Europeans, was not an organized rebellion, but rather "an outbreak of violence without leader and without objective beyond being motivated by a string of grievances."[162] Native Christians were targeted as well as the British. Wilayat Ali, husband of Fatima and father to seven children, was one of the faithful Christian martyrs who stood strong for Jesus Christ.

161. George Smith, *Twelve Pioneer Missionaries*, 135.
162. Rupert Colley, "Siege of Cawnpore Summary, History in an Hour, http://www.historyinanhour.com/2012/06/27/siege-of-cawnpore-summary/.

Wilayat Ali: Converted Muslim

Wilayat Ali was born in a well-respected Muslim family in Agra, India; his father had even made two pilgrimages to Mecca which gave him great favor among the Muslims in his community. So, family and friends were shocked when Wilayat began spending time with a British missionary who gently persuaded the kind young man to read the Bible. After struggling for a few years, Wilayat decided that the Christian Bible was the true Word of God. He turned to Christianity and spent hours studying under the missionaries in Agra. As was expected, his family and friends exploded in anger and revenge at his decision.[163]

"No sooner was he baptized than his own family and neighbours commenced to throw bricks into his yard, stopped him from getting water at the well, and attempted to poison him. A dish of food was sent to him, but his suspicions being aroused, he gave it to his dog, which died almost immediately. His younger brother commenced an action against him for a large sum of money, and while preaching...one evening, he was seized by two policemen [but later released]."

Their Lives Were in Continual Danger

Shortly after, Wilayat took his family to live in another town for safety. As his faith grew, he taught his wife to read and she was baptized as a Christian. When the British missionaries wanted to send a native preacher to a church in Delhi, they chose Wilayat for his faithfulness to the cross. The steadfast Christian man prayerfully weighed the dangers to himself and his family before accepting. Once he had decided, "he consulted no more with flesh and blood, but declared his readiness to go, though he might be called to lay down his life for his Lord and Saviour."

Wilayat's ministry in Delhi overflowed with the Lord's anointing. Large crowds listened attentively to him in the bustling public bazaars

163. Facts and subsequent quotations are all taken from Rev. M. A. Sherring, *The Indian Church During the Great Rebellion* (London: James A. Nisbet and Co., 1859), 42–46.

and in the quiet Christian churches. Even the Muslims of the city treated him with respect; one of the princes from the city's palace sneaking into his home in the darkness of night to hear him teach the Word. The rest of Wilayat's story comes from his wife's account.

Forces clash during the Revolution in India in 1857.
Photos.com\Thinkstock

The Lord's Work Cannot be Stopped

> On Monday, the 11th of May, about nine o'clock in the morning, my husband was preparing to go out to preach, when a native preacher named Thakoor, of the Church mission, came in, and told us that all the gates of the city had been closed, that the sepoys [East India Company soldiers] had mutinied, and that the Mohammedans of the city were going about robbing and killing every Christian. He pressed hard on my husband to escape at once, if possible, else that we would all be killed. My husband said, "No, no, brother, the Lord's work can not be stopped by any one."
>
> In the meanwhile, fifty horsemen were seen coming, sword in hand, and setting fire to the houses around. Thakoor said, "Here

> they come, now what will you do? Run, run: I will, and you had better come." My husband said, "This is no time to flee, except to God in prayer." Poor Thakoor ran, was seen by the horsemen, and killed.

In spite of the horror that was pressing down on his young family, Wilayat remained true to the Lord's call. He dropped to his knees and prayed, "Lord, many of Thy people have been slain before this by the sword, and burned in the fire for Thy name's sake. Thou didst give them help to hold fast the faith. Now, Lord, we have fallen into the fiery trial. Lord, may it please Thee to help us to suffer with firmness. Let us not fall or faint in heart under this sore temptation. Even to the death, oh, help us to confess and not to deny Thee, our dear Lord! Oh, help us to bear this cross, that we may, if we die, obtain a crown of glory."

Kissing Fatima and then each of his seven children, Wilayat encouraged them with a final passionate word:

> See that, whatever comes, you don't deny Christ, for if you confide in Him, and confess Him, you will be blessed, and have a crown of glory. True, our dear Saviour has told us to be wise as serpents, as well as innocent as doves. So if you can flee, do so; but, come what will, do not deny Christ.... Know that if you die, you die to go to Jesus; and if you are spared, Christ is your helper. I feel confident that if any of our missionaries live, you will all be taken care of and should they all perish, yet Christ lives forever. If the children are killed before your face, oh, then take care you don't deny Him who died for us! This is my last charge, and God help you.

I Once Was Blind but Now I See

The rebellious horsemen still galloped through Delhi looking for Westerners or Christians to put to death. As they approached Wilayat, the rebels cried out, "Kill Wilayat! Kill him! He is an infidel preacher who has destroyed the faith of our people by preaching Jesus Christ!" The horsemen pulled up to an abrupt stop and seized him. "Repeat the *Kalima* [Muslim Creed]," they demanded. But he calmly refused. As the rebels began firing into the air and shouting, Wilayat's children snuck out the back door of their home and took refuge with a neighbor.

Yes, I am a Christian, and am resolved to live and die a Christian.

"Who are you, and what are you?" the rebels demanded of Wilayat. "I was at one time blind," he answered, "but now I see. God mercifully opened my eyes, and I have found a refuge in Christ. Yes, I am a Christian, and am resolved to live and die a Christian." "Ah" said the rebel, "we see that he is a kaffir (infidel); let us kill him!" The rebels were suddenly distracted by two European men trying to flee the area; they turned to run after them before they escaped. Wilayat turned quickly to Fatima, "Flee, flee—now is the time, before they return." With tears, she ran to check on the safety of the children.

A crowd of Muslims soon appeared in the public square, dragging Wilayat on the ground while kicking him in the head. "Now preach Christ to us," they mocked. "Now where is your Christ in whom you boast?" Others cried, "Forsake Christianity and repeat the *Kalima*." About this time, Fatima snuck back into the shadows of the public square and heard her husband respond, "No, I never will; my Saviour took up His cross and went to God; I take up my life as a cross, and will follow Him to heaven."

Mockingly the crowd asked him if he was thirsty. He replied, "When my Saviour died He got vinegar mingled with gall: I don't need your water. But if you mean to kill me, do so at once, and don't keep me in this pain. You are the true children of the prophet Mohammed. He went about converting with his sword, and he got thousands to submit from fear; but I won't: your swords have no terror for me; let them fall, and I fall a martyr for Christ."

Just before an Indian rebel aimed a blow with his sword—which nearly severed Wilayat's head—the martyr spoke out loud "Lord Jesus, receive my soul!"

Fatima ran from the scene of her husband's death grieving but turning her attention to the children's safety. Frightened neighbors told her that they would no longer shelter her out of fear for their own lives. They begged her to recant her faith and return to Islam, promising her a monthly income to feed her family. "No," she replied tearfully. "I cannot forsake Christ. I will work to support myself and the children, and if I must be killed, God's will be done."

Fatima and her children escaped to an area outside of Delhi where she picked corn to support them. Once the British squashed the rebellion, Fatima reached a missionary from Agra who was still alive and well. Thankful that she was spared the massacres, he invited her to return to the mission with her children. Fatima wrote back gratefully, "I cried for joy, and thanked God, for now I knew what my dear husband said would be fulfilled—that if our missionaries were spared, I and the children would be provided for." [164] God had been faithful to the family of Wilayat Ali.

Over seventy British and Indian ministers and their families were killed during the Indian Mutiny. However, the cause of Christ remained strong. Missionaries, both Western and native, continued to preach the Word of God and also to teach the Indian people how to read and write in their own language. As Bibles were printed in various dialects, the cause of Christ in India continued to grow.

The Houghtons in Zanzibar, 1886

Standing on board the *SS Kerbala* as they sailed through the Red Sea, John and Annie Houghton stood holding hands and gazing out

164. Rev. M. A. Sherring, *The Indian Church*, 46–53.

over the rolling waves. They were over halfway to their destination at Mombasa [modern-day southern Kenya]. They were filled with both wonder and excitement at what awaited them in the British colony of eastern Africa.

Just a few weeks earlier, on October 22, 1884, the newly married couple set sail from Europe as Methodist missionaries to the Galla country of East Africa. The Galla (modern Orma) were the largest tribe on the African horn and were responding openly to the gospel message. Since the missionary settlement near the Galla wasn't ready for their arrival, the Houghtons ministered near Mombasa until January of 1886, when they finally made their way up the Tana River to Golbanti, near the coast of present-day Kenya. At the time, the Galla were considered the most powerful tribe in all of Africa. Earlier missionaries were convinced that "if the Galla converted to Christianity, Africa would become a Christian continent."[165]

Portrait of Anne Houghton as it appears in *Martyrs of Golbanti.*
Public domain.

Delighted to finally be at their mission destination, John and Annie quickly made themselves at home. On March 31, Annie wrote, "We are now building a new chapel, for the old one is scarcely fit to go into....

165. Shel Arenson, "Missionaries Murdered at Golbanti," *Old Africa Magazine*, January 9, 2009, 2016, oldafricamagazine.com/missionaries-murdered-at-golbanti/, accessed April 14, 2016.

When the new one is finished we hope for better times.... Mr. Houghton is the first European missionary, and myself the first white woman of any description that has been here; so we are quite isolated. Many of the men think Mr. Houghton a great man...equal with God. Of course he tells them differently."[166]

Early in their ministry, several of the natives eagerly accepted Christ as Savior; the time they spent with the Galla was full of hope for future blessings.

Maasai Warriors on the Move

The Galla had a fierce tribal enemy, the Maasai, who frequently raided their settlements and stole their cattle. The people were terrified of the tall, lance-bearing Maasai warriors. "The terror of their name is something awful," John wrote home after the first month of living in the settlement.[167]

On February 24, 1886, the Maasai swooped down on the undefended settlement, murdering nearly fifty innocent men and women, before carrying away a large number of their cattle. (A large part of the Maasai herd had been wiped out by disease.) Several of the new Christian Galla converts ran into the mission house and grabbed John's guns without telling him. They chased after the Maasai and shot at the fleeing warriors before four of the Galla were speared to death. The natives and the Houghtons buried the dead and prayed that the Maasai would not return.

Three months later, on a pleasant day in early May, Annie was standing in the doorway of their hut, watching for the arrival of her cook when she saw shadows in the forest. A girl who helped in the kitchen saw Annie gazing intently at the tree line. The girl gazed in the same direction and then screamed, "Yes, Bibi, those are Maasai!"[168] The young girl bolted to the forest, saving herself, but Annie ran straight for the chapel to warn John. Hearing Annie's screams, John ran from the chapel,

166. Robert Brewin, *The Martyrs of Golbanti* (London: Andrew Crombie), 87.
167. Ibid, 114.
168. Arenson, *Old Africa Magazine.*

grabbed her hand, and they both ran for the house where the guns were kept. Unfortunately, before they could reach it, they were surrounded by two groups of Maasai warriors.

The Maasai were convinced that the earlier gun episode had been planned by the Houghtons. In revenge, John and Annie were speared to death. The warriors scattered around the mission, killing whomever they could find, and finally destroying the contents of the Houghton's house. John and Annie had been in Golbanti for only five short months.

Portrait of John Houghton as it appears in *Martyrs of Golbanti*.
Public domain.

Decades followed the death of John and Annie Houghton; other missionaries took up their vision to proclaim Jesus in eastern Africa. The Christian population of Kenya continued to grow until today 82 percent of the Kenyan people are Christians. The Galla (Orma) are still the largest ethnic group in eastern Africa, and fifty percent of the tribe are Christians, with Protestant Christianity the fastest growing faith among them. The once fierce Maasai tribe, now numbering one million, still live in the region, and forty-five percent of their population are believers in Jesus Christ today.[169]

In the end, the victory belongs to Jesus.

169. Ethiopian Population Census Commission, "Summary and Statistical Report of the 2007 Population and Housing Census," United Nations Population Fund, http://www.csa.gov.et/newcsaweb/images/documents/pdf_files/regional/Oromya1.pdf.

Killed for Converting: Mirza Ibrahim, 1892

These things I have spoken to you, that in Me you may have peace. In the world you will have tribulation; but be of good cheer, I have overcome the world. (John 16:33)

Mirza Ibrahim, imprisoned in Tabriz (in modern-day Iran) for his Christian belief, knew that he had friends and powerful people lobbying for his freedom. But he didn't expect what happened next. Sitting quietly in his cell, as he did every day, he heard the feet of soldiers rushing toward his door. He stood up just before they burst in. "What is the matter?" he asked. "Just come," they said. Then one of them took a second look at him. "Let's clean him up." They took him to be bathed, and gave him new garments. Then, hastily, the group walked through the streets of Tabriz.

Mirza Ibrahim grew excited as he realized they were headed to the temporary residence of the Crown Prince. Now he knew why he needed to be presentable! With much solemnity, he was ushered into the royal presence. The Crown Prince looked at him and said amicably, "Mirza Ibrahim, I have heard your story and, though I think you are very foolish for declaring yourself a Christian, I do admire your courage. So today I intend to give you a great opportunity. If you will kneel here and do the *namaz* (a Muslim prayer), you may go—you are a free man."[170]

Mirza Ibrahim didn't blink an eye but took a gospel from his pocket and said, "Your Royal Highness, I know that you have the power of life and death over me, but here in the gospel I have found my Lord and Saviour Jesus Christ and new life in Him. Nothing that you could do, sir, could take away from me the life that I have found in Him. But as to doing the *namaz,* I regret that I can not perform the Mohammedan prayer because I am not a Mohammedan."[171]

---

170. Samuel M. Zwemer, *Heirs of the Prophets* (Chicago: Moody Bible Institute, 1946), 130.
171. Ibid., 130–131.

"Yes, Jesus; Though You Kill Me"

Mirza Ibrahim was a middle-aged Muslim living in the city of Khoi (located in modern-day Iran). He was seeking peace for his troubled soul, and found it in the gospel of Christ. ("Mirza" is a title of honor.) He publicly confessed his faith in Christ as his Redeemer in 1890. Because he was well-known in the city, his conversion caused an uproar. He was offered a comfortable post in the shrines if he would return. He refused. His wife left him, taking their children and all their property. And yet, eager in his faith, Mirza Ibrahim went out to the villages and preached Christ. Eventually, he was taken before the governor of Urumia (modern-day Urmia, Iran).

> The *Suparast* [governor] in the presence of a number of Mollahs and other Mohammedans inquired of him, "Why are you, a Moslem, teaching the Christian doctrines?" Mirza Ibrahim took his Testament from his pocket and said, "Is not this...a holy book?" The *Suparast* said it was. "Then am I not right in reading it and teaching it?" "But how about Mohammed?" "That is for you to say. My faith is in Christ and his word. He is my Saviour." At this the command was given, "Beat him."[172]

He was beaten, but it was nowhere near the end of his trials. He was thrown into prison, chained and bound, but still the city was not satisfied. A mob formed at the gates, threatening to murder him. The threat was so great that he was transferred to a prison in Tabriz. Before he left, fellow Christians gave him food, but he turned around and gave it to the hungry prisoners around him, certain that his Master would provide for him. Once they were in Tabriz, the governor there asked him, "Who oppressed you that you should want to leave Islam?" He replied, "No one; I became a Christian from conviction, because I was persuaded of its truth."[173]

---

172. Samuel Graham Wilson, *Persia: Western Mission* (Philadelphia: Presbyterian Board of Publication, 1896), 32, https://archive.org/details/persiawesternmis00wilsuoft.
173. Ibid., 35.

Mirza Ibrahim was brought to Tabriz the first week of June, 1892. Inside the prison walls, he was locked in a filthy, cold cell with the worst prisoners until Christian friends on the outside were able to collect the funds to have him moved to a carpeted, heated room. He was permitted to keep his New Testament for comfort and to receive letters.

> From the prison he wrote, "Our Lord Jesus has not promised us glory in this world; he has said we shall have tribulation."... Mirza Ibrahim fed upon the word of God and lived by prayer. He might have been released at any time by denying his faith.

Yet he stood firm.

In time the Muslim jailer began treating Mirza Ibrahim severely, beating him and casting him into the dungeon. His coat, bedding and sufficient food were taken from him. Still he remained true to Christ. One night Ibrahim began witnessing to a dozen wicked outlaws who were imprisoned with him in the dungeon. In a frenzy, they turned on the righteous man with uncontrollable wrath. They beat and kicked him and then took turns throttling him by the neck.

> "Is Ali true, or Jesus? Say Ali," they shouted. He answered, "Jesus is true. Yes, Jesus; though you kill me." They choked him until his eyes were almost out of their sockets, and he thought he would die. Greatly injured, he was taken from the dungeon. His throat swelled so that he could scarcely swallow or speak. [A doctor] went to see him, but found that...there was no hope for him.... He died Sunday, May 14th, having endured with the true spirit of a martyr the horrors and pains of a Persian prison for almost a year. The jailer immediately informed the crown prince of his death. He asked, "How did he die?" The jailer gave word, "He died a Christian." The prince answered simply, "Bury him."[174]

Mirza Ibrahim exchanged comfort, honor, prestige, and family for a prison, illness, abuse, and death. Yet for him, there was no other choice.

174. Ibid., 37–38.

Even in prison, like the apostle Paul, he witnessed of the Life-giver, Jesus Christ, to those around him. What a tribute to the convicting power of the Holy Spirit! Truly Mirza Ibrahim's whole heart changed to endure such persecution, and not give in—instead to bless those who persecuted him.

> *But I say to you, love your enemies, bless those who curse you, do good to those who hate you, and pray for those who spitefully use you and persecute you, that you may be sons of your Father in heaven; for He makes His sun rise on the evil and on the good, and sends rain on the just and on the unjust.* (Matthew 5:44–45)

Dangerous Unrest in China, 1870-1900

It was the summer solstice, June 21, 1870 in the northern Chinese city of Tianjin. As the afternoon wore on, a careful observer would have noticed a group of firemen quietly gathering together, their number growing by the minute although no smoke was in sight. As they walked down the main street, it became apparent that they weren't carrying buckets or ladders—but weapons.

They headed toward the French part of the city, their grisly intentions becoming clearer with each passing moment. The crowd swelled with furious force as anti-foreign fanatics joined its ranks—premeditated or not, the result was deadly. They broke into two mobs and headed simultaneously for the cathedral and the Hospital of the Sisters of Mercy.

> [The French consul] was at once attacked, murdered, and his body thrown into the river. Warming to their work, the infuriated mob attacked the cathedral, set it on fire, dragged forth two Roman Catholic priests…and cruelly murdered all of them, as well as many Chinese inmates. On the other side of the river, not more than twenty minutes' walk from the cathedral, a still more

savage mob attacked the Hospital and Church where the Sisters resided.[175]

Chapel of the Sisters of Charity after the Tianjin Massacre.
Wellcome Library via Wikimedia Commons.

These Catholic sisters not only conducted a hospital, but also an orphanage, where many Chinese children lived. The attack on them was gruesome. The nuns were insulted, stripped, ripped open and some cut to pieces. Nearly forty of the children in the orphanage were smothered to death in a locked vault. Older staff workers were sent to prison where they were tortured or killed. In all, on that June day, eight Protestant and eight Roman Catholic chapels were destroyed, hundreds of

175. George Candlin, *John Innocent: A Story of Mission-work in China* (London: United Methodist Publishing House, 1909), 172, https://babel.hathitrust.org/cgi/pt?id=mdp.39015026709637;view=1up;seq=228.

Christians and foreigners were killed, and missions all over the country were raided.

The Tianjin Massacre: Just the Beginning

The day became known as the Tianjin Massacre and it was only the beginning of a rising protest against Westerners in China. Unfortunately, it was the Christian missionaries who were serving God throughout inland China who paid the greatest price in the rebellious insurrections.

In the city of Tianjin, and throughout the northern provinces of China, pamphlets were scattered claiming that Christians, both Protestants and Catholics, kidnapped Chinese children and then killed them in order to use their body parts—eyes, hearts, etc.—for medicine. As preposterous as that sounds to us, it was believable to the Chinese who were extremely biased against the foreigners and who had actually used human body parts in medicines over the centuries. The Chinese had also reached a saturation point with the number of European nations who were conducting trade in Shanghai and the coastal cities of China and inflicting Western laws on the Chinese citizens. Northern China, especially, was filled with turmoil and unrest.

In the face of all of these factors, a fierce, intensely spiritual army arose called the Boxers—although their Chinese name is closer to "United Fists." As one contemporary visitor to the country described, "It was believed that the [Boxers] became inspired with the spirits of ancient gods. They fell on the ground and foamed at the mouth. They became rigid, and in that condition were not affected if boiling water was poured upon them or needles pierced their flesh. They believed themselves invulnerable...."[176]

Early in 1900, the Empress Dowager of China, incited by the European interference, issued an order to destroy every foreigner and all

176. Mary Bryson, *Cross and Crown* (London: London Missionary Society, 1904), https://archive.org/stream/crosscrownstorie00brysiala#page/n0/mode/2up.

Chinese in any way connected with them. It was the beginning of the Boxer Rebellion.[177]

The Boxer Rebellion 1899–1900

Wun-e stood against a mud wall in the middle of a dark night in Peking (modern-day Beijing). In the distance she could hear the Boxers shrieking and hunting down Christians. She had been abandoned by her Christian husband three days earlier out of fear of the murdering Boxers. He had fled at night leaving her—not with missionaries or Christian friends—but with mere acquaintances. When the Boxers did come, burning, looting, and killing, the acquaintances turned her out. "You will bring danger to us!" they cried.

Today, in spite of all that the Chinese communists have done to stop the spread of Christianity in China, there are more than 100 million Chinese citizens who proclaim Jesus Christ as Lord and Savior.

She began to weep, watching the fires in the distance. But even as Wun-e prayed for help, an old woman came seeking her. She knew Wun-e from the mission and wanted to offer her refuge.

"Come with us," the woman whispered kindly. "We will care for you, and no one shall harm you." But Wun-e refused. "If I come I will only bring you sorrow, for everyone here knows I am a Christian!" she cried. But the old woman insisted, and Wun-e took refuge in their home for three weary weeks while Christians and foreigners were hunted down and brutally killed all around her. Unfortunately, a man from the nearby mission school recognized her. Although most of the mission students were faithful—some dying a martyr's death—this

177. See my book *God's Generals: The Missionaries* for more details on the Christian missionaries and the Boxers.

one was eager for the destruction of the Christians. He ran to tell the Boxers, and Wun-e was immediately arrested on the charge of being a Christian.

"Do not admit your faith!" the old woman insisted as Wun-e was dragged from the house. "Just offer one small stick of incense! Please do not die." But Wun-e's resolve was not shaken.

She took to heart Jesus' words, *"And I say to you, My friends, do not be afraid of those who kill the body, and after that have no more that they can do"* (Luke 12:4).

> She was hurried along in a cart to the Boxer headquarters for that district. One can picture the girlish figure in the midst of a crowd of fierce-looking men and boys, maddened by the blood they had already shed. In answer to all their questions she answered quietly, "I am a Christian. I believe in Jesus. I cannot burn incense to idols." Apparently some of the Boxers were inclined to spare her life. She was so brave and calm that they were half afraid to harm her.
>
> "We do not believe she is a Christian," some of them said. "Her neighbours say she is not," referring to the testimony of the old people who had sheltered her. Others said, "See, there is no fear in her face. No, she is not a Christian!"
>
> "That is not true," replied Wun-e calmly. "I have been a Christian for years. I belong to a Christian family.... No one can doubt that I am a Christian too!" At this they all shouted with rage and declared she was not fit to live. [178]

Wun-e was beheaded by her cruel captors; her death during the weeks of carnage known as the Boxer Rebellion was only one of thousands:

> The Boxer Rebellion caused the death of over 5,000 [Chinese] Protestant Christians, and over 20,000 [Chinese] Roman

178. Bryson, *Cross and Crown*, 44–46.

> Catholics.... Besides these native Christians, the number of foreign missionaries put to death was 188, including many children. These numbers would have been very much larger but for the fact that in many centers there were brave and enlightened Chinese officials who risked their own life and their future chances of promotion to save the strangers from afar, and hurry them out of the country."[179]

Today, in spite of all that the Chinese communists have done to stop the spread of Christianity in China, there are more than 100 million Chinese citizens who proclaim Jesus Christ as Lord and Savior.

The Christian Church Tripled in the Next Century

The Boxer Rebellion took place in the early months of the twentieth century. In a sense, it was the opening act of destruction in a century that would see tens of millions of Christians murdered worldwide at the hands of communists, Nazis and tyrannical dictators. We know that more Christians died a martyrs' death in the twentieth century than all the previous nineteen centuries combined.

It was still a time of amazing Christian growth—in that same one hundred year period, the Christian population of the world more than tripled, from 500 million in 1900 to nearly two billion in 2000![180]

As we watch the Christian church grow in spite of all Satan's attempts to destroy it, we are encouraged that God is alive, that Jesus Christ is still building His church, and that the Holy Spirit is still sanctifying believers until Christ returns in all of His glory. Christians, we can count on it.

---

179. Ibid.
180. David B. Barrett & Todd M. Johnson, "Annual Statistical Table on Global Mission" *International Bulletin of Missionary Research*, January 2002. An updated table can be found at http://www.gordonconwell.edu/ockenga/globalchristianity/resources.htm.

"Look, he is coming with the clouds," and "every eye will see him, even those who pierced him"; and all peoples on earth "will mourn because of him." So shall it be! Amen. "I am the Alpha and the Omega," says the Lord God, "who is, and who was, and who is to come, the Almighty." (Revelation 1:7–8 NIV)

COMMUNISM: SATAN'S WEAPON OF MASS DESTRUCTION

9

COMMUNISM: SATAN'S WEAPON OF MASS DESTRUCTION

(AD 1900–2000)

The twentieth century opened with the rumblings of revolution in China and in Russia as well where Satan brandished a hideous new weapon of death: communism. Initially celebrated as a blissful state of economic equality, it quickly became what it really was—a totalitarian government system run by godless dictators. In every nation that fell to communist rebels, the result was the massive slaughter of human life such as the world had never seen before. In the Soviet Union, China, North Korea, Vietnam, Cambodia, tens of millions of people, including Christians, were ruthlessly murdered in the name of political ideology and atheism.

Communism became the driving force in Satan's newest attempt to wipe God's people from the earth. In the Soviet Union alone, twenty million Christians died at the hands of these militant atheists.[181] In China, the numbers were in the tens of millions just in the first half of the century. These are numbers we can hardly comprehend. Yet, even in the midst of wholesale massacres, once again the Christian church stood strong in Jesus Christ in the face of the godless enemy and continued to grow, even if it had to go underground for years.

We want to honor our brothers and sisters in Christ from the twentieth century who stood resolutely for truth in Jesus Christ while communism waged its unholy war. Were they foolish to stand against such evil when they knew it would cost them their lives? Not according to God's Word. In Revelation, a victorious Jesus brandishes His sword and promises us, *"Be faithful until death, and I will give you the crown of life"* (Revelation 2:10).

Westminster Abbey Honors Twentieth-Century Martyrs

In 1998, ten twentieth-century Christian martyrs were commemorated at Westminster Abbey in London with statues placed above the Abbey's west gate. Their names are Maximilian Kolbe, Manche Masemola, Janani Luwum, Grand Duchess Elizabeth of Russia, Martin Luther King, Óscar Romero, Dietrich Bonhoeffer, Esther John, Lucian Tapiedi, and Wang Zhiming. These ten men and women represent the millions who died from religious persecution and oppression in six continents. Among them are victims of communism, Nazism, and tyranny in Africa and South America. "There has never been a time in

181. "Christian Martyrdom," Todd M. Johnson, presentation at Notre Dame, November, 2012, with research from *World Christian Trends,* David Barrett and Todd M. Johnson (Pasadena, CA: William Carey Library, 2001).

Christian history when someone, somewhere, has not died rather than compromise with the powers of oppression, tyranny, and unbelief," the Reverend Dr. Anthony Harvey of Westminster Abbey, shared on the dedication day. "But the twentieth century, which has been the most violent in recorded history, has created a roll call of Christian martyrs far exceeding that of any other previous period."[182]

Western façade of Westminster Abbey,
showing the ten twentieth-century martyrs commemorated.
Violetastock\Thinkstock

These next chapters on martyrs of the twentieth century will represent the testimonies of a few of these men and women commemorated in Westminster Abbey, along with others, some famous, some not so famous, who laid down their lives for the kingdom of God.

> *Truly, truly, I say to you, unless a grain of wheat falls into the earth and dies, it remains alone; but if it dies, it bears much fruit."*
>
> (John 12:24 NASB)

182. "Martyrs of the Modern Era," BBC News, July 8, 1998, http://news.bbc.co.uk/2/hi/uk/129587.stm.

Grand Duchess Elizabeth of Russia: Princess to the True King

Princess Elizabeth of Hesse (known as Ella to her family) was a princess in every sense of the word. Born in 1864, she was the daughter of an English princess and a German prince and the granddaughter of Queen Victoria of England. Rather than being indulged by her royal surroundings, however, Elizabeth was raised in a godly German home where she and her siblings were required to sweep up their own rooms and to make regular visits with their mother to comfort wounded soldiers or carry food to the poor. Elizabeth understood that it was all an outreach of love in the name of Jesus Christ.

A Royal Love Story

Grand Duchess Elizabeth with her well-beloved husband, Grand Duke Sergei Alexandrovich of Russia. Public domain.

Princess Elizabeth was a beautiful and graceful woman—some historians have considered her the most beautiful woman in Europe at the time. Of course, she had many royal suitors who wanted to marry her, several of them highly favored by her grandmother, Queen Victoria. The most famous was her oldest cousin, Wilhelm, who shortly after became Kaiser Wilhelm II, king of Germany. Surprisingly, Elizabeth rejected every suitor until a Russian prince, the Grand Duke Sergei Alexandrovich, won her heart. Sergei was the younger brother of the Russian Tsar Alexander III and a "serious and religious" young man who loved God and the people of Russia. *That* was what the Christian royal princess was looking for. Elizabeth and Sergei were married in 1884 and began their married life in the courts of Moscow.

Although she could have spent her life in luxury, Elizabeth spent much of her time instead ministering to the less fortunate in the capital city, including soldiers returning from European wars. She and Sergei had no children of their own, but they reached out to embrace other children in their lives, including adopting her husband's niece and nephew who had lost their parents.

The Ugly Seeds of Revolution

Several years after Elizabeth's marriage, her youngest sister, Alexi, married the young Tsar Nicholas II, becoming the Empress Alexandra of Russia. Now both sisters were part of the royal Romanov family. In earlier years, this would have been a great honor. However, the royal court in Moscow was full of political strife. As the twentieth century approached, starving Russian peasants brought petitions to the royal court asking for better working conditions and more representation in the government. Unfortunately, their pleas were scoffed at by the inexperienced tsar. Because of this and many other circumstances, the seeds of Marxist revolution were planted and flourished.

Elizabeth's husband, Sergei, as governor of Moscow, made many enemies himself because of his unpopular policies. On February 18, 1905, as Sergei was leaving the Kremlin, a grim-faced revolutionary, Ivan Kalyaye, ran beside his carriage and tossed a small bomb inside. It landed on Sergei's lap and within seconds exploded, ripping the carriage to pieces. Elizabeth was numb with grief. Their love for one another had remained strong throughout twenty-one years of marriage. But instead of allowing it to devastate her, she turned to the Scriptures for her source of comfort and guidance. The night before Sergei's state funeral, she visited the imprisoned Kalyayev to offer him Christian forgiveness and to beg him to repent for his sins against God. Defiantly, Kalyayev cried, "I killed Sergei Alexandrovich because he was a weapon of tyranny! No! I will not repent."[183]

183. Edvard Radzinsky, *The Last Tsar: The Life and Death of Nicholas II* (New York: Anchor Books, 1993), 82.

"On the eve of revolution," one biographer wrote of Elizabeth, "she had already found a way out—forgiveness! Forgive through the impossible pain and blood—and thereby stop it then, at the beginning, this bloody wheel. By her example, poor 'Ella' appealed to society, calling upon the people to live in Christian faith."[184]

Honoring Jesus in Life

When Elizabeth married Sergei years earlier she became a member of the Russian Orthodox Church. After Sergei's assassination, she began to minister daily to the most destitute people of Moscow. She sold all of her worldly possessions including her royal jewels and used the money to build a hospital, a chapel, a pharmacy and an orphanage. In 1909, Elizabeth became a Russian Orthodox nun and established the Convent of Martha and Mary with a desire to reach thousands of Moscow's poor with the love of Christ.

Eight years later, the Communist Revolution, led by Vladimir Lenin, could no longer be contained. In March of 1917, Nicholas II abdicated the Russian throne, and several days later he, Alexandra, and their five children were escorted by Bolshevik guards over a thousand miles east of Moscow, supposedly for their protection from the revolution. In the early morning of July 17, 1918, the tsar, the empress and all five royal children were executed in the basement of a house in the town of Yekaterinburg, shot to death by their guards.

Praising Jesus in Death

Just a few weeks earlier, Lenin ordered the state police to arrest Elizabeth since she was also a part of the royal court. Lenin didn't care about her years of selfless service for Russia's poor. Her connection with the royal Romanov family was enough to fuel the Communist hatred. Elizabeth and another nun from the convent were arrested. They, along

184. Ibid.

with five royal princes who were cousins of the Tsar, were transported to the small mining town of Alapayevsk in central Russia.

On July 18, 1918, the morning after her sister, Alexandra, had been executed, the fifty-three-year-old Elizabeth stood before her communist captors. She and the other captives were taken to the edge of a mining shaft and beaten severely by the police.

The following is the personal account of the assassin, Vassili Ryabov:

> First we led Grand Duchess Elizabeth up to the mine. After throwing her down the shaft, we heard her struggling in the water for some time. We pushed the nun-lay sister Varvara down after her. We again heard the splashing of water and then the two women's voices. It became clear that, having dragged herself out of the water, the grand duchess had also pulled her lay-sister out. But, having no other alternative, we had to throw in all the men, also.
>
> None of them, it seems, drowned, or choked in the water and after a short time we were able to hear all of their voices again. Then I threw in a grenade. It exploded and everything was quiet. But not for long. We decided to wait a little to check whether they had perished. After a short while, we heard talking and a barely audible groan. I threw another grenade.
>
> And then, what do you think—from beneath the ground we heard singing! I was seized with horror. They were singing the prayer: "Lord, save your people!"
>
> We had no more grenades, yet it was impossible to leave the deed unfinished. We decided to fill the shaft with dry brushwood and set it alight. Their hymns still rose up through the thick smoke for some time yet.
>
> When the last signs of life beneath the earth had ceased, we posted some of our people by the mine and returned to Alapaevsk by first light and immediately sounded the alarm in the

> cathedral bell tower. Almost the whole town came running. We told everyone that the grand dukes had been taken away by unknown persons![185]

When the seven bodies were discovered a few months later by supporters of the royal family, it appeared that most of the prisoners had died a slow death, either from their injuries or the smoke from the fire.

The Legacy of a Princess

Out of fear that the prisoners' bodies would be mutilated after death, the rescuers traveled further east with their coffins, finally burying them in the Russian Orthodox Mission cemetery in Beijing, China. An exception was made for the Grand Duchess Elizabeth whose body was transported to Jerusalem and buried in a Russian Orthodox cemetery there. For her faithfulness to Christ at the dawn of the communist terror, Elizabeth was chosen as one of the ten twentieth-century martyrs to be memorialized above the Great West Door of Westminster Abbey.

Elizabeth's true legacy is shared with nearly twenty million unknown Christian martyrs who were exiled to die in Siberian labor camps or were executed by firing squads through seventy years of forced atheism in the Soviet Union. We are so thankful that the Lord God knows each one by name.

Communist Revolution Ends in Failure

Although Lenin called the Communist promotion of atheism "the cause of our state," and Joseph Stalin launched a "five year plan of atheism" in a violent attempt to destroy every remnant of Christianity; their plans ended in failure. The love for Jesus Christ in the heart of the Russian people was not snuffed out no matter how vehemently

185. Archimandrite Nektarios Serfes, compiler, "Murder of the Grand Duchess Elizabeth," from Andrei Maylunas and Sergi Mironenko, *A Lifelong Passion* (New York: Doubleday, 1997), 638–639, http://www.serfes.org/lives/grandduchess/murder.htm.

the government worked to destroy it. After years of Soviet domination, the people still hungered for the Word of God and the fellowship of Christian believers. The underground church grew in every city and in every labor camp throughout the vast Soviet Republic. When the Soviet Union was dissolved in 1991 and the doors were opened to the gospel once more, the Russian people flocked to churches to be baptized and to join in Christian celebrations.

The Convent of Saints Mary and Martha in Moscow, founded by Elizabeth.
ValerijaP\Thinkstock

In Russia today, over 60 percent of the population consider themselves Christians—Orthodox, Catholics and Protestants.[186] Unfortunately, persecution still exists under Russia's government and seems to be on the rise, but the body of Christ remains strong and is growing in faith and power.

Communism Floods into China

Tragically for the people of China, the communist rebellion and its focus on atheism quickly infiltrated mainland China. By 1923, China's

186. See http://www.pewforum.org/2011/12/19/global-christianity-exec.

revolutionary leaders had established an official Communist Party. Violent communist rebels roamed throughout China bringing terror and death, while Christian missionaries, especially from the China Inland Mission, were busy spreading the gospel of Jesus Christ to a spiritually hungry Chinese population. Millions of those Christians, both foreign missionaries and Chinese believers, lost their lives as communism overran the country.

John and Betty Stam: "Whether in Life or in Death"

Tsingteh's city streets were filled with the screams of the dying, the shattering of heirlooms and the crumbling of family homes framed against the caustic laughter of the Communist rebels waving their machetes high in the air. What had been a thriving marketplace, a Chinese town of neighbors and tradesmen, was transformed into a graveyard where angry Communist rebels trampled on the bodies of the villagers. Desperate prisoners, released from the town's jails by the rebels, joined the Communists in their brutal rampage.

What had been a thriving marketplace was transformed into a graveyard where angry Communist rebels trampled on the bodies of the villagers

The morning after the terror, two young American missionaries, John and Betty Stam, were lined up with a hundred Chinese captives for a forced march to the next village. Betty cradled their three-month old baby girl, rocking her in the morning sunlight that glinted off the rusted and bloodstained machetes around them. The baby's sudden cry of hunger broke through the muffled voices of their captors. In seconds, a rebel leader stalked toward the American couple, his intent clearly written in every line of his hate-filled face.

"Let's kill the baby," he growled to a comrade. "It is too much trouble to take her along." Betty, with her heart beating wildly, cradled the infant to comfort her, whispering soothing words into the baby's ear while silently crying out to Jesus for His mercy.

"Stop!" A Chinese man in a tattered prison uniform turned back to confront the rebel, his former rescuer. "This baby has done nothing worthy of death!" he spoke compassionately, his eyes darting from Betty's pleading face to the blue-eyed baby in her arms.

A thirst for vengeance was thick in the Communist's soul. "Then, will you trade your life for this white American baby?" he smirked. Without flinching the prisoner answered boldly, "I am willing." In a flash, the rebel's blood-streaked hand tightened around his weapon and, with a sharp movement, he hacked the baby's rescuer to death right before Betty's tear-filled eyes.

Just two weeks earlier, John and Betty Stam with their three-month-old daughter, Helen, had entered this quiet village nestled in the mountains of eastern China to establish a new Christian mission. Now, they faced the hatred of the Communist rebels armed only with their unwavering faith in the God who never makes mistakes.

Serving Jesus Christ with a Whole Heart

It was in the 1890s when Peter Stam, John's father, strode down the ship's swaying gangplank and stepped onto Ellis Island, New York, and into a whole new world. The young immigrant from Holland was one of thousands entering the US in the closing years of the nineteenth century. Since he wanted to learn English as quickly as possible, Peter accepted a Dutch/English New Testament from a female street evangelist. His goal was to learn a new language; her goal was to welcome a new convert to Jesus Christ. Both of their goals were realized.

By the time Peter completed his English studies by reading that Bible, he had accepted Jesus Christ as Lord of his life. He and his wife settled in Paterson, New Jersey, where they built a successful contracting business and had nine children. Peter's fifth son, John Cornelius Stam, was born on January 18, 1907. He was a young man who was destined to follow Jesus to the other side of the world, and to inspire thousands of young missionaries to serve Jesus Christ *no matter the cost.*

In addition to running a flourishing business, Peter Stam founded an outreach mission, The Star of Hope, to share Christ's love with the less fortunate in Paterson. It was the first of many ministries for Peter Stam, his children, his grandchildren, and his great-grandchildren extending even to today.[187] Serving the people of Paterson alongside his father, John Stam felt a call to serve Jesus Christ with his whole heart, soul, mind and strength.

One Million Lost Souls a Month

At age twenty-one, John left the security of his family's ministry and traveled halfway across the country to enroll in Moody Bible Institute. He had saved up some money for school, but when it ran out it was time to learn that God was a mighty Provider whether the need was large or small. Walking down a windy Chicago street one afternoon, John saw a five dollar bill lying on the sidewalk. It was just enough to buy a couple of wool shirts and socks for the frigid Chicago winter. "Every time I pull these socks on during these cold nights, they preach a sermon to me on the Lord's wonderful power to provide whatever my needs might be," he later wrote to a friend.[188]

John Stam was a tall and outgoing student on Moody's campus, compassionate and fun-loving. Although many students would be staying in the US to preach, he believed that God's call for him was to China's lost, where "one million souls a month slipped into eternal darkness." Was it the Holy Spirit speaking to his heart? John walked eagerly into his first China Inland Mission (CIM) meeting at Moody. The CIM was a Spirit-anointed ministry reaching out to China's hundred million citizens with

187. See "Meet Us," CarlStam.org, http://www.carlstam.org/meetus.html.
188. Kathleen White, *John and Betty Stam (Men and Women of Faith)* (Bloomington, MN: Bethany House, 1990), 33.

the gospel. It was founded by a British missionary, Hudson Taylor, sixty years earlier.

Not long after joining the CIM meetings, John's attention was drawn to a dark-haired, blue-eyed graduate student named Betty Scott. Although more reserved than John, Betty had an enthusiasm for China that swept up everyone in her path; she brought life to the meetings with personal stories of her missionary childhood on the Chinese mainland. Within just a few weeks, John and Betty's friendship began to blossom into a lasting love.

At Any Cost

Elizabeth (Betty) Scott was born on February 22, 1906, the oldest of five children. Her father, Dr. Charles Scott, was a well-liked college professor with a longing to work in the mission field. The family moved from Michigan to China and were stationed in the eastern seacoast town of Tsingtao (modern-day Qingdao), overlooking the Yellow Sea where their ministry to the Chinese flourished.

> *It's clear to me that the only worthwhile life is one of unconditional surrender to God's will, living in His way, trusting His love and guidance.*

In the fall of 1926, Betty returned to the United States to attend Wilson College, an all-female Presbyterian school in Pennsylvania. At Wilson, her relationship with Jesus became the central focus of her life. "I have now surrendered myself to the Lord more than I ever realized was possible," Betty wrote. "It's clear to me that the only worthwhile life is one of unconditional surrender to God's will, living in His way, trusting His love and guidance."[189] Her life verse became, *"For to me, to live is Christ and to die is gain"*

189. Mrs. Howard Taylor, *The Triumph of John and Betty Stam*, (Chicago: Moody, 1923), 35.

(Philippians 1:21 NASB). After graduation from Wilson, Betty enrolled in Moody Bible Institute "to learn how to win souls to Christ."[190]

"I Want Something Really Worthwhile to Live For"

John and Betty believed that the Holy Spirit had brought them together, but they wanted to hear God's voice clearly—should they minister as husband and wife or as single missionaries for Christ? This young couple was wise beyond their years. It is so important for ministers of the gospel to be certain of the will of God when it comes to a marriage partner. John and Betty understood the importance of not rushing into something that was not ordained by Him. The Word of God was clear: *"Seek first the kingdom of God and His righteousness, and all these things shall be added to you"* (Matthew 6:33). So they diligently sought God's direction.

Since Betty was a year older than John, she applied to the China Inland Mission first and was immediately accepted. She left for China in the fall of 1931 while John was finishing his senior year at Moody. Before she sailed back to her childhood home Betty wrote,

> *I want something really worthwhile to live for.* I want to invest this one life of mine as wisely as possible, in the place that yields the richest profits to the world and me...wherever it is, I want it to be God's choice for me and not my own.... Christ said, *"He that would find his life shall lose it"* and proved the truth of this divine paradox at Calvary. I want Him to lead me and His Holy Spirit to fill me.[191]

Advance in Face of the Impossible!

At the end of John's senior year at Moody, his fellow students elected him the graduation speaker with a class motto "Bearing Precious Seed." John encouraged his fellow graduates:

190. Ibid, 36.
191. White, 96.

> Now is the time to reach men whose minds are swept of old beliefs, before Communistic atheism, coming in like a flood, raises other barriers far harder to overcome—and before this generation passes into Christless graves.... Shall we beat a retreat and turn back from our high calling in Christ Jesus; or do we dare to advance at God's command in face of the impossible?"[192]

John's rousing message rang as a clear battle cry to the cheering students. And it rang just as clearly a few years later in an isolated cluster of pine trees in China where John and Betty Stam won their eternal victory in Jesus.

"For This Purpose I Came to This Hour"

Within a month of graduation, in July of 1932, John was accepted by the CIM and sailed on the *Empress of Japan* to join Betty in China. He had no idea where she was stationed in the vast inland mission field. When his ship docked in Shanghai several weeks later, he was thrilled to find that Betty was visiting her missionary parents in the city. To the young couple this unplanned reunion was God's final green light—there were no more barriers to keep them from sharing a ministry to the Chinese as husband and wife.

Before they married, John was required by CIM to complete his language training in the city of Anking. During that cold winter, John's fellow trainees noticed his intense dedication to Jesus. "John seemed to know the Lord more intimately, more practically than the rest of us. When I was discouraged, he helped me to find the joy of the Lord."[193]

At the end of his language training, John was excited to receive his first assignment—the next year, he and Betty were to launch a new mission station in Tsingteh, a small city located in the mountains west of Shanghai. John wrote home to his parents, "I thought again of the words of the Lord Jesus '*For this cause I came to this hour*' (John 12:27) and I

192. Taylor, 54–55.
193. Ibid., 73.

realized that for me, too, all the background of life and training has been to prepare me for this hour." The CIM wanted John to be mentored by a more experienced missionary couple, Walter Birch and his wife, before they left for Tsingteh, so he moved first to Suancheng.

Empress of Japan liner, on which John Stam sailed to China.

An Exciting Vision for the Gospel

John's tall frame, happy smile, and hearty handshake were a welcome sight to the Chinese people who were drawn to his message of Christ's love. He began open air preaching in the crowded city and then invited flocks of interested listeners to his weekly Bible studies. It was a fruitful time of ministry. During those same months, Betty's outreach in Yingshan was flowing in the power of the Holy Spirit. She wrote in excitement, "Oh, John, how the people streamed in yesterday after our arrival! They were everywhere, in the chapel, in the courtyard, in our room—everywhere! And they will hear the love of Christ preached daily!"[194]

On October 23, 1933, John and Betty married, honeymooned, and then were off to spend a year of ministry in Suancheng with the Birches.

194. Ibid., 67.

The two couples shared a home, meals, God's Word, and fellowship. They launched out on short evangelism trips into the surrounding Chinese villages, sharing the message of Christ's sacrificial love in village after village; the townspeople responded eagerly with a desire to hear more.

"This work is the most encouraging in our field!" Betty wrote to her parents who were stationed in Tsinan. "God willing, we will go 'over the border' again, stay longer and preach the Gospel in many villages in the large mountain valleys, and in the small hamlets perched among the mountain slopes."[195] With their vision for spreading the gospel, John and Betty's hearts nearly burst with excitement at the white field for harvest.

Jesus Doesn't Send Us Out Alone!

The wedding of John and Betty Stam in Jinan, Shandong.
Courtesy of Archives of the Billy Graham Center, Wheaton, Illinois.

In the Gospels, Jesus never sent His disciples out alone. Personally, I don't believe that even married couples should go into the mission field without another Christian couple for spiritual and physical

195. White, 83.

support. God provided that for John and Betty Stam. When they were in Suangcheng it was the Birches. As they got closer to the mission station in Tsingteh, God brought an older Chinese couple, the Wangs and a Chinese evangelist, Pastor Lo, into their lives for spiritual support.

The Wangs, earlier converts through the CIM, were stationed just twelve miles from Tsingteh in the village of Miaosheo. Pastor Lo traveled as an evangelist/pastor throughout the entire region. Together with John they would work as a team to reach the unsaved people of Anhwei Province. As they prepared for Tsingteh, John and Betty rejoiced that their first year of marriage had been blessed with so many Chinese lives surrendered to Christ.

God's Precious Gift

God wasn't finished with His blessings. On September 11, 1934, Betty gave birth to a baby girl with dark curly hair and deep blue eyes at the Methodist Hospital in Wuhu, fifty-eight miles north of Suancheng. John wrote home to his parents about the birth of Helen Priscilla: "We have translated Helen's name as nearly as we could to 'Ai Lien.' Lien means 'a chain or link' so that her name in Chinese means 'Love Link.' She has been dedicated to serve the Lord."[196]

Two weeks later, John traveled to Tsingteh for his first official visit to their missionary station. The time had come to launch the mission, but would it be safe to bring his family? Large sections of China were caught in the throes of the Communist rebellion and it seemed that no one was safe from rebel terrorism. John paid an official visit to Mr. Peng, the Chinese district magistrate in the city. Peng assured John that there was no threat of violence from Communist rebels in Tsingteh. He even offered the family his protection. "If there is any trouble, you can come to my yamen [official residence] for shelter," he said.[197] Satisfied with Peng's answer, John spent hours reaching out to the local Chinese,

196. Taylor, 96.
197. White, 91.

distributing Bible tracts, and preparing for his family's long-anticipated arrival.

John, Betty, and Helen left Wuhu for the seventy-mile journey to their new home. Mother and baby had a bumpy ride—pushed the entire way in a wheelbarrow, China's primary mode of rural transportation at the time! The little Stam family finally reached Tsingteh around November 23, 1934. Their home was a roomy Chinese house big enough to hold future Bible studies with their Chinese converts. They had a sweet Christian cook and a young Chinese girl to help them with the daily chores while they focused on new friendships and evangelism. The young couple was ready to make a difference in their little city. But they would soon touch the worldwide church in ways they never imagined.

Communist Terror Attack

On the morning of December 6, Communist rebels who were familiar with the isolated mountain trails behind Tsingteh coordinated a sneak attack on the city. Arriving undetected, they scaled the eastern walls of Tsingteh with nothing but a small guard of soldiers to stop them. As the rebels, two thousand strong, poured into the city, the guards retreated in fear. Instead of giving the protection he had promised, Magistrate Peng disguised himself as a farmer and fled through the western gate of Tsingteh, forgetting all about the young American missionaries in his terror.[198]

Betty was giving Helen her early morning bath when a frightened Chinese believer burst in the front door announcing that Communist bandits were overrunning the city. John ran out to the main street to see if the information was true. Breathless, he raced back into the house and told Betty to pack some things quickly; the rebels were causing destruction throughout the city. They could hear firing in the streets and shrieks of terror. Within minutes, all means of escape were closed.

198. Taylor, 99.

Without panicking, John and Betty knelt down to pray with their two female servants asking the Lord for His protection and wisdom. A loud battering sounded at the door and John had no choice but to go and open it. He was calm and friendly to the rebel leader and his men, and Betty walked out of the kitchen offering cakes for them to eat. Any attempt at civility was useless. The rebels demanded all of their food and money. Then they bound John's hands behind his back and marched him to the temporary headquarters set up in the city.

The Chinese servants sobbed and begged the men to release the missionary mother and child into their care. But they refused to listen.

By this time, the number of rebels had increased from two thousand to six thousand, and they were attacking the citizens of Tsingteh without mercy. Betty prayed that John would return quickly, but instead, rebel guards came back to the house to arrest her and the baby. The Chinese servants sobbed and begged the men to release the missionary mother and child into their care. But they refused to listen. Betty whispered in the young girl's ear, "It is better if you stay here. If anything happens to us, look out for the baby."[199]

When John was permitted to return to their house to collect some clothing and supplies for Helen, he spoke quiet words of faith to the Chinese women, "Don't be afraid; God is on the throne. These things do not matter—our heavenly Father knows."[200]

"We Were Just Too Late"

That afternoon, John had the chance to scribble a hasty letter to the CIM superintendent, not knowing whether it would reach anyone. He closed the letter with these words:

199. Ibid., 101.
200. Ibid., 102.

Things happened so quickly this a.m. They were in the city just a few hours after the ever-persistent rumors really became alarming, so that we could not prepare to leave in time. *We were just too late.*

The Lord bless and guide you, and as for us, *may God be glorified whether by life or by death.*

In Him,
John C. Stam[201]

"We Are Going to Heaven"

Early the next morning, the Communist troops evacuated Tsingteh, heading for Miaosheo. They pushed John and Betty, with baby Helen cradled in her arms, into a long line of Chinese captives for the forced march. The baby began to cry and one of the rebels threatened to kill her. It was then that the prisoner begged for Helen's life and was brutally murdered before Betty's eyes as described at the beginning of the chapter.

As they approached Miaosheo, the Stams prayed for the protection of the Wang family wherever they might be hiding. The young family was forced inside the village post office under guard while the rebels pillaged the village. The postmaster, his voice quivering with pity for the Stams and fear for his own life, asked John, "Where are you going next?" John's answer was simple and was repeated throughout the Christian world after his death. "We do not know where they are going, *but we are going to heaven.*"[202]

The Stams were moved to the large house of a wealthy man who had fled. Husband, wife, and baby were pushed into a narrow courtyard bedroom where John was tightly bound to the end of the bed. Surprisingly, Betty was given the freedom to lie on the bed and take care of her

201. John Stam, "John & Betty Stam," CarlStam.org, www.carlstam.org.
202. Taylor, 104.

baby. It was the last night that Helen would see her mother's tender smile.

There is no record of John and Betty's conversation through that long, dark night. The young couple, just twenty-seven and twenty-eight years old, knew that they were not alone as they faced the Communist hatred. The God who called them to China was forever by their side. I'm sure that they prayed to their heavenly Father for His protection, especially for baby Helen. Their relationship with Jesus was strong—*whether in life or in death*, they knew they belonged to Him and His kingdom.

The Holy Spirit Covered Their Eyes

In the early morning hours, not knowing what the day would bring, Betty must have held Helen up to John's wistful face so that he could kiss her with a father's tender love. Betty fed her baby girl and tucked her into the infant sleeping bag, placing her precious life in the hands of an almighty God.

Without warning, the Communist guards burst through the bedroom door. Stripping John and Betty of the coats that were keeping them warm, they bound their hands behind their backs and grimly walked them toward the door. No one asked about baby Helen. No guard turned around to look at the small bundle lying still on the bed. Did the guards ignore it? Did the Holy Spirit shield their eyes so that they couldn't see? What kept the baby girl sleeping as the guards stomped across the floor and shouted commands to their captives? God's grace kept baby Helen hidden quietly inside her winter bunting as her parents bravely marched from the room without looking back.

To Be Present with the Lord

As John and Betty were led through the streets of Miaosheo, they remained calm, even smiling gently at the frightened men and women who were forced to watch the execution of the Western missionaries.

We know what happened in the next few hours because spectators standing nearby shared details of the missionaries' final moments.

The Stams were marched up a small hill to a clump of pine trees. The bandits shouted at the frightened bystanders proclaiming the superiority of the Communist message over Christianity. One man, a Chinese medical worker, stepped out from the crowd, refusing to remain silent at the execution of the innocent couple. He risked his life trying to save theirs. Dropping to his knees, the worker begged the rebels to release the missionaries into his care. One bandit leader kicked the man aside, but he continued to cry out for their freedom. Angered, the rebels jerked the Chinese worker to his feet and arrested him. (Shortly after, they searched his home, discovered a Bible, and executed him later the same day.)[203]

As he dropped to his knees, the townspeople marveled that the missionary had such a look of joy on his face as though gazing at "an unseen Presence."

As the rebel guards stopped at the foot of the pine trees, John asked once for the release of the medical worker. The only reply was a brusque Chinese command for John to kneel. As he dropped to his knees, the townspeople marveled that the missionary had such a look of joy on his face as though gazing at "an unseen Presence."[204] Seconds later a sword slashed through the air and John's head was severed. Trembling slightly, Betty dropped to her knees as well and lay across her beloved husband's body. Another swipe of the sword and her body draped lifeless at his side.

Nothing brings us comfort like the Word of God. Paul reminded the Corinthian Christians centuries earlier, "*We are…well pleased rather to be absent from the body and to be present with the Lord*" (2 Corinthians 5:8). In mere seconds, John and Betty left the hostility of Chinese

203. Ibid., 107.
204. Ibid., 108.

rebellion and hatred for the sweet presence and majesty of the King of Kings and Lord of Lords. But this was not the end of their story. God intended to use John and Betty Stam to further His kingdom throughout the world in ways they could not have foreseen.

A Miraculous Rescue

The numb townspeople left the execution scene and hid in their homes, frightened by what might happen next. If they remembered baby Helen, no one dared to look for her. Darkness fell and they spoke in hushed whispers about the missionaries' deaths while a little baby lay crying alone in a dark, deserted house.

What happened to baby Helen? God had already provided for her protection. Weeks earlier, John had asked Pastor Lo to travel to Miaosheo to preach at that Sunday's meeting. Lo, his wife, and their four-year-old son were crossing the hills nearby when they heard the rebels terrorizing the village. They stayed hidden in the forest for two days—cold, wet, and hungry. When word came that the young American missionaries had been executed, a heartsick Lo scrambled from his hiding place and snuck into town to see if the horrifying news was true.

It was mid-morning the day after the murders when Lo crept into Miaosheo. Most of the people were still behind closed doors, but one old woman ventured outside. In tearful whispers, she pointed to the deserted house where the foreign baby was still alive. Lo entered the front door and searched from room to room until he heard a baby's faint cry. Rushing to the courtyard bedroom, he found Helen still snuggled in her sleeping bag safe and warm, although hungry after thirty hours alone. The grieving Lo was overjoyed to find her alive. Betty had tucked a clean baby gown, some diapers, and John's letter to the CIM in the bunting. Most importantly, deep inside the sleeping bag, the wise young mother had pinned two five dollar bills which became a lifeline to get Helen to safety.[205]

205. Ibid., 110.

"This Is All We Have Left"

How would they get the beautiful, blue-eyed American baby through nearly one hundred miles of Communist-infested country to the safety of Wuhu? With the money Betty left, Pastor Lo hired two young men to help with the journey. He placed baby Helen and his young son, who had become sick from exposure, into two rice baskets hanging from the ends of a bamboo pole. The hired helpers would take turns carrying the little ones all the way to Wuhu. Before they left Miaosheo, Lo and the Wangs purchased two coffins, wrapped the missionaries' bodies in white cloth and placed them in the coffins to be buried. Immediately after, Pastor Lo left for Wuhu with his wife and the children. All along the way, young Chinese mothers willingly nursed the American missionary orphan.

Halfway through their journey, the Lo's stopped in Suancheng for a rest. Late that night, George Birch heard a knock at the door of the mission compound. A travel-weary Mrs. Lo stood before him with an outstretched bundle. "This is all we have left." Mr. Birch took the bundle in his arms, pulled back the blanket, and was shocked to see a sleeping Helen Priscilla.

Word had already reached the CIM superintendent and Betty's grieving parents of the brutal death of the young couple. When Pastor Lo finally reached Wuhu safely, a telegram was sent to Betty's parents in Tsinan and John's family in America that that their granddaughter had been miraculously saved.

Did God Make a Mistake?

John and Betty Stam were buried in Miaosheo, China, near the pine trees where they had given their lives for Jesus. Today, their gravestones still bear their life verses: on John's, "That Christ may be magnified whether by life or by death" (see Philippians 1:20); on Betty's: "For me to live is Christ and to die is gain" (see Philippians 1:21).

Did God make a mistake? John and Betty were ready to live or die for Christ, but they were just beginning their ministry in China. God rescued baby Helen; why not her parents? We know that He had the power to deliver John and Betty as well. There are some things we won't understand until we reach heaven, but we do know that what Satan meant for evil God used for great good. The Stam's testimony and their martyrdom became a tremendous seed for missionary growth throughout the world.

The Stams' testimony and their martyrdom became a tremendous seed for missionary growth throughout the world.

After news of John and Betty's murder reached the Moody Bible Institute, hundreds of students committed their lives to missionary work, some joining China Inland Mission to take the Stam's place. Books were published about their life stories and sent to Christians around the world. Ten years later, when John's youngest brother was at Wheaton College in Chicago, hundreds of his classmates were preparing for missionary service because of the courageous testimony of John and Betty Stam. Among those classmates was a young couple, Billy Graham and his wife, Ruth, who dedicated the rest of their lives to evangelistic service to the same Lord and Savior. In the 1940s, Wheaton graduates Jim and Elisabeth Elliot also entered the mission field, inspired by the courageous commitment of John and Betty Stam to Jesus Christ.

God's Ministry in China Grows

After the Communist takeover in 1949, when all Western missionaries were forced to leave China, the CIM continued to evangelize throughout Southeast Asia, changing their name to OMF International. In 2015, OMF celebrated one hundred and fifty years of spreading Christ's gospel in Asia thanks to the vision of their founder, Hudson

Taylor, and thousands of Christian missionaries who faithfully embraced that vision—including John and Betty Stam.

Naturally, people have wondered what happened to baby Helen after the martyrdom of her parents. Helen grew up with her mother's family and chose to live a quiet Christian life in America out of the limelight of her well-known missionary parents. Her desire for privacy was honored, so very little information is available about her today.

"Whom Shall I Fear?"

John and Betty Stam served God in a dangerous part of the world, but they were centered on His purposes for their lives on earth. Instead of living in fear, they had faith in God's plan. Christians today are serving Christ in an equally dangerous world. God promises in His Word that He will be our Light and our Deliverer. We must focus on God and His eternal purposes for us and not the world's idea of safety from our enemies. We are so often invested in this life, but we are pilgrims just passing through, living to make a difference for Jesus' sake. *"The Lord is my light and my salvation—whom shall I fear? The Lord is the stronghold of my life—of whom shall I be afraid?"* (Psalm 27:1 NIV).

Wang Zhiming: "Listen to the One Above"

A small group of Chinese children stood quietly outside of the Communist detention center in the town of Wuding, China. "We would like to see our father," one brave son requested of the Red Guards standing in front of the prison gates. It was a familiar scene. The children often visited the camp, hoping to get even the smallest glimpse of their father, Pastor Wang Zhiming.

Laughter filled the air as the revolutionary soldiers taunted the children, sneering at their innocent faces. "Your old man was a bad guy. He believed in God...God is not the savior! Chairman Mao and the

Communist Party are the saviors of the people. Your father is going to be executed. Do you believe in God or in Chairman Mao and the Communist Party?"[206]

Once again the children walked sadly away. All their efforts to see their father after nearly four years in prison still unfulfilled.

China's Plan to Wipe Out Christians

Wang Zhiming was born in 1907 in Wuding, Yunnan Province, a small village tucked in the mountains of southwest China. Faithful Christian missionaries visited the region when he was a boy, and he and many villagers responded to the gospel and became born again. When the communists forced the missionaries out of Yunnan in 1944, Wang was ordained and became their pastor. Shortly after, because of his wisdom and faithful leadership, he was appointed as the general superintendent of all the Christian churches in the area.

Wang Zhiming had a heart for Christ, and he wanted to see the church grow without constant persecution from the Red Guards. He tried his best to lead the people without becoming an enemy of the Communist government. By then, the Christian church had been struggling against Communist persecution for forty years.

In the mid-1960s, China was plunged into the Cultural Revolution, headed by dictator Mao Zedong. The Cultural Revolution was Chairman Mao's vicious attempt to wipe out all remaining influence of Western culture, capitalism, and Christianity. Mao's Red Guard began cleansing the population of Christian witnesses. Pastor Wang refused to take part in public denunciations of Christians, stating, "My hands have baptized many converts, and should not be used for sinfulness."

206. Nigel Tomes, "Wang Zhiming, Chinese Christian martyr, 1973" Church in Toronto Blog, churchintoronto.blogspot.com/2012/01/wang-zhiming-chinese-christian-martyr.html, excerpted from Liao Yiwu, *God Is Red: The Secret Story of How Christianity Survived and Flourished in Communist China* (New York: HarperOne, 2011), 107–112.

Death to the Christians!

Wang was denounced as a counter-revolutionary, falsely accused of being a spy and of secretly murdering seven Red Guard soldiers. He was arrested in 1969 and held in a Communist prison for four long years, where he was regularly abused and starved. His wife and children were denied visiting rights.

Close-up of statue of Wang Zhiming in Westminster Abbey (far right).
Andrea Shaffer\Flikr

"Death to the Christians!" became an increasingly common slogan among the Communist soldiers of China. It is the same cry we have heard from centuries of anti-Christian persecution, and the same cry we hear in too many countries in the world today! We need to remind ourselves that no matter what people group or what ideology shouts these inflammatory words, Satan is behind them all with his plan of rebellion against God and His church.

In December of 1973, Red Guards showed up at the Wang home with the dreaded announcement: "Wang Zhiming will be executed tomorrow, December 29, 1973. You may visit him today." We have the details of what happened in the last two days of Wang Zhiming's life because his son, Wang Zisheng, gave an interview to a fellow Chinese believer many years later.[207]

"Listen to What 'The Above' Tells You!"

The son, Wang Zisheng's, story began at the prison that day:

> When we saw my father, his hair had turned gray; he was thin, like a skeleton. Each time he moved, the shackles around his ankles clanked loudly. As he hobbled toward us, we all cried.... Seeing our whole family crying and sobbing, one guard howled at us: "Stop crying! Hurry up and talk to your father one by one. Time is limited."
>
> My mother nodded at my father and said, "You are the one who used to do all the talking. We listen to you first." My father smiled.... "I haven't been able to reform my thinking," my father said. "Since I cannot be changed, I am responsible for, and deserve, what I receive. But for all of you, don't follow me. *Listen to what 'the above' tells you.*"[208]

The family instantly understood what their beloved husband and father was saying to them; he would pretend to be guilty and deserving of death, but they were to continue to follow the voice of Jesus Christ "the above" no matter what the consequences might be. His faithful words, after four years of abuse, warmed their hearts.

At this point, a prison officer made a cruel announcement, "Wang Zhiming has been sentenced to death. The execution will be carried out tomorrow after a public trial. The criminal's body shall be handled by

207. Nigel Tomes, "Wang Zhiming."
208. Ibid.

the government. Family members don't need to be involved…the government has decided to blow up his body with explosives."

"No!" his wife cried. The Zhiming family was heartbroken. Their beloved father would experience such a horrific death and they would have no opportunity to give him a Christian burial. After begging the Red Guards to let them bury Zhiming's body, they returned home. Throughout the night they prayed fervently, along with the Christians of Wuding, that the Lord would change the method of execution and allow them to bury their father in peace.

"God Has Heard Our Prayers!"

Zishang's story continued, "Early the next morning, a village official came and told us to borrow a horse-drawn cart. He said we could go to Father's public trial, which would be attended by 10,000 people. Afterward, we could, in his words, 'drag home the body of the counterrevolutionary.'" The family was grateful that the Lord had intervened. Slowly they walked to the prison stadium singing hymns along the way. When they arrived, they were greeted by armed Red Guards who aimed their guns at the family and barked their orders:

"Don't move. Squat down with your hands clutching your heads." The family knelt with their back to the prisoners and judges. Whenever the guards were distracted, they would quietly turn their heads to get glimpses of their father. He stood on the stage with his hands and legs bound by ropes. Blood was streaming down the corner of his mouth. Later, the family learned that a

Later, the family learned that a guard had used his bayonet to cut Zhiming's tongue out to prevent him from preaching or calling on the name of Jesus before the large crowd.

guard had used his bayonet to cut Zhiming's tongue out to prevent him from preaching or calling on the name of Jesus before the large crowd.

Once again, as in so many stories of martyr's deaths, a frenzied crowd was riled up by the propaganda of its leaders and cheered in anticipation of the Christian's execution.

After false accusations were made against Zhiming, a leader grabbed the microphone and announced:

> "Wang Zhiming has been sentenced to death; the execution will be carried out immediately." Soldiers raised Father into the air so everyone could see him. The crowd roared. They raised their fists high and shouted in a frenzy, "Down with...," "Smash...," and "Long live Chairman Mao!"

Thankfully, Wang Zhiming was not executed with a bomb tied to his waist that day in December of 1973. Instead, he was carried to a truck and driven by a Red Guard escort to a private spot where he was shot to death without the cruel shouts of the crowds still resounding in his ears.

Friends from the village borrowed a cart and retrieved Pastor Wang Zhiming's body. When the family saw their husband and father, they wept with sorrow and yet celebrated with joy that he was now safe in heaven. They wiped his blood-stained face with a clean cloth, covered him with a family quilt and had a Christian burial for him near the outskirts of the village. It was a bittersweet moment for his congregation as they rejoiced that their beloved pastor was now at rest in the arms of Jesus.

China's Attempt to Eliminate Christianity Was a Failure!

So how successful was the Chinese Communist government in wiping out Christianity in Yunnan Province? It was a failure. The end result of the suffering by Wang Zhiming and other Christian leaders of the region was steady church growth. At the time of Zhiming's death, there were 2,795 Christians in the village of Wuding. By 1980, the church had grown to over 12,000 believers! Today, it is estimated that Wuding has over 30,000 Christian worshippers meeting in more than 100 places of worship.[209] The Chinese Communists continue their persecution of Christians to this day, but believers have grown in numbers and in their faithful stand for the Lord Jesus Christ.

Wang Zhiming received two honors after his death that the humble pastor would never have expected. In 1981 he became the only Christian martyr of Mao's Cultural Revolution to have a monument of honor erected at his gravesite. It still stands today. Then, in 1998, he was memorialized in Westminster Abbey as one of the ten twentieth-century Christians representing a century of global martyrdom in the Christian church. In spite of all that China tried to do to stop the gospel, God received all the glory and honor from Wang Zhiming's life and death. *"Not to us, LORD, not to us but to your name be the glory, because of your love and faithfulness"* (Psalm 115:1 NIV).

209. Rodney Stark and Xiuhua Wang, *A Star in the East: The Rise of Christianity in China* (West Conshohocken, PA: Templeton Press, 2015), 60.

NAZISM: THE COST OF DISCIPLESHIP

10

NAZISM: THE COST OF DISCIPLESHIP

(AD 1900–2000)

While communism was ravaging Asia in the early part of the twentieth century, a new form of tyranny descended on Europe: National Socialism. In Germany it was commonly known as Nazism, fed by the venomous hatred of Adolf Hitler. His desire to overrun the world fed his socialistic atheism and became a three-pronged attack: (1) to become the Führer and dictator of Europe and Russia; (2) to change the church to fit his image as lord; and (3) to destroy the Jews, God's chosen people. During Hitler's dictatorship, known as the Third Reich, it is estimated that six million Jews and five million non-Jews—many of them Christians—died at the hands of the Third Reich. However, in spite of the Nazi's demonic agenda, the kingdom of God still stood strong when the conflict was over.

One man among those millions who stood with courage against the Nazi regime was Dietrich Bonhoeffer. He had a world-renowned platform, but he still died in the grey darkness of a Nazi concentration camp, standing until the very end of his life for the truth found in Jesus Christ alone.

Dietrich Bonhoeffer: Only Jesus Knows the Journey's End

"If we answer the call to discipleship, where will it lead us?
To answer this question we shall have to go to Him,
for only He knows the answer. Only Jesus Christ,
who bids us follow Him, knows the journey's end.
But we do know that it will be a road of boundless mercy."
—Dietrich Bonhoeffer, 1938[210]

The air in his cell was dank, heavy with the smell of his unwashed body and the musty scent of mold. With each weary breath, he inhaled the faint metallic taste of metal bars and rusted hinges; expelling the air brought little relief.

Dietrich lifted a dirty hand and ran it through his ash blond hair. Peeling his glasses from his face, he cleaned the rims of his spectacles with the last clean patch of cloth from his shirt and placed them atop the Bible resting on the slab of wood that served as his desk and chair.

He smiled faintly at the small enclosure that had been his home for eighteen long months when the faint echo of footsteps reached him.

210. Dietrich Bonhoeffer, *The Cost of Discipleship* (New York: Simon & Schuster, 1959).

With practiced ease, Dietrich slid on his glasses and waited in the silence. The whisper of metal sliding across metal, the cautious opening of the prison door, and Sergeant Knoblauch, the German guard who had faithfully befriended him, stood before him just as he promised.

"Pastor Bonhoeffer," the soldier whispered, his Berliner accent a biting tongue in Bonhoeffer's jail cell.

The pastor smiled at one of God's gifts to him in the months he had dwelt in captivity. "Yes, my friend. I am here."

The man's voice was anxious, "Please, sir, you must tell me now! The plans are all but finished; if we are to escape we must act quickly!" His eyes darted down the menacingly plain architecture, envisioning himself behind a similarly barred wall if anyone lurked and listened. "Please, are you with me?"

Dietrich sighed softly, watching his last ember of hope for survival fading away. *How easy, O Lord, would it be to accept!* Then, in a moment of heart-wrenching truth, the faces of his family flashed before him, his brother Klaus and his sisters' husbands, Hans and Rudiger, already behind bars. His beloved fiancée, Maria, frightened daily by the Gestapo's menacing threats. Every precious face he envisioned would be mutilated, every life vengefully taken if they found his prison cell empty.

"No," Bonhoeffer firmly replied. "I cannot go. I must stay."

An Uncompromising Stand Against Evil

Dietrich Bonhoeffer was a Christian hero of uncompromising courage, daring to publicly oppose the ruthless evil of Adolph Hitler's Third Reich. It is hard to do justice, in just a few pages, to the many ways Bonhoeffer defended the gospel of Christ while exposing the Nazi persecution of Christians and Jews to the outside world. This chapter is a glimpse into the life of a twentieth-century spiritual warrior who relentlessly pursued God and doggedly opposed Hitler even while most of Germany's pastors were submitting to the Nazi tyranny.

God had given Bonhoeffer a prophetic gift, allowing him to see the deeper truth of what was happening to Germany and the German church before any of his contemporaries. Dietrich was a man who fixed his spiritual eyes "*not…at the things which are seen, but at the things which are not seen. For the things which are seen are temporary, but the things which are not seen are eternal*" (2 Corinthians 4:18).

Bonhoeffer, a twenty-six-year-old theologian, pastor, writer, and teacher, laid it all down at the foot of the cross to confront godless Nazism. He could have chosen another way—he didn't have to make a public stand against Hitler's demonic aggression. He was repeatedly urged by family and friends to travel to the United States and weather the war in safety, returning to pick up the pieces of the German church when the Nazi regime was finally destroyed. But he wouldn't consider it. Just like the godly leaders of the Reformation, Bonhoeffer's place belonged with the persecuted Christians and Jews of his homeland; he would continue fighting to bring the Third Reich to its knees.

Why Is Bonhoeffer Important?

Why is Dietrich Bonhoeffer's story so important to Christians today? Because Bonhoeffer was a believer who refused to compromise his faith in the midst of a godless contemporary culture. In spite of relentless pressure from the Nazi government and the German church, Bonhoeffer defended the truth of God's Word even when it cost him his life.

Today, we live in a world of compromise. Many pastors and their congregations are choosing the easy way, submitting to the culture, and dissecting God's Word in order to reject the Scriptures that oppose the popular sin of the day. Atheists and elitists are trying to eliminate Christian truths from society, from education, and even from the church, trying to force true believers to hide within their own church buildings. Adolph Hitler and the Nazi regime did the same thing; their anti-Christian culture snuck up on the German people like a thief in the night. Bonhoeffer is an example of a man of God who had the courage in the name of Christ to say, "Enough and no more!" We need to have that same courage today!

Born into German Prosperity

Dietrich Bonhoeffer was born in Breslau, Germany (modern-day Wroclaw, Poland), on February 4, 1906, just moments before his twin sister Sabine. They were the sixth and seventh children born into the brilliant Bonhoeffer family. Their father, Karl, was a university professor and the leading psychiatrist/neurologist in Germany and their mother, Paula, was one of a few German women at the time who had earned a college degree. Dietrich's oldest brother, Karl-Friedrich, was a world-renowned physicist who worked with Albert Einstein and was one of the first scientists to split the atom. His brother, Klaus, was a highly respected German attorney.

Karl Bonhoeffer, Dietrich's father.
Public domain.

The Bonhoeffers lived in an exclusive part of Berlin surrounded by German doctors, renowned scientists, gifted musicians, and university professors, many of them Jewish. From a very young age, Dietrich was an exceptionally talented pianist. Perhaps his future was in the world-renowned Berlin Philharmonic Orchestra, his mother thought. Imagine his family's surprise when fourteen-year-old Dietrich proudly announced that he wanted to study theology instead. Why would he waste his genius on theology? The Bonhoeffer family seldom attended church, even though Paula had taught her children some biblical truths. But in the end, the close-knit family supported Dietrich's decision to pursue his chosen career.

At seventeen, Dietrich entered the University of Tübingen and a year later transferred to Berlin University. In 1927, at age twenty-one, he received his doctorate in theology. But what would he do for the next four years? The German Lutheran Church wouldn't ordain anyone below the age of twenty-five. Bonhoeffer had no way of knowing it, but it was God preventing him from pursuing a theological career. The Almighty had another path for Dietrich Bonhoeffer's life—beginning with a personal appointment with Jesus Christ.

Spiritual Revival in Harlem

After spending months traveling through Italy and northern Africa with his brother, Klaus, and then teaching classes in Barcelona, Spain, Dietrich decided to spend a year studying at the Union Theological Seminary in New York City. He arrived in New York harbor in August of 1930. His first weeks in New York were a great disappointment.

"In New York they preach about virtually everything," Bonhoeffer wrote. "Only one thing is not addressed...the gospel of Jesus Christ, the cross, sin and forgiveness, death and life."[211] In the name of progressive humanism, most of his theology professors had abandoned the Bible for social doctrine, and the churches that he visited were more like social clubs than places of worship. "In place of the church as the congregation of believers in Christ there stands the church as a social corporation," Bonhoeffer wrote, "filled with programs and social engagements."[212] Unfortunately, there are many churches throughout America today that still struggle with a lack of Jesus' presence. When will they learn that without the presence of the living God, their church will become just another human failure?

211. Eric Metaxas, *Bonhoeffer: Pastor, Martyr, Prophet, Spy* (Nashville, TN: Thomas Nelson, 2011), 107.
212. Ibid.

Thankfully, God's hand was leading Bonhoeffer on a path he had never walked before—one of spiritual revival. Among Dietrich's closest seminary friends was Frank Fisher, an African-American student who spent his Sundays serving at the Abyssinian Baptist Church of Harlem. At the time, it was one of the largest Protestant churches in America with ten thousand members, predominantly black.[213] In Harlem, four thousand miles from Berlin, Dietrich Bonhoeffer experienced a personal revelation of Jesus Christ.

Jesus Can Change a Life

Walking into the expansive, crowded sanctuary, Bonhoeffer was astounded by the singing and hallelujah choruses of the lively congregation. For the first time, he heard an impassioned message from the pulpit proclaiming Jesus Christ as the center of every part of a Christian's life. The Abyssinian congregation was filled with people who had known oppression and suffering, many whose parents had been slaves, but they worshipped the living God with their whole hearts—in spirit and in truth.

Bonhoeffer was inspired by the sights and sounds of spiritual worship and responded to the anointed preaching with a joyful heart. In Harlem, his eyes were opened to a simple, yet life-changing, truth: the heart of Christianity was the Lord Jesus Christ. The role of a disciple was to pick up his cross and follow the Master daily, no matter the circumstances. Theology, religion, moral rule—none of it was the same as the power

In London on the way back from America to Germany, July 1939.
Public domain.

213. See http://abyssinian.org/about-us/history/.

of a personal relationship with Jesus: *"Christ in you, the hope of glory"* (Colossians 1:27).

After that initial visit, every Sunday would find the fair, blonde-haired German theologian leading Sunday school for a class of young boys and later joining in the joyful clapping of the black spirituals. He observed, "Here, one can truly speak and hear about sin and grace and the love of God." For eight months, Bonhoeffer saw the true gospel as it was lived out by an oppressed people who were alive in Christ. His Christian journey would never be the same.

Germany's Destruction from Within

Returning to Germany in 1932, Dietrich was no longer interested in a theological career. After his ordination as a Lutheran pastor, he began teaching a confirmation class of boys in the poorest section of Berlin. At the same time, he and the rest of the Bonhoeffer family grimly watched the rising threat of the Nazi Party. Dietrich was exceptionally passionate in his opposition to Hitler's National Socialist party. Although he didn't realize how vital his future role would be, the twenty-six-year-old Bonhoeffer could clearly see the peril of a German ruler who glorified himself as the savior of his people.

On January 30, 1933, Adolf Hitler was elected chancellor of Germany, an event that would cost the world twelve years of unspeakable human suffering. Two days later, on February 1, Bonhoeffer broadcast a radio speech he had written just before the election. With a clear, calm voice, he warned the German people of a political ideology rising in popularity called the "Führer Principle," that elevated the national leader over the authority of almighty God. Half way through the broadcast, his radio transmission was suddenly cut off.[214] Dietrich's controversial role as a "prophet" to the people of Germany had begun.

214. Eberhard Bethge, *Dietrich Bonhoeffer*, ed. by Victoria Barnett (Minneapolis, MN: Fortress Press, 2000), 259–260.

Heil Hitler!

Adolph Hitler's sinister plans for Germany were carried out with lightning speed. As an American citizen it is hard to comprehend what happened in just a few short months. We must all pray that it never happens here! Hitler was a scheming leader who created a frenzied loyalty in the German people by playing on their fears of a common enemy. First Hitler began a rumor: the godless Communists living in Germany were on the brink of overthrowing the government just as they had done in Russia.

Two weeks after Hitler won the election, the Reichstag Building (where Germany's Parliament met) was mysteriously burned to the ground. A Communist dissident found nearby was arrested, tried, and convicted. (To this day many believe that the fire was started by the Nazi leaders themselves.) Hitler and his cabinet members used the fire to incite a country-wide panic that the Communist takeover had begun. Hitler immediately requested that the Reichstag (Parliament) pass the Reichstag Fire Decree which gave Hitler the authority to suspend the civil rights of all German citizens until further notice.

Rather than attempting to *abolish* German rights and privileges, a move that would have raised a protest from the people, Hitler moved to *suspend* them, until a time national security was reestablished. Except that Hitler never intended for that time of national security to occur. By February 27, 1933, the rights of all German citizens had been erased. Imagine the United States Congress voting to suspend our American Bill of Rights—freedom of religion, freedom of the press, freedom to assemble, freedom to bear arms—and *poof*, they are gone for good.

The destruction of the German democracy continued to spin madly out of control. One month later, in March of 1933, Hitler persuaded the Reichstag to pass the Enabling Act, which gave the chancellor the power to pass laws by decree, bypassing the Reichstag completely. It effectively wiped out Germany's parliamentary system. Democracy in Germany had come to an end. By March 23, 1933, a little less than two months after his election, Adolf Hitler was the sole dictator of Germany![215]

The Malicious Attack on the Jews Begins

Now that Hitler had arrested or deported most of the Communists in Germany, he moved to his real national enemy—the Jews. For years, Hitler had believed that the Jews were an inferior race and the cause of all of Germany's financial and social problems. He promoted the Aryan ideal, a doctrine of racial purity that claimed that all non-Jewish Caucasians, especially those with blond hair and blue eyes, were a master race. The Aryans were the true German people, appointed by God, and all non-Aryans were to be rejected and pushed out of Germany. (As the satanic influence over Hitler grew, his policy of forced emigration of the Jews changed to a policy of total extermination.)

In April of 1933, Hitler released the Aryan Paragraph, a policy which demanded that Jewish workers be fired from all government jobs. That same month, the first boycott of Jewish stores, doctors' offices, and attorneys' offices began. Jewish students were forced to leave German schools and to establish segregated schools of their own. In May, Jewish professors were dismissed from German universities, and Jewish books confiscated in Berlin were burned. In September, the Jews were banned from taking part in many cultural activities. By the end of 1933, Jewish journalists had lost the right to publish anywhere in the Third Reich, and all church groups for the young were forced to join the Hitler Youth. In the next two years, the Jews became ostracized from all of German society.[216]

Remember our earlier chapters on Roman persecution? The policies in Germany in 1933 are so similar to the policies that were enforced in Lyon, France, before the execution of the Christian martyrs

215. United States Holocaust Memorial Museum, "Nazi Rule," Holocaust Encyclopedia, www.ushmm.org/wlc/en/article.php?ModuleId=10005143, accessed May 20, 2016.
216. "Nazi Germany 1933–1939," United States Holocaust Memorial Museum, https://www.ushmm.org/learn/holocaust-encyclopedia, May 20, 2016.

in the Colosseum. Satan's malicious plan to wipe out God's people has not changed since the garden of Eden; it has been an insidious thread throughout the course of history. He uses power-hungry people to persecute believers, driving them out of society and then to their deaths. Solomon's wisdom reminds us that there is nothing new on this earth: *"What has been will be again, what has been done will be done again; there is nothing new under the sun"* (Ecclesiastes 1:9 NIV).

Bonhoeffer's house in Berlin.
Axel Mauruszat\Wikimedia Commons

What power did Hitler use to make such radical, racially-motivated changes so quickly? Without a doubt, Hitler's most powerful weapons were the relentless propaganda of the Nazi Party and the Führer's public speeches, which created an atmosphere of mass hysteria. Each time Hitler spoke his demonic lies against the Jewish people, he claimed that he had been sent by "God's providence" to restore the greatness of Germany. As though under a wicked spell, the German people embraced his message.

Where Was the Christian Church?

In the midst of Hitler's evil, where was the Christian church? Where were the Lutheran pastors who had spent four hundred years teaching the truths of Martin Luther's Reformation? Where were the German evangelical church leaders?

They were silent.

Bonhoeffer's voice was one of the first to raise the alarm about Hitler's treatment of the Jews; he demanded that the German pastors stand up in protest. He gave a clear warning: "Silence in the face of evil is itself evil. God will not hold us guiltless. Not to speak is to speak! Not to act is to act!"[217]

Bonhoeffer's voice was one of the first to raise the alarm about Hitler's treatment of the Jews; he demanded that the German pastors stand up in protest.

Tragically, most of Germany's church leaders were just as deceived as the German people. They accepted Hitler's lies and preached from their pulpits that he was an Aryan savior sent from God to erase the German shame of losing World War I.

In the spring of 1933, as Hitler was declaring himself the Führer, twenty-seven-year-old Bonhoeffer preached a message in direct opposition to Hitler's lies. Standing in the pulpit of Trinity Church in Berlin, he announced, "The church has only *one* altar, the altar of the Almighty...before which all creatures must kneel.... The church has only *one* pulpit, and from that pulpit, faith in God will be preached, and no other faith, and no other will but the will of God."[218]

217. While widely attributed to Bonhoeffer, this quotation does not appear in any of his published works.
218. Metaxas, 144.

Hitler's False Nazi Church

Under Hitler's rule, the Evangelical Church in Germany became a distorted shadow of Christianity. Hitler was determined to draw all of the evangelical churches into one Reich Church led by Nazi doctrine, with Hitler as its leader. The members of Hitler's state church were known as the new "German Christians." They rejected the historical fact that Jesus was a Jew and claimed He was an Aryan Christ who offered the gospel only to the Aryan people! How could anyone who read the Bible claim that Jesus was not a Jew, unless they had been deceived by Satan himself?

The most fervent Nazis in this "German Christian" movement went so far as to reject the entire Old Testament, as well as the book of Hebrews and other portions of Paul's writings, denying that they were part of the Bible. This is how people can be led into false doctrine once they replace Jesus Christ with any other idol or accept only certain portions of the Scripture as God's Word. False doctrine can spread like a plague among Christians who do not abide in Christ, study the truths of God's inerrant Word, or stay in tune with the Holy Spirit.

The Nazis forced all Jewish Christians to leave the German churches and set up segregated places to worship. Christian pastors of Jewish descent had their ordinations revoked, including Dietrich's friend, Franz Hildebrandt. Bonhoeffer was infuriated with both the treatment of the Jews and the silence of the German pastors. He had close Jewish friends and neighbors including his twin sister's husband, Gerhard Leibholz, a brilliant German attorney. Bonhoeffer had seen enough. He joined with other Christian leaders to force the German pastors to make a choice between truth and falsehood.[219]

Thankfully, God always has a remnant of His faithful people. In Hitler's Germany that remnant was led by Dietrich Bonhoeffer and several other Christian leaders including Martin Niemöller, Gerhard

219. John Malkov, "Dietrich Bonhoeffer Biography & Chronology," dbonhoeffer.org, http://www.dbonhoeffer.org/Biography.html.

Jacobi, and Karl Barth. Together, they stood for truth in Jesus Christ, called the German church into account, and exposed the false doctrine of the new Nazi Church. They founded an organization called the Pastor's Emergency League, with Martin Niemöller as their unofficial leader. He sent letters to all of the pastors in Germany asking them to join. Out of eighteen thousand pastors, two thousand signed the Pastor's Emergency League charter.

You may not have heard of Martin Niemöller before, but you have probably heard his famous quote on the cowardice of his countrymen to stand against the growing Nazi evil:

> First they came for the Socialists, and I did not speak out—
> Because I was not a Socialist.
> Then they came for the Trade Unionists, and I did not speak out—
> Because I was not a Trade Unionist.
> Then they came for the Jews, and I did not speak out—
> Because I was not a Jew.
> Then they came for me—and there was no one left to speak for me.[220]

The Confessing Church Is Born

The Lutheran Synod was eager to silence Bonhoeffer's opposition to the Nazi Church, so they sent the young pastor to London to lead two German congregations. But their plan backfired; Bonhoeffer was anything but quiet. For a year and a half, he preached to his congregations and throughout England on the lordship of Jesus Christ above all secular rulers, and he warned many British pastors of Hitler's growing persecution of the German Jews. One man in particular, Anglican Bishop

220. This version of Niemöller's poem is taken from the Holocaust Encyclopedia, "Martin Niemöller," United States Holocaust Memorial Museum, https://www.ushmm.org/wlc/en/article.php?ModuleId=10007392. However, because the poem was taken from his lectures given in early postwar period, many versions of it exist.

George Bell, became Bonhoeffer's lifelong friend and, along with several other British leaders, was Bonhoeffer's future underground connection to expose the Nazi's war crimes to the rest of the world.

In 1934, the Pastor's Emergency League became an official new church in Germany, the Confessing Church. It was founded by Bonhoeffer and the other Christian leaders in order to be a true representation of Jesus Christ and the Bible in Germany and to denounce the heresies of the pro-Nazi "German Christianity." The new church proclaimed the following truths:

That Jesus was the only way to God and salvation: "*I am the way, and the truth, and the life.* ***No one comes to the Father except through Me***" (John 14:6 ESV). "*Truly, truly, I say to you, he who does not enter the sheepfold by the door, but climbs in by another way, that man is a thief and a robber*" (John 10:1 ESV).

That Jesus Christ and the Word of God are to be obeyed above Hitler: "Jesus Christ, as he is attested for us in Holy Scripture, is *the one Word of God* which we have to hear and which we have to trust and obey in life and in death. We reject the false doctrine, that the church... would have to acknowledge as a source of its proclamation, [anything] besides *this one Word of God,* [or any] other events and powers [Hitler], figures and truths, as God's revelation."[221]

Bonhoeffer: Prophet to a Nation

Dietrich Bonhoeffer could see with spiritual eyes what others could not easily see. Even his closest friends and family did not recognize the menacing evil of the Third Reich as clearly as Bonhoeffer. All of his later biographers affirmed that Bonhoeffer's vision of Germany was that of a prophet. His brother-in-law wrote, "Dietrich Bonhoeffer was one of the few that understood, even before Hitler came to power, that National

221. "Theological Declaration of Barmen," excerpt from Arthur C. Cochrane, *The Church's Confession Under Hitler* (Philadelphia: Westminster Press, 1962), 237–242, emphasis added.

Socialism was a brutal attempt to make history without God and to found it on the strength of man alone...."[222]

Bonhoeffer's desk.
Axel Mauruszat\Wikimedia Commons

In the spring of 1935, Bonhoeffer returned home from England, his concern for Germany mounting. The Confessing Church opened a seminary in Finkenwalde, eastern Germany, so that the truth of God's Word could still be taught, and Bonhoeffer became their primary instructor. In 1936, as a result of his leadership in this "rebellious church," the Nazis declared Bonhoeffer "an enemy of the state," revoking his privileges to teach in all German universities. Dietrich used his extra time well and wrote his most famous work, *The Cost of Discipleship*. Based on the Sermon on the Mount, the book challenged Christians to live as true followers of Jesus Christ, no matter the cost.

222. Gerhard Leibholz, "Memoir," in Bonhoeffer, *The Cost of Discipleship* (New York: Simon & Schuster, 1959).

The book began with Bonhoeffer's famous explanation of the "costly price" of God's grace compared to the cheap grace of those who refused to walk as true followers. He wrote,

> *Cheap grace* is the deadly enemy of the Church. We are fighting today for costly grace.... *Cheap grace* is the preaching of forgiveness without requiring repentance, baptism without church discipline, communion without confession. Cheap grace is grace without discipleship, grace without the cross, grace without Jesus Christ.
>
> "*Costly grace* is the treasure hidden in the field...the pearl of great price. Costly grace confronts us as a gracious call to follow Jesus. It is costly because it compels a man to submit to the yoke of Christ and follow Him; it is grace because Jesus says: '*My yoke is easy and my burden is light.*' Above all it is costly because it cost God the price of his Son."[223]

I pray that the church will listen to this message on grace from Bonhoeffer today.

"When Jesus Calls a Man..."

"When Jesus calls a man," Dietrich Bonhoeffer wrote, "he bids him come and die." To Bonhoeffer this was also the true cost of discipleship.

He wasn't writing about physical martyrdom at the time, but the dying every Christian must experience: dying to self, to fleshly desires, to selfish ambitions. It's the discipleship Jesus spoke of when He said, "*If anyone desires to come after Me, let him deny himself, and take up his cross, and follow Me*" (Matthew 16:24). It's what the apostle Paul meant when he said, "*I have been crucified with Christ; and it is no longer I who live, but Christ lives in me*" (Galatians 2:20).

---

223. Bonhoeffer, *Cost of Discipleship*, 44–45, emphasis added.

Every time Bonhoeffer published a new book, the German Gestapo responded with increased persecution. Following the publication of *Discipleship*, Dietrich was forbidden to live or work in Berlin. Within days of that order, the Gestapo was marching up the seminary steps in Finkenwalde.[224]

With his twin sister Sabine Leibholz in London, July 1939.
Public domain.

"Where is Pastor Bonhoeffer?" the plainclothes agents demanded. "We have orders from the Führer! This false seminary is now closed!" The seminary students were escorted from the building and the Gestapo agents quickly barred the large oak doors of the Finkenwalde Seminary. Twenty-seven Confessing Church pastors were arrested at the same time, including Martin Niemöller. (By God's grace, Niemöller survived seven years in concentration camps and was finally freed by

224. Malkov, "Dietrich Bonhoeffer."

the Allied troops in 1945. He lived for several more decades after the war.)

Bonhoeffer remained undaunted—not even the feared Gestapo could stop him from teaching about Jesus Christ and the truth of His Word. Defying the Führer again, Dietrich took the seminary "underground" and conducted what became a "seminary on the run" for two more years.

The Terrible "Night of Broken Glass"

The entire Bonhoeffer family was vehemently opposed to Adolf Hitler. His sister Sabine's family was in grave danger since her husband and children were Jewish. After Germany's takeover of Austria in 1938, Dietrich was convinced that the German Jews would soon be destroyed in an avalanche of bloodshed and death. One evening in September, 1938, Dietrich convinced Sabine and Gerhard to flee Germany with their two young daughters before it was too late. His discernment saved their lives.

Two months later, Nazi leaders orchestrated a national night of terror. November 9, 1938, became known as *Kristallnacht*, or the Night of Broken Glass. Over two hundred and fifty Jewish synagogues were burned; dozens of Jews were murdered; thousands of Jewish businesses and homes were destroyed; and glass littered the streets of a nation, while the German police stood watching. Early the next morning, thirty thousand Jewish men were rounded up, herded into cattle cars and shipped off to concentrations camps. Immediately after, Hitler declared that the Jews were forbidden to leave Germany, and the Secret Service permanently closed the borders to prevent any Jewish escapes. The Holocaust had begun.[225]

---

225. United States Holocaust Memorial Museum, "Introduction to the Holocaust," Holocaust Encyclopedia, www.ushmm.org/wlc/en/article.php?ModuleId=10005143, accessed February 24, 2016.

War's Darkness Overshadows the World

"To lift one's hands against the Jews is to lift one's hands against God Himself!" Bonhoeffer declared after the night of terror for God's chosen people. He recalled Zechariah 2:9: *"He who touches you touches the apple of His eye."*

> *"To lift one's hands against the Jews is to lift one's hands against God Himself!"*

The Second World War officially began when Germany invaded Poland in 1939. There was no way that Bonhoeffer was willing to put on a German army uniform and fight for Hitler's regime. So, at his family's urging, he left for the United States. As soon as he stepped on American soil, he knew it was not God's will; he belonged with the people of Germany. Bonhoeffer wrote, "I must live through this difficult period in our national history with the people of Germany. I will have no right to participate in the reconstruction of Christian life in Germany after the war if I do not share the trials of this time with my people."[226]

Bonhoeffer Becomes a Double Agent

When Dietrich arrived back in Germany, he still faced the problem of military service for the Third Reich. At that time, Germany was conscripting most men into service. His brother-in-law, Hans von Dohnanyi offered him an unusual solution: join Hans in working for the German Military Intelligence, the *Abwehr*. It would save Dietrich from serving in the army.

On the surface, his official role would be as a "goodwill ambassador" for Germany, traveling to Switzerland to promote the German cause. In reality, as von Dohnanyi explained, Bonhoeffer would be entering a world of espionage against the Third Reich. Known only to a close

226. G. Leibholz, "Memoir," 18.

group of military leaders, Admiral William Canaris, the head of the *Abwehr*, was also one of the top leaders of the German Resistance plotting to end Hitler's reign over Germany. Von Dohnanyi, formerly an attorney for Germany's Supreme Court, was one of Canaris' top aides and the "intellectual" leader of the Resistance.

Since becoming the head of the *Abwehr* in 1935, Canaris had found many subtle ways to subvert the Führer's schemes to overtake Europe. Canaris convinced General Franco of Spain to reject Hitler's invitation to join the war as Germany's ally. He also gave Hitler false information that convinced the dictator not to invade Switzerland.[227] Canaris, and his deputy, General Hans Oster, welcomed Bonhoeffer and his international contacts in England and the United States. Bonhoeffer's assignment was to use his friends in church leadership, including his close friend Bishop George Bell of England, to convince the Allies that there was a German Resistance scheming to end Hitler's reign of terror.

The years of 1940 to 1943 were filled with the pain of war. Even though Bonhoeffer worked for the *Abwehr*, the Gestapo continued to harass him for his Christian beliefs. In 1940, Bonhoeffer was prohibited from preaching or speaking in public any longer. In 1941, he published a small book entitled, *The Prayer Book of the Bible*, encouraging Christians to pray to God directly from the Psalms as Jesus had two thousand years earlier. Because it was part of the Old Testament, the Nazis were livid! As a result, Bonhoeffer was forbidden to publish anything else in Germany under the threat of imprisonment.

The *Abwehr* Helps Jews to Escape

As the war escalated, Hitler was no longer content with just killing German Jews; his new satanic policy was the annihilation of the entire Jewish population of Europe. Through grotesque death camps like Auschwitz and Dachau, he almost succeeded. The SS (German secret

227. See "Willaim Canaris," Jewish Virtual Library, http://www.jewishvirtuallibrary.org/jsource/Holocaust/canaris.html.

police) began the use of gas chambers and mass exterminations from 1942 until the end of the war. By the end of the Holocaust, it is estimated that ninety percent of all Polish Jews and two-thirds of the Jews of Europe had been killed.[228]

What was the reaction of the German Resistance to this horrifying genocide of innocent people? For one, they worked tirelessly on a new plot to assassinate Hitler and his Reich leaders. Several attempts to assassinate the Führer had already failed, but this wouldn't stop the resistance leaders from attempting once again. Hans von Dohnanyi kept very detailed accounts of the Nazi atrocities to use against the war criminals once the fighting was over. He also kept notes on the work of the *Abwehr* to stop Hitler. His accounts were named the Zossen files and were hidden in the *Abwehr* offices in Zossen, Germany. A number of *Abwehr* agents helped by plotting to save Jews whenever they could. Dietrich and Hans even aided a group of Jewish citizens escape to Switzerland disguised as *Abwehr* agents. They were successful and the escaped Jews were never discovered.

Finding Love in the Midst of War's Horror

When Dietrich wasn't on an *Abwehr* mission, he occasionally visited the Pomeranian estate of a close family friend, Ruth Kleist-Retzow. On one visit in 1942, he met Ruth's granddaughter, Maria von Wedemeyer, an intelligent young woman who was planning to study mathematics at a German university when the war finally ended. The two spent long hours discussing the horrors of the war, God's plan for personal salvation, and the restoration of Germany in the future. At eighteen, Maria was only half Dietrich's age, but the two fell deeply in love. At thirty-six, Bonhoeffer had been a confirmed bachelor, spending his time and energy defending the gospel of Christ from Satan's attacks on the church and on Germany. Now, deeply in love, Dietrich

228. See "The Final Solution," Jewish Virtual Library, http://www.jewishvirtuallibrary.org/jsource/Holocaust/killedtable.html.

proposed and Maria accepted in January of 1943. Unfortunately, their happiness was short-lived.

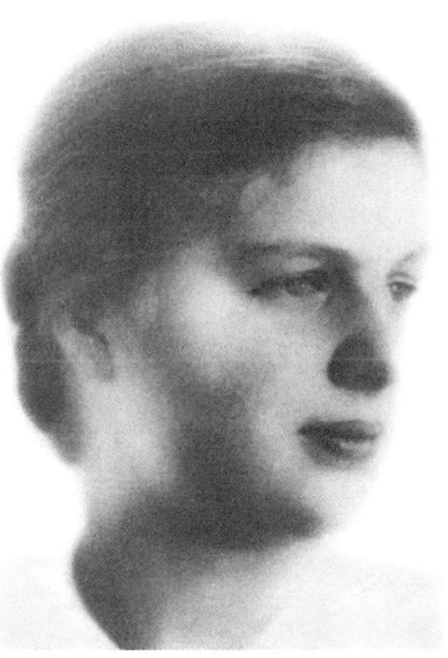

Maria von Wedemeyer,
Bonhoeffer's fiancée, 1942.
Public domain.

In April 1943, a black SS vehicle pulled up in front of the Bonhoeffer family home in Berlin. Paula Bonhoeffer peered out of the front window, immediately fearful for the Bonhoeffer men who had become so involved in the fight against Hitler. Stomping across the porch to the wooden front door, the agents knocked loudly, demanding entrance. "Pastor Bonhoeffer, Herr von Dohnanyi, you are both under arrest for currency violations and for conspiracies against the state. Please come with us now!"

What currency violations? When Dietrich and Hans helped the Jewish refugees escape disguised as *Abwehr* agents, they also wired money to Switzerland so that the escapees had a way to survive. Although their rescue of the Jews was never discovered, sending money outside of Germany was illegal. For this monetary crime, Bonhoeffer and von Dohnanyi were sent to prison. They were now under the power of the Third Reich.

Dietrich was held in the Tegel Prison in Berlin. Although in a solitary cell, he was eventually allowed occasional visitors. In the eighteen months he was imprisoned there, Maria visited him seventeen times, always hoping that month would bring a fair trial and freedom.

A cell in Tegel prison.
Public domain.

Few letters were permitted from the prison, but Bonhoeffer's sympathetic guards were blessed by his prayers and acts of kindness. They smuggled his letters and writings in and out of his cell, especially many to Eberhard Bethge, his close friend and former seminary student. After the war, those letters were released as *Letters from Prison,* edited by Bethge. In one letter Bonhoeffer wrote, "A person's strength comes solely from being united with the will of God."[229]

During his first weeks in Tegel Prison, Bonhoeffer was interrogated daily by the Gestapo about the Resistance movement. He acted puzzled by the whole line of questioning and never revealed a single name. Soon the agents abandoned their interrogations, and Dietrich spent his time in the Scriptures and writing. Unfortunately, von Dohnanyi was treated much more severely. He was ruthlessly interrogated and tortured because of his suspected activities within the German Resistance. He became seriously ill in prison and was eventually paralyzed from the waist down. His goal was to resist his captors and hang on by God's

229. Metaxas, 409.

grace until Admiral Canaris could obtain his freedom or the war would end. It was a devastating blow to both Bonhoeffer and von Dohnanyi to hear that Hitler had become suspicious of the *Abwehr,* fired Canaris, and ordered the agency to shut its doors.

In the courtyard of the Wehrmacht Detention-Berlin, Tegel, the summer of 1944.
Public domain.

Operation Valkyrie: Failed Assassination of Hitler

On July 20, 1944, the final and most famous attempt on Hitler's life, named Operation Valkyrie, was carried out by Colonel Claus von Stauffenberg, a German officer and Resistance leader. There were two bombs hidden in von Stauffenberg's briefcase that he would carry into a war meeting with Hitler and his staff. Unfortunately, Von Stauffenberg only had enough time to set the timer on one bomb before placing his briefcase under the conference table near Hitler. Exactly ten minutes after Von Stauffenberg excused himself from the meeting, he heard a terrific explosion and believed that the Führer was dead.

The explosion was extensive, killing several Nazis members, but Hitler escaped with only a few scratches. He had been protected by a thick oak table leg that separated him from the blast. Why this man, so obviously led by Satan, was allowed another year to continue the war is one of those things we will not understand this side of heaven. Within days, von Stauffenberg and thousands in the German Resistance who were suspected were executed. The following morning, Bonhoeffer heard Hitler's speech about the failed assassination attempt on a small prison radio. At that moment, he knew that his life would be forfeit.

The Gestapo Discover the Zossen Files

After the Valkyrie plot, an incensed Hitler ordered the Gestapo to conduct an intensive search for all other German "traitors." The closed *Abwehr* offices in Zossen were searched from top to bottom. Even though the Zossen files had been well-hidden by von Dohnanyi, the Gestapo agents discovered the secret documents filled with incriminating evidence of the German resistance. On October 5, Admiral Canaris and General Hans Oster were arrested along with Dietrich's brother, Klaus, and his brother-in-law, Rudiger Schleicher. Knowing that Bonhoeffer would be incriminated next, Sergeant Knobluch at the Tegel Prison tried desperately to convince the German pastor to escape while he still had the chance. Just as I described in the chapter's beginning, so many Bonhoeffer family members were now in the hands of the Gestapo that Dietrich refused to save himself at their expense.

On October 8, 1944, Gestapo agents burst into Bonhoeffer's prison cell at Tegel and dragged him out in front of the sympathetic guards. He was transported by car to the dark basement cell of the Reich Security Head Office, the Gestapo's high security prison in Berlin. For the next four months, deprived of any contact with the outside world, Bonhoeffer knew nothing of the safety of his family or Maria. Surely he prayed from the psalms that had comforted him in the past: "*My soul waits in silence for God only; from Him is my salvation*" (Psalm 62:1 NASB).

On February 3, 1945, Bonhoeffer and a group of prisoners were unexpectedly moved to Buchenwald concentration camp where they each had a cell mate and the opportunity to encourage one another daily. They knew the war was racing to an end because the Allied bombings could be heard from their prison cells.

On April 5, with the Americans and Russians both closing in on Berlin, and the war lost for Germany, Hitter made a cruel and vengeful decision. In a rage after reading Admiral Canaris' diary, he demanded the execution of every man involved in Admiral Canaris' resistance movement. They were to be executed within earshot of the approaching Allied bombers who could have granted them their lives and their freedom.

"For Me It Is the Beginning of Life!"

During the first days of April, Bonhoeffer had been moved with fifteen other prisoners to a school house in the village of Schonberg. They were grateful to be placed in one large schoolroom together. On Sunday morning, April 8, the men asked Dietrich if he would lead a worship service for them. Bonhoeffer preached that morning from 1 Peter 1:3: "*Blessed be the God and Father of our Lord Jesus Christ, who according to His great mercy has caused us to be born again to a living hope through the resurrection of Jesus Christ from the dead"* (NASB). Bonhoeffer explained to his fellow prisoners what this Scripture meant to someone who was surrendered to Christ—that an eternity with Jesus was his greatest hope.

> He had hardly finished his last prayer when the door opened and two evil-looking men in civilian clothes came in and announced: "Prisoner Bonhoeffer. Get ready to come with us." Those words "Come with us"—for all prisoners they had come to mean one thing—the scaffold.[230]

As Bonhoeffer was led past the grieving men, he turned to a fellow prisoner and gave him a message for his friend George Bell in England, "This is the end—for me it is the beginning of life." Those are Dietrich Bonhoeffer's last recorded words.

"I Have Fought the Good Fight"

That day Dietrich was taken to Flossenburg concentration camp and given a mock trial. In the early morning hours of April 9, 1945, Dietrich Bonhoeffer and five other male prisoners were led naked into the Flossenburg courtyard to stand in a line in front of the gallows. It was Hitler's personal command that they be disgraced before their execution. I'm sure it wasn't lost on Bonhoeffer that his Savior hung on the cross naked as well.

The other prisoners executed with Bonhoeffer included Admiral Canaris and General Oster. We don't know what words Bonhoeffer may have spoken the morning of his execution, but perhaps they were similar to Paul's word to Timothy at the end of his life:

> *For I am already being poured out as a drink offering, and the time of my departure has come. I have fought the good fight, I have finished the course, I have kept the faith; in the future there is laid up for me the crown of righteousness, which the Lord, the righteous*

230. Metaxas, 528.

Judge, will award to me on that day; and not only to me, but also to all who have loved His appearing. (2 Timothy 4:6–8 NASB)

The concentration camp Flossenberg.
Public domain.

Dietrich Bonhoeffer, faithful disciple of Jesus Christ until the end, was dead to this world, but alive in Jesus Christ. Two weeks later, on April 23, 1945, the US Army marched into Flossenberg and freed the prisoners who remained. One week after that, on April 30, the madman Adolf Hitler listened to Satan's hissing temptations one last time and ended his own life. The Third Reich had finally come to an end.

"I Will Confess Him Before My Father"

The Bonhoeffer family paid a great price for their resistance to Hitler. The same day that Dietrich was executed, a paralyzed Hans von Dohnanyi was carried in a stretcher to the gallows and hung at Sachsenhausen concentration camp. On April 23, Dietrich's brother, Klaus, and brother-in-law, Rudiger, were taken outside of the Lehrerstrasse Prison in Berlin and shot for their resistance against the Führer.

Sabine received the news of her brothers' deaths from a pastor in London at the end of May. His comfort to her was the Word of God which assures us: "*Therefore everyone who confesses Me before men, I will also confess him before My Father who is in heaven. …He who has found his life will lose it, and he who has lost his life for My sake will find it*" (Matthew 10:32, 39 NASB). Sabine and her family returned to Germany after the war and lived well into their nineties. Their family thrived because of the love and care of Dietrich so many decades earlier.

Dietrich's parents had the rumors of their son's death confirmed when they heard a radio broadcast of his memorial service from Holy Trinity Church in London on July 27, 1945. Bishop George Bell eulogized his dear friend, "Wherever he went and whoever he spoke with—whether young or old—he was fearless, regardless of himself; he devoted his heart and soul to his parents, his friends, his country as God willed it to be, to his Church and his Master."[231]

Dietrich Bonhoeffer's Legacy

"Life only really begins when it ends here on earth—all there is here is only the prologue before the curtain goes up."
—Dietrich Bonhoeffer

Bonhoeffer's legacy is of a Christian who—by God's grace—had the strength and courage to stand for Christ in the face of the "isms" of this world—theological liberalism, communism, racism, and, eventually, Nazism. He gave a dauntless challenge to the church to remain true to the Word of God and to never let the enemy have a foothold in our faith. The German church had already lost its first love, Jesus Christ, before

231. Metaxas, 537.

Hitler ever came on the scene. That made it much easier for them to be seduced by his satanic lies. Without the church standing for righteousness, Hitler's evil nearly swallowed Germany whole.

Bonhoeffer always argued that Christians should not retreat from the world but stand as a powerful force for God within the world. He wrote to his friend Eberhard from the Tegel Prison,

> The Christian cannot simply take for granted the privilege of living among other Christians. Jesus Christ lived in the midst of his enemies. In the end all of His disciples abandoned Him. On the cross He was all alone, surrounded by criminals and the jeering crowds. He had come for the express purpose of bringing peace to the enemies of God. So Christians, too, belong not in the seclusion of a cloistered life but in the midst of enemies. There they find their mission, their work.[232]

Some liberal Christians have tried to make Bonhoeffer a spokesperson for liberal theology. I don't believe this is a true picture of his Christian faith. I might not personally agree with every doctrine that he believed, but I recognize that he was a man whose life was centered on one Person—the Lord Jesus Christ. For Bonhoeffer, Christ was the Center of all things and the cost of discipleship was to truly pick up one's cross and follow Him daily. For his role as a twentieth century martyr, Bonhoeffer was also memorialized over the West Gate of Westminster Abbey.

Of the millions of believers who were dying at the hands of the Nazis, Bonhoeffer wrote, "One day we shall know and see what today we believe; one day we shall hold a service together in eternity."

---

232. Dietrich Boenhoeffer, *Letters and Papers from Prison*, Eberhard Bethge, ed., (Minneapolis, MN: Fortress Press, 2010).

GOSPEL POWER IN THE THIRD WORLD

11

GOSPEL POWER IN THE THIRD WORLD

(AD 1900–2000)

Operation Auca: Reaching the Unreachable

He makes His ministers a flame of fire.' Am I ignitable, Lord? God...saturate me with the oil of the Spirit that I may be a flame for You.... Make me Thy Fuel, O Flame of God!"
—Jim Elliot, 1948[233]

233. Elizabeth Elliot, *Through Gates of Splendor* (Carol Stream, IL: Tyndale, 1996 [1956]), 18.

Jim Elliot gave his wife a quick kiss before jumping eagerly into the bright yellow Piper plane idling on the runway. He had prayed for this day for six years: the day that he and his team would conduct a mission to an unreached tribe in the middle of the Amazon rainforest. Elliot and pilot Nate Saint, along with fellow missionaries Ed McCully, Pete Fleming and Roger Youderian, were embarking on the mission of a lifetime: they had dubbed it Operation Auca.

After months of dropping gifts to the fierce Auca Indians and receiving gifts from them in return, the missionaries believed it was God's time to meet this "Stone Age" tribe face-to-face. On January 3, 1956, Nate flew the eager young men from their missionary outpost in Arajuno, Ecuador, to a small beach hideaway on the shores of the Curaray River.

The beach sand was hot and alive with pestering bugs, but the men didn't care. They spent two days erecting a protective tree house and preparing for signs of Auca visitors. Suddenly, on Friday, January 6, three Auca natives—a man and two women—stepped out of the dense underbrush and stood on the opposite river bank. The air was tense with excitement. The Auca visitors spent a day with the American men communicating in exaggerated gestures and awkward Auca phrases. Things were going so much better than the missionaries had dared to dream!

Radio Silence

On Sunday morning, January 8, Nate flew his Piper over the beach site. Banking a little to the west, he spotted a small group of Auca men heading for the beachhead. Whooping in excitement he shouted first to his four friends waiting with anticipation on the beach below, and then to his wife, Marj, over the plane's radio: "This is it! This is it! Pray for us. Next broadcast will be at 4:30!"[234]

---

234. Russell T. Hitt, *Jungle Pilot* (Grand Rapids, MI: Discovery House Publishers, 1997 [1959]), 277.

Marj Saint hovered over the radio waiting for word of the day's triumph. Four-thirty arrived…and passed…the minutes slowly ticking by. Marj held her breath, waiting for the familiar crackle of the radio. Nate had never missed a broadcast check-in during their eight years in Ecuador.

5:30.

6:30.

Radio silence.

Jim Elliot: "He is No Fool…"

"He is no fool who gives what he cannot keep to gain what he cannot lose."

—Jim Elliot, October 28, 1949[235]

Elliot wrote this famous quote while he was still a student at Wheaton College, fervently seeking God's will for his future. He was only twenty-eight years old when his life, along with his missionary friends, ended abruptly in the Ecuadorian jungle in the most famous martyrdom account of the twentieth century. But Jim Elliot was no fool. He knew that man's greatest wisdom was to seek and obey the will of God—His specific will for each of His followers on earth.

Elliot was a young man bursting with energy, passion, and confidence in Christ. "Wherever you are, *be all there,*" he recorded in his college journal. "Live to the hilt every situation you believe to be the will of God."[236] His personality reminds me of the bold example of the apostle Peter. Jim was a born leader who was always the first to enthusiastically respond to God's voice. Like Peter, Jim would have stepped out of the boat and into the swelling waves to answer Jesus' call; he would have

235. Elizabeth Elliot, *Shadow of the Almighty* (New York: HarperCollins, 1989 [1958]), 108.
236. Elliot, *Through Gates of Splendor*, 8.

impulsively cut off the servant's ear in a garden full of shouting Roman guards or run full tilt into Christ's empty tomb on Resurrection morning. He also would have been the first to say, as Peter did, "*Yes, Lord. You know that I love you*" (John 21:16 NASB).

Jim Elliot at Wheaton College.
Courtesy of Archives, Buswell Library, Wheaton College, Wheaton, IL.

Training in Body, Mind and Spirit

During Jim's years at Wheaton, he focused all of his time and energy preparing for the mission field, majoring in Greek to train his theological skills and joining the wrestling team to train his body for the rigors of missionary life. From his freshman year, the popular student leader knew that God had called him to surrender his life to a special call, and he was determined that nothing would stand in his way. He ministered with his closest college buddy, Ed McCully, who would join him later in South America. At the end of Jim's sophomore year, he met Dr. Wilfred Tidmarsh, a British missionary who had worked for twelve years among the Quichua Indians of Ecuador. After months of prayer, Jim believed that he shared the same call: "I feel quite at ease saying that tribal work in the South American jungles is the direction of my missionary purpose...and I am quite confident that God wants me to begin jungle work as a single man."[237]

God had slightly different plans for the young missionary, although Jim wouldn't catch on for a few years. At Wheaton he met Elisabeth Howard, a tall, compassionate young woman who was also passionate about serving Jesus on the foreign field. The two became close friends and then fell in love, but Jim was still determined to serve the Lord in the jungle as a single man. He laid his feelings for Elisabeth at the foot of the cross and left them there for the next few years. After graduation, when Jim received an invitation from Dr. Tidmarsh to serve as his replacement to the Quichua tribes, he was ecstatic! Knowing that Jesus did not send His disciples out alone, Jim prayed for another single Christian man to go with him.

Pete Fleming: Obedience to the Call

Pete Fleming, a friend of Elliot's from his home state of Washington, answered the Lord's call to go with him to the Quichua Indians. Pete wrote in his journal, "I think the call to the mission field is no different than any other means of guidance. A call is nothing more nor less than obedience to the will of God, as God presses it home to the soul by whatever means He chooses."[238]

A call is nothing more nor less than obedience to the will of God, as God presses it home to the soul by whatever means He chooses

At first glance, Pete seemed to be an unlikely young man to end up in the primitive rainforest. He was a philosophy major with a master's degree in literature, but he loved the Lord with his whole

237. Elliot, *Shadow of the Almighty*, 88.
238. Elliot, *Gates of Splendor*, 10.

Jim Elliot with daughter Valerie.
Courtesy of Archives, Buswell Library, Wheaton College, Wheaton, IL.

heart and had pledged his life to reach the lost for Christ. Pete's ability to learn new languages was a priceless gift on the mission field. Once he decided to travel with Jim to the Quichua, he broke off his engagement with Olive Ainslie, his high school sweetheart. (A couple of years later, Pete proposed to Olive for the second time and they were married.)

On February 21, 1952, Jim and Pete finally arrived at the Quichua mission station in Shandia and began training with Tidmarsh. Working from sunup to sundown, the eager young men constructed new mission buildings, led an elementary school for boys, held open-air church services, and baptized new converts. By December of that year, Ed McCully, with his wife Marilou, joined Jim and Pete in Shandia. Jim welcomed his old college buddy with open arms.

Ed McCully: Reckless Abandon to Christ!

An athletic six feet, two inches tall, Ed McCully excelled at everything: he was a championship football player, a track star, a national champion as a Hearst Public speaker, and president of the student body at Wheaton. After graduation, he entered Marquette Law School, and his life was set on a straight course to worldly success—until God stopped him in his tracks and radically changed the direction of his life. As he studied God's Word, Ed's heart burned with a passion to dedicate his life to spreading the gospel on foreign fields. "I have one desire now,"

Ed wrote, "to live a life of reckless abandon for the Lord, putting all my energy and strength into it."[239]

Ed met Marilou shortly after he left law school. They married in 1951 and spent a year studying at the School of Missionary Medicine in Los Angeles before sailing for Ecuador. Once they arrived, the initial mission team was set. Jim, Ed, and Pete developed a ministry plan: Shandia would remain the central station with smaller outposts built deeper in the jungle. The McCullys and Pete would stay in Shandia while Jim established an outpost and village school in the village of Puyupungo. Shortly before this, Elisabeth Howard moved to Ecuador to serve in another part of the country. Finally convinced that he could fulfill his missionary call and still have a wife, Jim and Elisabeth were married on October 8, 1953 (Jim's twenty-sixth birthday). The following year, Elisabeth gave birth to their baby daughter, Valerie, and Marilou delivered the McCully's second son, Michael. Life in Ecuador was full.

Reaching a Murderous Tribe for Christ

> [It is] *my ambition to preach the gospel, not where Christ has already been named, lest I build on another man's foundation.*
>
> (Romans 15:20 ESV)

I believe it is in the heart of every missionary and evangelist to preach the message of Christ's salvation to those who have never heard it before. Jim Elliot and his friends were no different. When Jim met Tidmarsh for the first time, the older missionary talked about a small, violent tribe hidden in the jungles of Ecuador who had no contact with the outside world—the Quichuas called them *Auca* which translates to *savage*. Anthropologists considered the Auca one of the most violent tribes in the world. Feuds would flare up between Auca families, and the smallest act of violence would launch a stream of revenge killings by ten-foot wooden spears thrown with deadly precision. With seventy-four

239. Elliot, *Gates of Splendor*, 42.

percent of the tribes' deaths the result of tribal murder, the Auca were destroying their own people.[240]

The Quichua Indians feared the Auca, but from the first time Jim Elliot heard about the mysterious tribe, his heart was set on fire. Perhaps this was the answer to Jim's lifelong prayer: to bring the message of salvation in Christ to a people who had never heard it before. He shared his vision with Pete and Ed, and it became the center of their prayer life. "Lord, if it is Your will, open a door to reach the Auca."

While they waited for God's answer, their ministry to the Quichuas grew; the three men distributed medicine, taught in the schools, held Bible conferences and rejoiced as they baptized new believers. They also became acquainted with two more American missionaries, Nate Saint and Roger Youderian, who would become the final team members of Operation Auca.

Nate Saint: Pilot Extraordinaire

The remains Nate Saint's Piper airplane on display.
Missionary Aviation Fellowship\Wikimedia Commons

The yellow Piper plane soared over the lush rainforest until it reached a small break in the tree line. Below him, Nate Saint located

240. John W. Cowart, "Auca Martyrs," 2005, http://www.cowart.info/AucasTheWorstPeopleOnEarth.htm.

a large mission station surrounded by a series of small houses. Slowly, he began to fly in tighter and tighter circles using the force he created to lower a basket filled with medical supplies straight into the hands of the missionary family waiting below. Once the basket was emptied, the plane soared off into the tree-lined horizon once again, heading toward the home airstrip. Mission accomplished.

Nate Saint had dreamed of being a pilot ever since he was a boy. By the time he was a young man, missionary aviation in the South American jungles became his heart's desire. As a jungle pilot for the Missionary Aviation Fellowship (MAF), Nate was the lifeline between isolated missionaries, their necessary supplies, and the outside world. His "spiraling-line technique" described above was his unique invention to deliver essential supplies to isolated missionaries; it is still used by MAF pilots around the world today.[241]

"Watching and Praying for that Day"

Nate Saint and his wife, Marj, were an inseparable ministry team. Inside Marj's wedding ring, Nate had the reference "Psalm 34:3" inscribed. The full verse reads, "*O magnify the* Lord *with me, and let us exult his name together.*"[242] While Nate served the Lord in the air, Marj manned the radio and was Nate's "eyes on the ground." The couple arrived in Ecuador in 1948, four years before Elliot and the others. They were stationed, along with their three small children, at Shell Mera, a small village constructed by the Shell Oil Company which included a well-maintained airstrip. Shell Oil had deserted the entire site after eleven of their oil workers were speared to death by the Auca.

Nate became friends with Jim, Pete, and Ed as soon as they landed in Quichua country. When Nate heard of Jim's interest in reaching the Auca, he was all in! Several years before the Elliots' arrival, Nate had written to his parents about the murderous tribe, "We expect the

241. Elliot, *Gates of Splendor*, 55.
242. Hitt, *Jungle Pilot*, dedication page.

airplane will play an essential part in reaching these people one day with the Gospel. *We're watching and praying for that day.*"[243]

Roger Youderian: Decorated WWII Paratrooper

Roger Youderian, the last man to join the Auca missionary team, was no stranger to courage in the face of danger. Dropped from an airplane over a war-torn Europe in WWII, he was also decorated for his heroic action in the Battle of the Bulge.[244] In 1952, Roger, his wife, Barbara, and their two children moved to the Ecuadorian rainforest to live among the primitive Jivaro tribe. The Jivaro were famous for their tribal custom of shrinking human heads.

Nate was the only team member who knew Roger. When Nate invited him to join in their outreach to the Auca, his response after prayer was a resounding, "Yes!" Nate knew Roger's commitment to the Lord was strong. "I will be led and taught by the Holy Spirit," Roger wrote. "The Holy Spirit can and will guide me in direct proportion to the time and effort I expend to know and do the will of God."[245]

They were set—five American missionary pioneers—always looking beyond the horizon for what lay ahead. This time it would be the Auca.

"The Time We Have Waited For!"

"Hey, Ed! How'd you like to go look for your neighbors?" Nate Saint flashed a wide grin as he watched Ed leap off his chair in excitement. There was nothing Ed would rather do than fly over the jungle looking for signs of the Auca villages. Ed and Marilou were now living in the Arajuno outpost on the outskirts of Auca territory. It was September 19, 1955, and it would be a fateful day of discovery.

243. Ibid., 132, emphasis added.

244. Elliot, *Gates of Splendor*, 72.

245. Ibid., 149.

The men flew in the yellow Piper until their gas supply was low and the sun was hanging just above the horizon. Suddenly they spotted a small clearing near the Curaray River. "This was it!!" Nate Saint wrote later that night. "We had enough gas to hang around for a few minutes. All told, we must have seen fifteen clearings and a few houses. It was an exciting time! The time we had waited for!"[246] The small Auca village was located just fifteen minutes by plane from the Arajuno outpost.

For the American missionaries, the Auca were now the focus of daily life. By early October, they decided to develop a plan to reach the infamous natives. Why were they so dedicated to bringing the gospel to this small tribe secluded in the rainforest? Any time they were questioned by their wives, they answered directly from the book of Revelation, where every tribe was present at God's heavenly throne. *"After this I looked, and there before me was a great multitude that no one could count, from* ***every nation, tribe, people and language****, standing before the throne and before the Lamb. They were wearing white robes and were holding palm branches in their hands"* (Revelation 7:9 NIV). The men were of one mind and spirit—this was God's Word for them.

Launching Operation Auca

Hovering over an aerial map of the region, Jim, Nate, and Ed studied the best way to launch an outreach to the Auca. (Pete had returned to the United States for a short period to marry Olive; Roger was still at the Macuma station with the Jivaros.) Serious about their mission, the men dubbed the outreach Operation Auca. The first step was for Jim to travel to a nearby village to learn friendly Auca phrases from Dayuma, a native woman who had fled the Auca warriors to save her life. Jim learned *Biti miti punimupa,* which translates to, "I like you; I want to be your friend" and the Auca words for "What's your name" and "Let's get together."[247]

246. Hitt, *Jungle Pilot,* 259.
247. Elliot, *Gates of Splendor,* 128.

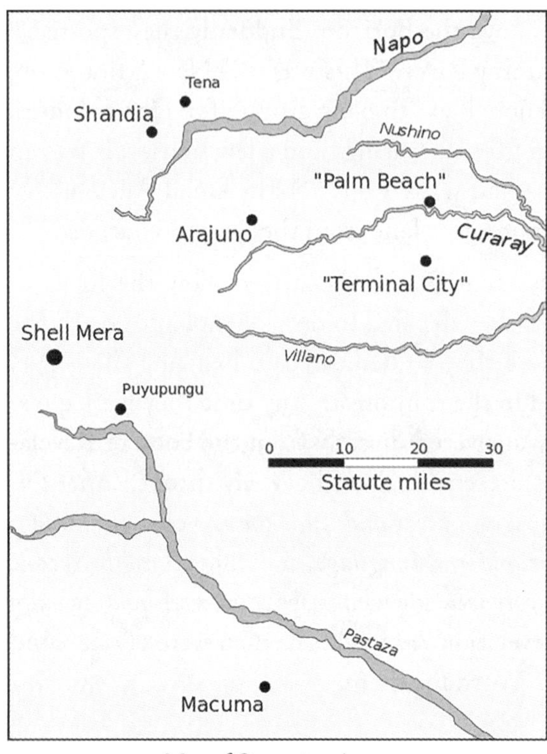

Map of Operation Auca.
By Nathaniel Sheetz, derivative work.

The second step was to drop gifts into the Auca village in an attempt to build a bridge of friendship. With Nate's "spiral-line technique," they could place the gifts directly in the natives' hands. Each week, the bright yellow Piper would fly over the Auca village delivering different gifts: a man's bright red t-shirt, a machete, a pair of trousers, a cooking pot, a yellow shirt with beads. At the sound of the approaching plane, the natives would rush out of their longhouses to get a clear view of the white men.

As the plane circled to drop a basket with gifts, Jim or Ed would use a battery-powered loudspeaker to call out of the window, "We are your friends! We like you!" The natives would smile and wave in return. After several weeks, the Auca began to put return gifts in the basket; the most memorable was a small parrot that became young Steve Saint's pet for several years. The plan was working perfectly!

"Phase Two Is a Go!"

On December 23, 1955, all five men met for prayer. It was time to take Operation Auca to phase two: a face-to-face meeting with the warlike tribe. Flying over the Curaray River, Nate spotted a sandbar and a beach near one of the Auca villages that he could use as an airstrip. They nicknamed the landing site "Palm Beach," and the nearby Auca village they called "Terminal City."

Each man was assigned a final task; Jim devised a tree house out of tin sheeting to be built thirty-five feet above the beach for protection against tropical thunderstorms or Auca attacks. Roger collected medical supplies; Ed found gifts for the natives. Pete had been undecided about going on this first face-to-face trip but made a last minute decision to go, leaving his young bride in Shell Mera with Marj Saint. On January 2, Jim packed his knapsack with last minute items. Elisabeth was hit hard with the realization that she may never see her husband again—but Jim was so focused on the mission that he only gave her a quick kiss goodbye and with a final wave soared away in the yellow Piper.

The next day, Nate flew one man at a time to the beach along with their supplies. Jim, Ed and Roger quickly built the tree house where they would sleep each night. Although they made a commitment that they would never shoot the Auca, they brought along firearms to scare them away if necessary. Taking no chances that a flash flood would strand the plane on the beach, Nate flew the Piper back to Shell Mera each evening, taking Pete with him.

Face-to-Face with the Auca!

On Friday, January 6, the long awaited first contact was made. Three Auca natives, one young man and two women, walked through the jungle underbrush and approached the missionaries from the opposite bank of the Curaray River. When they hesitated at the sight of the white men, Jim rolled up his pant legs and waded across the low point of the river with an outstretched hand leading them back to "Palm Beach."

The younger man and woman acted like a couple so the men nicknamed them Delilah and George. George, whose real name was Nankiwi, was fascinated by the airplane and gestured that he wanted to fly in the "Yellow Wooden Bee" as the Auca called it. While Nate flew over Terminal City, Nankiwi leaned out of the open window and excitedly waved to his friends below. The missionaries applauded his excitement. They had no way of knowing that Nankiwi would be a deadly threat in the following days.

"This Is *the Day!"*

Saturday was a quiet day with no sign of Auca visitors. The men were certain that the next day—Sunday, January 8—would be *"the day."* As Pete and Nate climbed into the Piper on Sunday morning, Pete called to their wives, "So long, girls. Pray. I believe today is the day!"[248] A little later that morning, as Nate cruised over the jungle treetops, he spotted a group of Auca males heading toward Palm Beach.

"This is it! This is it!" Nate waved excitedly to his waiting friends on the sandy beach. "This is it!" he exclaimed over the plane radio to Marj. "Looks like they'll be here for the early afternoon service. Pray for us." His last words before ending the transmission were, "This *is* the day! Will contact you next at four-thirty."[249]

For the five hopeful American missionaries, four-thirty never came. Within minutes of the Auca party's arrival on the beach, the five were speared, and their bloodied bodies tossed into the muddy Curaray River.

"Lord, Has Anyone Escaped?"

The radio remained silent. Four-thirty came and went without Nate's next report, and Marj's uneasiness grew. What could have happened? The five young wives gathered at Shell Mera, their headquarters. Marj never left the radio. Through the night, they prayed. Early the next morning, Johnny Keenan, Nate's aviation partner with MAF, flew over the beach site. The first thing he saw sickened his stomach. The Piper sat on the beach with the plane's bright yellow skin stripped off and

248. Ibid., 190.
249. Ibid.

lying in pieces on the sand. There were no signs of the men. A flyover the next day brought the sight he was dreading. A man's body in jeans and a white t-shirt floating face down in the Curaray River. A little farther downstream, he spotted another body. "Lord, has anyone escaped?"

The US Embassy in Ecuador and the US Air Rescue Service in Panama were contacted. The missionary radio station HCJP in Ecuador flashed the news around the world: "Five Men Missing in Auca Territory!" Christians worldwide began to pray. A rescue party of Quichua Indians, Ecuadorian soldiers, and US military trekked warily through the jungle for three days to reach the tree house and plane. The US Navy flew a helicopter in, piloted by Major Nurnberg, to help with the search. Aboard the helicopter was a well-known photojournalist with *LIFE* magazine, Cornell Capa.[250] The whole world would soon read the personal story of five Christian men willing to give their lives for the salvation of the Auca. "*Greater love hath no man than this, that a man lay down his life for his friends*" (John 15:13 KJV).

"By Life or Death, May God Get the Glory"

While they were waiting for news of their husbands' fate, the Lord gave Barbara Youderian a Scripture for the wives to lean on: "*For this God is our God for ever and ever; he will be our guide even unto death*" (Psalm 48:14 KJV). Elisabeth Elliot wrote in her journal during those tense days of waiting, "Jim was confident, as I was, of God's leading. There are no regrets. Nothing was more burning in his heart than that Christ should be named among the Aucas. By life or death, oh, may God get the glory to Himself."[251]

The search party reached Palm Beach five days after the men were murdered. From his helicopter, Major Nurnberg spotted their bodies floating in the Curaray River. After five days in the warm jungle water, the men were disfigured beyond recognition, identified only by their clothing and personal belongings. Ed McCully's death was certified by

250. Ibid., 229–236.
251. Hitt, *Jungle Pilot*, 281.

the discovery of his watch and wedding ring, but his body couldn't be reached; it had washed away in the river current. The other four men were brought ashore and buried in a solitary grave dug hastily at the foot of the tree house. Overhead a violent tropical storm with torrential rains blackened the skies. It was as though the jungle itself grieved at the loss of these faithful young men.

Overhead a violent tropical storm with torrential rains blackened the skies. It was as though the jungle itself grieved at the loss of these faithful young men.

Major Nurnberg flew back to Shell Mera to break the tragic news to the young widows who were now single mothers of nine small children. The major was amazed at their level of faith as the women turned to Jesus for their comfort and their strength. The next afternoon, he flew them over Palm Beach and the solitary grave so that they could say goodbye to the husbands they loved.

What Went Wrong?

Everything had gone so well with the months of gift exchanges and the Friday Auca visit; so what went wrong? Why had the warriors viciously attacked their white visitors? For years, the missionary families pieced together parts of the story, but they never had all the answers. Nearly forty years later, in 1995, Nate Saint's son, Steve, and his family went to live with the Auca tribe for a year and finally learned the whole truth from the men who were responsible. Most of those spear-throwers, Gikita, Kimo, Dyuwi, and Mincaye, had accepted the message of Christ's salvation years earlier and were now Christian elders in the village. Together they shared the story,

"George" or Nankiwi had gone down to the beach on January 6 out of curiosity; he wanted to see the white men and the bright yellow plane.

Huaorani (Auca) face paint.
Kate Fisher\Flickr

The young woman, "Delilah," was his girlfriend, and the older woman, Mintaka, was their required chaperone. After Nankiwi had taken his airplane ride, he and "Delilah" were bored and wandered back toward their village leaving Mintaka behind. While walking through the jungle, Nankiwi and Delilah ran into her brother and a group of Auca warriors. As soon as her brother saw the young couple without a chaperone, he became enraged. Realizing that he was about to be speared, Nankiwi blurted out a twisted lie—insisting that the white visitors were about to kill and eat them, so they had "run into the jungle to save their lives." Gikita, the leader, had been suspicious of outsiders his entire life and took Nankiwi at his word.[252]

The following fateful morning, six ferocious Auca warriors with faces painted, screaming words of vengeance, led a surprise attack on the unsuspecting American missionaries spearing them without mercy. In just a few nightmarish minutes, Satan used the evil of one man's lie to end the lives of five faithful believers. But what Satan had meant for evil, God meant for much good. This is not the end of the Auca story!

The Miracles of Operation Auca

The greatest miracle was the forgiving hearts of the five widows. Four of them remained in Ecuador for many years, continuing missionary work among the natives. In God's perfect timing, two years after the

252. Steve Saint, "Did They Have to Die?," *Christianity Today*, September 16, 1996.

men were murdered at Palm Beach, Rachel Saint and Elisabeth Elliot were invited to live in the Auca village of Tiwaeno and teach the natives about Jesus and the outside world! Courageously, Elisabeth went, trusting the Auca with her life and the life of three-year-old Valerie. They lived with the Waodani, as the Auca call themselves, for two years and learned to love them. As the natives opened their hearts to Jesus, Elisabeth had the thrill of experiencing the miraculous answer to the five martyrs' fervent prayers.

Modern-day Huaorani (Auca) children.
Adrienne\Flickr

Marj Saint ministered in Quito, Ecuador for ten years before marrying Abraham Van Der Puy, the president of the HCJB World Radio. For six years, Marilou McCully ran a home for missionary children in a small Quechua village before returning to the state of Washington with her three sons. There's a school named after Ed and Marilou in that village today. Barbara Youderian returned to live with the Jivaros for several years before returning to the States. Olive Fleming returned to Seattle soon after the deaths and married Walter Liefeld, a Bible professor, three years later. Nate's sister, Rachel, spent the rest of her life in the

Waodani village. She worked with Bible translators to produce a New Testament in the Waodani language.

A modern-day Huaorani (Auca) leader.
Kate Fisher\Flikr

Even before she returned to the States, Elisabeth Elliot wrote two books about Operation Auca, *Through Gates of Splendor* and *Shadow of the Almighty*, giving the world a poignant account of the five young men who sacrificed their lives so that the Auca might spend eternity with Jesus. She remarried to Lars Gren, spent forty-five more years in Christian ministry, and was named one of the most influential Christian women of the twentieth century before she passed away in 2015 at eighty-eight years old.

Miracles that Multiplied!

Marj Saint and her three children visited the Waodani village and Rachel Saint many times over the years. Ten years after their father's death, two of Nate's children, Steve and Kathy, were water baptized by Kimo, one of the men who had speared their father. In 1995, when

Steve and Ginny Saint went back to live among the Auca for a year, three of Steve's four teenaged children were baptized by the same Kimo and shy Dyuwi; both native men were teenagers themselves when they speared the missionaries to death forty years earlier. God's forgiveness had come full circle.

While living among the Auca that year, Nate learned of an astounding miracle that the warriors experienced on that fateful Sunday morning. As the men lay dying on the beach, the Auca warriors were overcome by sparkling lights in the sky just above the treetops, and they heard beautiful music coming from the lights. One woman, Dawa, who was hiding in the bushes, said she saw *cowadi,* white strangers, singing above the treetops. Had they seen and heard a choir of angels?[253]

During Steve's visit with them at the time, Steven Curtis Chapman, the Christian singer, was there as well. As Chapman played Christian music from a tape player, Kimo stopped and said, "That is just as I heard it." With further questioning, Kimo and Dyuwi explained in detail the lights appearing in the trees that convinced them that killing the *cowadi* had angered the gods. As the music played, Kimo and Dyuwi cried out, "That is it! That is the music we heard that morning on the beach!"

The miracles continued, Mincaye, who had speared Nate Saint, traveled throughout the United States with Steve sharing the inspiring story of how *Wangongi,* the Creation God, had changed the lives of the murdering Waodani for eternity. In 2005, Steve Saint produced a movie of Operation Auca entitled *End of the Spear* to inspire other Christians to answer God's call to the tribes and to the nations. Nate Saint, Jim Elliot, Pete Fleming, Ed McCully and Roger Youderian would have been thrilled to see that their prayer-covered mission produced such a great victory. Who can count the number of Quichua and Waodani souls

253. "Operation Auca: The Miracle of Five Martyred Missionaries." http://christianitymiracles.blogspot.com/2013/05/operation-auca-miracle-of-five-martyred.html.

rejoicing in heaven and on earth today because these five young men heard the command of their Savior to "Go!"—and obeyed.

This is a prayer written by Nate Saint in the final days of his life: "May God continue to put His good hand on the project.... At present we feel unanimously that God is in it. May the praise be His and may it be that some Auca, clothed in the righteousness of Jesus Christ, will be with us as we lift our voices in praise before His throne. Amen." [254]

Nate Saint's prayer was answered for all eternity.

Paul Carlson: Healing Hands for Africa

The torrential rains of the Congo had been falling for days. The mission hospital at Wasolo was filled to capacity with the sick and injured. It would be a long week for the hospital staff. Suddenly, a small truck careened to a stop outside of the hospital station and a Congolese man bolted to the missionary door, "Bumba has fallen!" he shouted. "You must leave!" Paul Carlson raced to the radio transmitter tucked into the corner of the kitchen. Messages from other mission stations filled the airwaves,

"Get out! Get out of there, Three Nine...get out! Do you read me?" The other missionaries were pleading with the Carlson family to flee at once. But leaving the Wasolo station that day was not easy. Their vehicle was in another city, a day's journey away, picking up much-needed supplies, and there was a hospital full of desperately sick people waiting for Dr. Paul's help.[255]

Paul and Lois Carlson looked at one another with questioning eyes. Their two children and the other mission workers were depending on them to make the right decision. "We will put it in God's hands," was Paul's response, "and we will leave it there."

---

254. Elliot, *Gates of Splendor*, 140, emphasis added.
255. Lois Carlson Bridges, *Monganga Paul* (Chicago: Covenant Publications, 2004), 110.

An Independent Republic of Congo

In 1960, the Democratic Republic of Congo in central Africa gained its freedom from Belgium. Knowing that the new Congolese government would probably be an epicenter of violence, seven hundred Belgium doctors fled the country. They left empty hospitals and clinics with no one to heal the sick or aid the dying.

In that same year, Paul Carlson was finishing his surgical residency at Harbor General Hospital in Torrance, California, just outside of Los Angeles. After years of intense study, he could have opened a prosperous surgical practice anywhere in southern California. However, Paul wasn't interested in a privileged lifestyle. Ten years earlier, he had shared with his wife, Lois, that his heart was dedicated to medical missions. If he could find a way, he wanted to use his medical skills wherever God led him.

Early in 1961, the Carlsons received a flyer in the mail from the Christian Medical Society with an appeal for doctors willing to go on short term medical mission tours in the Democratic Republic of the Congo. By July 18, 1961, Paul was sitting on a plane, embarking on a four-month medical mission to the Congo.[256]

Wasolo: the Lost Corner of Africa

Paul was assigned to Wasolo, a village sitting high on top of a hill in an obscure northeastern corner of the Democratic Republic of Congo— "a long distance away from everywhere!"[257] Wasolo was in such a hidden area of the jungle that earlier Belgium citizens had dubbed it "le coin perdue" or "the lost corner." With his easy manner and warmth, his excellent medical abilities, and his compassion for the needy, Paul was a perfect candidate for the mission field. At the end of the four-month assignment, the Evangelical Church of the Ubangi Province asked him to return as their missionary doctor. Paul knew that he and Lois would

256. Bridges, 34.
257. Ibid., 41.

need to pray and to find financial support, but his heart was already in Wasolo.

Paul Carlson.
Courtesy of Covenant Archives and Historical Library, North Park University, Chicago.

After prayer, the couple was certain that God was calling them to medical missionary work. Their home denomination, the Evangelical Covenant Church, raised the mission funds to send them back to Wasolo. The Carlson family, including ten-year-old Wayne and six-year-old Lynette, would be making their new home among the needy people of the African Congo. Medical and church friends were shocked that Paul would walk away from a prosperous life as a surgeon in the US, but his heart was fixed on a much higher calling: "Here there are so many to do the work—over there so few. I am needed."[258]

Monganga Paul

The Carlson's long flight to the Congo ended with Wayne and Lynette staring out of the airplane window fascinated by the deep greens of the jungle and the winding blue ribbon of the Ubangi River far below.

258. Ibid., ix.

As the plane's tires squealed to a stop on the runway, the family nearly burst with excitement. What would they find in Wasolo?

"Monganga Paul is here! Monganga Paul is here!" A crowd of Congolese natives stood in front of the Wasolo hospital cheering at the doctor's return. *Monganga* in Lingala means "doctor." In the four months Paul had lived among them, he had fallen in love with the Congolese people and they had fallen in love with him. The joy of his heart was to see their lives transformed through medicine and the gospel of Jesus Christ.

When the Carlsons arrived in Wasolo in the early months of 1963, Paul was the only doctor at the eighty-bed facility in Wasolo, but he had four trained nurses working on his team. The doctor/patient ratio in the province was 1 to 100,000! On a typical day, Monganga Paul would see two hundred patients, working from early morning until late at night. His ministry to the people, both physically and spiritually, was personally exhausting but flourishing.

Political Upheaval in the Congo

The following year, on June 30, 1964, the United Nations peacekeeping troops pulled out of the Congo, leaving the nation as a free independent state. A new government had been elected, but as soon as the UN troops were gone, a rebel group known as the Simbas (wild lions) began to incite the people to a government coup. In that same month, Paul spoke at a regional Christian conference, warning his audience of the political unrest and challenging his brothers and sisters in Christ to search their hearts for their commitment to Jesus: "We do not know what will happen in 1964—in 1965—we do not know if we will have to suffer or die during this year because we are Christians. But it does not matter! Our job is to follow Jesus. Will you follow Jesus this year?"[259] Less than two months later, Paul Carlson had to stand in faith upon those very words.

---

259. Ibid., 106.

Map of Congo
Artindo\Thinkstock

Escaping Wasolo

After the UN forces left, the National Congolese Army tried to hold back the Simba militants. But the army was too small and inexperienced to withstand the onslaught. By early August, Stanleyville (modern Kisangani), the capital of the Democratic Republic of the Congo, was taken by rebel forces. Stanleyville was a long way off from Wasolo, so Paul still had hope that no one would even remember their little corner of the Congo nation.

On August 20, Paul and his nurses were unpacking boxes of medical supplies sent from the Christian Medical Society. It was then that the truck driver pulled up to the hospital, warning them that the city of Bumba had been taken and that they must escape immediately! The heavy rains of the Congo had been falling, and their truck was not at the mission camp, so the family waited. Two days later, Paul went into the nearby town of Yakoma only to find it deserted. The rebels were on their way and the townspeople had fled. Climbing out of his truck in Wasolo, Paul found Lois and spoke quietly so that the children wouldn't be frightened. "Start packing. We will go tonight."[260]

Unfortunately, the torrential rains of the Congo wouldn't let up. For a week, the Carlsons remained in their home, unable to get out by truck. Paul continued his medical work unruffled. By September 3, the word came through radio emissions: "You must evacuate the women and children." It was two weeks since they had received their first warning to flee. The next morning, Paul took Lois, the two children and his American nurse, Jody, down to the Ubangi River. They crossed the river, along with hundreds of other refugees, to the safety of another country, the Central African Republic, on the other side.

Captured by Rebels!

After Paul sent his family across the border to safety, he returned to Wasolo to continue his hospital work. One more life saved...one more baby brought safely into the world...one more surgery to heal a wounded body. By the next Wednesday, he planned to leave Wasolo and join his family for good.

On Tuesday, the rebels were in Yakoma just minutes from the Wasolo hospital by truck. That night Paul sent out a message by wireless radio, "I must leave this evening. It is time that I leave my station."[261] But by then it was too late; the area was full of Simba rebels. The next morning, while Paul was in the middle of surgery, the militants burst into the hospital, capturing Carlson and shooting two of his nurses to death. Throughout the next two months of his captivity, Paul would

260. Ibid., 111.
261. Ibid., 106.

hear constant threats of his execution. He wrote a letter to Lois in September which was given to her later:

> For me to live is Christ and to die is gain—this becomes more real each day. I've had beatings and known what it means not to know the future for tomorrow. Where I go from here I do not know, only that it will be with Him. If by God's grace I live, although I doubt it, it will be to His glory.... I'm praying that through this we might see revival in our churches in the Ubangi, in the hearts of all of us, and in our Congolese brothers too.[262]

Weeks earlier, Paul had written to his home church, "Let's pray for revival. Only through revival—a refreshing of the church—will we receive growth and win Christians who can stand and face the future."

From that point on, Lois had no idea where Paul was or if he was alive. She was forced to move with the children further into the Central African Republic for safety. Still she waited for word of Paul. In late September word came that Paul and three captured priests were being moved to Stanleyville for some sort of trial. The Simba leader, Christophe Gbenye, wanted to make an example out of the Christian men by accusing them of being mercenary soldiers plotting against the Congolese people. Strangely, even though he was in captivity, they allowed Paul to continue giving medical help to the sick soldiers and other prisoners.

Falsely Accused by the Enemy

Gbenye was a shrewd rebel leader who wanted to frighten the people of the Congo into submission. He knew that Monganga Paul was well-loved among the people of his country, so he devised a new plan to try to turn their hearts against him. The Simba leader falsely accused Dr. Paul of being a military agent of the United States, renamed him Major Paul Carlson, and brought him to trial once again as an American spy. On

262. Ibid., 137.

November 16, Lois received word that "Major" Carlson had been tried, found guilty and sentenced to be executed.

On Tuesday morning, November 24, the prisoners were awakened early in the morning by the loud droning of airplanes overhead. Frantic Simba guards opened up the prison doors and herded the captives out into the city streets. Above, Belgian paratroopers were dropping from American planes into the city in an attempt to rescue the captives. Frightened and confused rebels began to fire their weapons in the air and then indiscriminately into the crowds of prisoners. Pandemonium broke out. Prisoners fell to the ground, some dead, others pretending to be dead in the hope of later escaping.

In the confusion, a small group of prisoners led by Paul Carlson ran to a wall behind a nearby house to escape. Only one person could scramble over the wall at a time. Always putting others before himself, Paul slowed down to allow another prisoner, Chuck Davis, the room to scale the wall first. When Davis turned to give Carlson a hand up, a young Simba rebel fired five shots, and Paul slumped over, then fell to the ground. At thirty-six years old, Monganga Paul was dead. Davis and the prisoners with him began to weep at the loss of this dearly loved man of God. Davis escaped his prison guards and spent time with Lois later, sharing the last weeks of Paul's life.[263]

Frightened and confused rebels began to fire their weapons in the air and then indiscriminately into the crowds of prisoners. Pandemonium broke out.

Telegrams poured in to Lois from all over the world—from President Lyndon B. Johnson, from the United States Ambassador to the Democratic Republic of Congo, from the President of the Central African Republic. Lois decided that Paul should be buried in Karawa in the Congo near the people he loved. He sacrificed his life to take care of them,

263. Ibid., 153.

whether rebel soldier or Congolese native, until the last possible moment. His headstone, written in the native Lingala, reads "*Greater love hath no man than this that a man lay down his life for his friends*" (John 15:13 KJV). At his funeral, one friend joined in the eulogy, "Monganga Paul came to do two things, he came to teach us the Good News and he came to heal our diseases. Whoever shot Paul didn't kill him; he killed us."[264] The December 4, 1964 front cover of *TIME Magazine* featured Paul Carlson's picture and the byline *The Congo Massacre* with his story.

Monganga Paul's Legacy

Paul Carlson served for less than two years in the heart of Africa, but the impact of his life and death on the Congolese people cannot be measured. He was a true follower of Jesus Christ—loving and healing those who cried out for help in a desperate country.

Over fifty years later, people are still being healed—both physically and spiritually—because of his legacy. In Paul Carlson's honor, a hospital and church were set up in his name in the area around Wasolo. Shortly after returning to the United States, Lois and other members of the Evangelical Covenant Church founded a Paul Carlson Partnership to continue Paul's work. They partner with the Covenant Church of the Congo (CEUM) to bring the gospel of Christ and medical services to the Congolese people. Miraculously, through fifty years of unrest and persecution in the Congo nation, the CEUM today has 247,507 church members, 1,574 pastoral workers, and 1,647 churches. The CEUM also services five hospitals, 108 clinics, and 80,000 students in Christian schools in northeastern Congo.[265] Isn't it amazing what God can do with one life surrendered to Him? "*For it is God who works in you both to will and to do for His good pleasure*" (Philippians 2:13).

264. Ibid.,137.
265. See "A Presence in Congo," *Covenant Companion*, November 1, 2014, http://covenantcompanion.com/2014/11/01/a-presence-in-congo/.

Archbishop Oscar Romero: Shot While Serving the Lord

It had been a day full of laughter and shared testimonies of faith. Oscar Romero, the archbishop of San Salvador, had spent the afternoon with Christian friends and fellow priests. They shared a common faith in Christ and a common hope for the freedom of El Salvador from the violence of drug cartels and murderous street gangs. The fellowship was filled with the sunny, bright hope of a better tomorrow for their country torn apart by violence.

After cleaning up from the afternoon festivities, Archbishop Romero drove to the Hospital of Divine Providence in the middle of San Salvador, the capital city of El Salvador, a country whose name means *The Savior*. He was going to celebrate mass in the small chapel on the hospital grounds. It was a Monday evening, so the congregation was small and quiet. The day before, he had shared a message with thousands in the Metropolitan Cathedral of the Holy Savior, his home church. This quiet Monday night sermon would be his last.

The Supernatural Reform of a Christian Heart

Oscar Arnulfo Romero was appointed the archbishop of San Salvador on February 23, 1977. His faith was strong in Christ and the believers of San Salvador were happy with his appointment. However, Marxist segments of the government and liberal, radical priests were disappointed—even angry. They were pushing a new doctrine they called "liberation theology," which was founded more closely on the words of Karl Marx than the words of Jesus Christ. It was a Marxist attempt to bring freedom to the oppressed people of El Salvador. Romero disagreed with this false message.

According to his longtime secretary Msrg. Jesus Delgado, Romero had very little use for a theology that preached communist violence rather than peace through Jesus Christ. While courageously outspoken against the poverty and social injustice of El Salvador,

Romero believed that a transforming faith in Jesus was what the people of his nation needed to give them freedom. Romero preached from the pulpit, "The most profound social revolution is the serious, supernatural, interior reform of a Christian." "A personal encounter with Jesus" was the transformation that the people of El Salvador needed.[266]

Romero had built up an enormous following among his countrymen for his courage and his faith. He broadcast his weekly sermons across the country, messages that were a combination of Christian hope for the future and defiance of the cartels and gangs who were murdering Salvadoran citizens daily.

"I Have to Walk the Same Path"

On March 12, 1979, Rutilio Grande, Romero's close friend and fellow priest, was assassinated for trying to help the poorest people in San Salvador. Romero rushed to the crime scene to find his dear friend still lying on the ground. Rutilio's death had a profound effect on Romero. Romero later wrote, "When I looked at Rutilio lying there dead, I thought 'if they have killed him for doing what he did, then I too have to walk the same path.'" Romero pleaded for government intervention in finding

The Archbishop Oscar Romero with Pope Paul VI.
Public domain.

266. Alvaro de Juana, "Archbishop Romero had no interest in liberation theology," *Catholic News Agency*, February 21, 2015, http://www.catholicnewsagency.com/news/archbishop-romero-had-no-interest-in-liberation-theology-says-secretary-79788/.

his murderers, but the government turned a deaf ear and the Marxist-leaning press was silent.

Romero began to speak out even more courageously against the poverty, social injustice, assassinations and torture taking place in his country. The international community encouraged him in his fight, awarding him with a nomination for a Nobel Peace Prize. But it wasn't international honor that spurred Romero on; it was a love for his fellow countrymen and a desire to see them set free in Christ that was the power behind his plea for action.

Killed During Communion

The last home of Romero.
By Jrh008 via Wikimedia Commons

On March 24, 1980, Oscar Romero walked into the chapel at the Hospital of Divine Providence to celebrate mass for a small and faithful congregation. After sharing a sermon on the power of Jesus Christ to change lives from the inside out, the sixty-two-year-old archbishop walked quietly to the front of the altar to prepare for communion. As he stood in prayer with his back to the congregation, a shot rang out from the front door of the chapel. Romero slumped over, his blood staining the carpet of the chapel floor. The best friend that the poor of El Salvador had was lying dead in a small hospital chapel in San Salvador.

During his Sunday sermon the day before, Romero had broadcast a message to all Salvadoran army soldiers who were Christians, challenging them to obey God's Word first and to refuse to carry out the government's orders to violate and kill the people of El Salvador. He was probably killed for this message.

Oscar Romero was buried in his home church, the Metropolitan Cathedral of the Holy Savior in San Salvador. His funeral on March 30 was attended by more than 250,000 mourners from all around the world. It was considered the largest demonstration of love and support for God's message of hope and freedom in the history of Latin America. But the hatred and unrest of the country would not be easily silenced. During the funeral, a bomb exploded on the Cathedral Square and shots were fired from a nearby building. A mass stampede followed and forty people were killed. No one ever found out who interrupted the funeral services, although it is suspected government soldiers were the culprits. The assassins who killed Romero were believed to be members of a Salvadoran death squad, but no one was ever bought to justice.[267]

Where Is Our Hope?

Today, over thirty-five years later, El Salvador is still embroiled in political turmoil and violence. So are the people there without hope? Did a Christian leader like Oscar Romero die in vain?

The hope of the church of Jesus Christ is to preach the gospel message of salvation in Jesus Christ alone and pray that the nation will be

267. Anne-Marie O'Connor, "Participant in 1980 assassination of Romero in El Salvador provides new details," *Washington Post*, April 6, 2010, http://www.washingtonpost.com/wp-dyn/content/article/2010/04/05/AR2010040503234.html.

Pastel portrait of Archbishop Oscar Romero.
By J. Puig Reixach, www.puigreixach.net

turned around by spiritual revival from within. In the most recent years, El Salvador has shown signs of Catholic and evangelical Christian life everywhere. Churches own roughly thirty media outlets in El Salvador, including some of the largest in the country. The evangelical megachurches, such as the Baptist Tabernacle and Elim, own TV stations, radio stations, and newspapers proclaiming the message of Jesus Christ daily. These two churches alone draw as many as 70,000 believers to services each Sunday.[268]

Two decades after his death, Oscar Romero was honored by the Anglican Church of England with a statue in Westminster Abbey declaring him one of the ten most influential martyrs of the twentieth century. But Romero did not die for the honor of men; he lived and died to accomplish God's purposes in his small South American country and to see the people of El Salvador finally live in a nation that lives up to its original namesake, "The Savior."

Who shall separate us from the love of Christ? Shall trouble or hardship or persecution or famine or nakedness or danger or sword?

268. Paul Glader, "Christianity is Growing Rapidly in El Salvador," *Washington Post*, April 8, 2015 https://www.washingtonpost.com/news/acts-of-faith/wp/2015/04/08/christianity-is-growing-rapidly-in-el-salvador-along-with-gang-violence-and-murder-rates/.

As it is written: "For your sake we face death all day long; we are considered as sheep to be slaughtered." No, in all these things we are more than conquerors through Him who loved us. For I am convinced that neither death nor life, neither angels nor demons, neither the present nor the future, nor any powers, neither height nor depth, nor anything else in all creation, will be able to separate us from the love of God that is in Christ Jesus our Lord.

(Romans 8:35–39 NIV)

TODAY'S GLOBAL WAR— WHAT CAN WE DO?

12

TODAY'S GLOBAL WAR—WHAT CAN WE DO?

Dear friends, do not be surprised at the fiery ordeal that has come on you to test you, as though something strange were happening to you. But rejoice inasmuch as you participate in the sufferings of Christ, so that you may be overjoyed when his glory is revealed. If you are insulted because of the name of Christ, you are blessed, for the Spirit of glory and of God rests on you.... However, if you suffer as a Christian, do not be ashamed, but praise God that you bear that name. (1 Peter 4:12–14, 16 NIV)

The Global War on Christians: The Greatest Story Never Told

What is happening with Christian persecution around the world today? Why doesn't the average Christian know more details about the persecuted church? Why is it a story that has remained in the dark for so many years? Perhaps it was too painful to look at, or we just didn't have enough credible sources? Or perhaps, since the mainstream media ignored it, we thought it wasn't really happening? And so it became the *Greatest Story Never Told!*[269] But I hope that is changing rapidly today. And I would like this book to be a part of that change.

In this final chapter, we want to look carefully at the global war on Christians as it affects so many regions of our globe. Most importantly, we want to answer the compelling question of our time: What can we do to make a difference? This last chapter is a rallying cry for the body of Christ to stand beside the persecuted church throughout the world.

Before we go on, I want to remind you that the global war on Christians today is not just about radical Islam, even though radical Islam is certainly an enemy of Christians and of Jews. We have already discovered that this global war against God's people has been Satan's plan from the very beginning—Satan wants to attack God's people though oppression and persecution and, ultimately, to eliminate us from the face of the earth!

Coursing through this history of the Christian martyrs, we have seen that Satan will use whatever ideology is available to accomplish his goal.

Coursing through this history of the Christian martyrs, we have seen that Satan will use whatever ideology is available to accomplish his goal: the Romans, the Turks, the apostate church, Nazism, communism, despotism, and now radical Islam. Throughout the centuries, the people and the ideology have changed, but Satan's ancient and rebellious goal to destroy God's kingdom has remained the same, and his spirit of antichrist continues to roam the earth in a desperate attempt to accomplish his destructive plan.

269. John L. Allen, Jr., *The Global War on Christians* (New York: Image Publishers, 2016), 244.

Thank God, Satan will not be victorious. We are assured that *"He who is in you is greater than he who is in the world"* (1 John 4:4). And we have repeated one compelling Scripture throughout this book that remains a beacon of hope and faith for every single believer. *"I **will** build My church,"* Jesus promised, *"and the gates of hell **shall not** prevail against it"* (Matthew 16:18 ESV).

The Statistics Will Astound You!

Did you know that there are 2.2 billion people on the earth today who consider themselves Christians? (Of course, only God knows the true conversion of each heart in every Christian denomination. We can leave that in His hands.) Of those 2.2 billion people, over 76 percent or 1.7 billion Christians live in countries that are highly restricted or completely restricted from religious freedom for their people. In addition, of the 196 nations that exist in the world today, in 139 of them Christians endure harassment, persecution, or worse on a regular basis. That's over 70 percent of the nations of the world!

Who provides these revealing statistics on the global war against Christians? There are a number of Christian organizations that have dedicated all of their resources to serving the persecuted church. They also supply Christian and secular organizations with reliable information and statistics on the level of Christian persecution throughout the world, such as the Center for the Study of Global Christianity at Gordon-Conwell or the evangelical organization Open Doors USA that supplied the statistics that I listed above. Open Doors also produces a "World Watch List" each year that ranks the top 50 countries in the world where Christian persecution occurs.[270]

"It's a Dangerous Thing to Be a Christian in This World!"

This statement was made by Rutilio Grande only days before he was assassinated for his faith in El Salvador in 1977.[271] Yes, it is a dangerous

270. See https://www.opendoorsusa.org/christian-persecution/world-watch-list.
271. Allen, *Global War*, 46.

thing to be a Christian today. The statistics and stories in this last chapter will prove that statement is true. According to Open Doors—which serves the persecuted church in over 60 countries—there are over *100 million Christians* right now, as you read this page, who are in danger of being harassed, persecuted, tortured or killed for their Christian faith somewhere in the world.

In the Western church, we do not live in a world that is this dangerous. In spite of the ever-increasing animosity towards Christian beliefs in our society, we do not live in this life-and-death kind of culture... yet. One thing that most Western Christians don't realize is that *two-thirds* of the world's Christians live outside of the US and Europe! Only 10 percent of the world's Christians are Americans.[272] This should be a real eye-opener for those who believe that God is only interested in what goes on in the American church! Ninety percent of the people who make up Jesus Christ's bride are now located in other parts of the world, particularly the rapidly growing Protestant and Pentecostal churches of Africa and Asia.

The Lord has blessed us in countless ways in the United States throughout our two-hundred-and-forty-year history. We have an immeasurable opportunity to use our blessings to minister life to our brothers and sisters in Christ who are suffering persecution worldwide. "*Therefore, as we have opportunity, let us do good to all, especially to those who are of the household of faith*" (Galatians 6:10).

So What Can We Do to Help?

The first and most important thing we can do as Christians is to pray. "*The effective, fervent prayer of a righteous man avails* [accomplishes] *much*" (James 5:16). We will spend time in this chapter praying for our persecuted world. But there is a greater need for the body of Christ to pray fervently *on an ongoing basis*. At the beginning of His ministry,

272. Ibid., 16.

Jesus announced that He had come to earth to heal the brokenhearted and set the captive free:

> *The Spirit of the Lord is upon Me, because He has anointed Me to preach the gospel to the poor; He has sent Me to heal the brokenhearted, to proclaim liberty to the captives and recovery of sight to the blind, to set at liberty those who are oppressed.*
>
> (Luke 4:18)

As His body, we can be Christ's hands and feet to be used in the same way to help our suffering brothers and sisters.

Prayer for the Regions of the World

Father God, as we look with grieving hearts at the persecution of Christian brothers and sisters throughout the world, we pray that you will minister to them in their time of trials and suffering. Please, Lord, give them supernatural and natural ways of escape from the hands of those who seek to slaughter and imprison them. Holy Spirit, speak to them in these times of confusion and fear and guide them to freedom.

Lord Jesus, show us how to be Your hands and feet for the suffering church. Send us to bring healing to the broken-hearted and liberty to the captives in Your name. Show us what our brothers and sisters in Christ need the most to bring them comfort and freedom from oppression. Give us, Lord, eyes to see and ears to hear what Your Spirit is saying to the free church (Matthew 13:16), so that we might come alongside our persecuted brothers and sisters and make a true difference in their lives. We call out for Your guidance, in Jesus' name. Amen.

We can't pray well or give assistance if we aren't informed. The following pages give a brief review of the persecuted church and what the saints are enduring in different regions of the world.

Map of the Middle East.
Ruslan Olinchuk\Thinkstock

The Middle East

With the rise of ISIS, radical Islam, and the implementation of Sharia law (which forbids any religion but Islam), the Middle East has become a hotspot for Christian persecution. In the early twentieth century, Arab Christians made up 20 percent of the Middle Eastern population. The Middle East had been their home since the founding of Christianity, and they survived Islamic rule in the Middle Ages and in the Ottoman Empire. But today Christianity is being extinguished at an alarming rate throughout the Middle East. So many Christians have fled or been massacred that only 5 percent of the Arab population is Christian today, and those who remain are seeking ways to escape the genocide.[273] Christian converts from Islam are far more at risk than established Christian families. Countless new converts are silently murdered by their fathers and brothers in Muslim "honor killings."

Afghanistan

Afghanistan is one of the "World's Worst Countries" in which to be a Christian, ranked #4 in Open Doors' World Watch List. There is no visible Christian church in Afghanistan and Christian aid workers in particular are at risk from radical Islamists.

"We only die once, so it might as well be for Jesus."

South African Christian Werner Groenewald and his two teen-aged children, Jean-Pierre and Rodé, were killed in late November 2014 in an attack in Kabul. Werner had been helping uneducated Afghans through extended education projects since 2002. Three Taliban radicals burst into Werner's home dressed as policemen, shooting Werner first and then his children before setting the house

273. David Willey, "Rome Crisis Talks on Middle East Christians," BBC News, October 10, 2010, http://www.bbc.com/news/world-middle-east-11509256.

on fire. Werner's wife, Dr. Hannelie Groenewald, who also served the Afghan people, was working at her clinic at the time of the attack. Werner and his family had dedicated twelve years of service to the poor of Afghanistan. In his last message to his international co-workers, he closed the session with these words: "We only die once, so it might as well be for Jesus."[274]

Iraq

Iraq has been the home to Christians since the early days of Christianity, but the Iraqi church is now on the verge of extinction. In 2003, there were 1.5 million Christians in Iraq. Today, there is an estimated 300,000—and the number is shrinking every month.[275] One grieving Christian, living in the midst of the death and destruction, stated, "The attack on Christians continues and the world remains silent. *It's as if we have been swallowed up by the night.*"[276]

It is vital to let the world know that this Christian genocide is real, so that our brothers and sisters can be comforted knowing that we hear their cry and that we have not forsaken them.

Iran

Since the surge of the Islamic State throughout Iran, Christianity is considered "a condemnable Western influence, an imminent threat to the Islamic identity of the Republic."[277] It is impossible to know even a fraction of the persecution taking place under the secrecy of Iran's government, especially between family members who maliciously kill Muslim converts to Christianity. However, it is undeniable that pastors of the growing house church movement have been martyred for their faith.

---

274. Persecution Blog, Voice of the Martyrs, December 01, 2014, http://www.persecutionblog.com/2014/12/christian-humanitarian-workers-killed-in-afghanistan.html.
275. Giles Fraser, "Christians in Iraq: should they stay or should they go?" *The Guardian*, March 24, 2016, http://www.theguardian.com/commentisfree/belief/2016/mar/24/christians-in-iraq-should-they-stay-or-should-they-go.
276. Allen, *Global War*, 138, emphasis added.
277. "World Watch List: Iran," Open Doors, 2016, https://www.opendoorsusa.org/christian-persecution/world-watch-list/iran/.

Ghorban Tourani, an Iranian Christian convert, established a Christian house church in his Islamic hometown of Golestan, Iran, sharing God's Word despite multiple death threats—until he was abducted and murdered on November 22, 2005.[278]

Syrian refugee children live in an abandoned warehouse near Saida, Lebanon.
Anthony Gale\Flikr

Syria

Syria has remained in the center of world news since the civil war began in 2011. Syria's national struggle has developed into an international war between the dictator Bashar al-Assad, his loyal army, Syrian rebels, US and Russian military forces, and now ISIS. What a powerful mess! In the midst of the unbridled hatred and military power, the people of Syria, both Christians and non-Christians alike, face a daily life of death and destruction. In the spring of 2016, both the European Parliament and the United States Congress and State Department finally recognized the slaughter of millions of Christians in Syria and Iraq as deliberate religious genocide. Syrian Christians have been slaughtered by the thousands by

278. See "The Martyrs of the Iranian Church," Elam, https://www.elam.com/article/martyrs-iranian-church-ultimate-price.

military troops and by Islamic extremists through crucifixions, beheadings, and firing squads, as we read about in the first chapter.

Pakistan

Pakistan is the world's second-largest Muslim country, and Taliban insurgents are regaining influence as the government weakly responds. There are an estimated 2.5 million Christians in Pakistan who are marginalized, ostracized by family, and becoming increasing fearful for their safety.

An example of Islamic radicalism: On August 1, 2009, there were riots in the town of Gorja, Pakistan, where eight Christians were killed in mob violence, including six family members who were burned alive in their home. The dead included four women and one seven-year-old child. Three thousand incensed Muslims descended on the city of Gorja, incited by false accusations that the Qur'an had been burned at a Christian wedding a few weeks earlier. The militants destroyed at least 100 Christian homes, using a special fuel that was difficult to extinguish, trapping and injuring Christians behind the flames. The evening before, on July 30, the same Islamic jihadists had destroyed fifty Christian homes and two churches in a nearby village using the same fuel.[279] Each year the number of Christian martyrs in Pakistan increases. In 2013, a suicide bombing at a church in Peshawar left more than 100 people dead.

Jordan

For a long time, Jordan was one of the most liberal countries in the Middle East in its free exercise of religion with the largest Arab Christian population. However, times are changing. The Jordanian government has been willing to host a large number of Middle Eastern refugees, which leads to economic, political, and religious pressure. The 150,000 Christians currently living there are in grave danger from the arm of Islamic persecutors.

279. Fareed Khan, "Eight Christians Burned Alive in Punjab, Pakistan," *Asia News*, August 2, 2009, http://www.asianews.it/news-en/Eight-Christians-burned-alive-in-Punjab-15943.html.

Saudi Arabia

In Saudi Arabia it is against the law to practice any religion outside of Islam. However, Saudi's youth culture is changing dramatically—pushing some toward radical Islam but also emboldening others to convert to Christianity. Christians in Saudi Arabia must become part of a very secretive underground church. Several Middle Eastern countries claim in writing to have religious freedom, but it's not the case in actual practice.

Kuwait, Jordan, and Azerbaijan

Kuwait, Jordan, and Azerbaijan all have constitutions that allow for religious freedom, but they are strongly Islamic and, as the rest of the Middle East, becoming increasingly restrictive.

Prayer for the Middle East:

Lord, you have created the nations of the world. As Psalm 86:9 says, "All nations whom You have made shall come and worship before You, O Lord, and shall glorify Your name." *We bring the nations of the Middle East before You today. You chose that part of the world to begin human life on this earth. Please move once again by the power of Your Holy Spirit and free our brothers and sisters in Christ who are trapped there in the turmoil of hatred and war. Create a way of escape for the captives so that they will not be captured and killed by the ones who seek to destroy their lives. I pray that their testimony for Jesus may remain strong and that all of the glory from their witness would go to You.*

Please lift the veil of deception from the jihadists' eyes so that they will stop the gruesome killing and sexual enslavement of both Christians and non-Christians, who have been at their mercy. Create a miracle, Lord; change the leadership of those nations so that they would pursue peace. We also pray for the peace of Jerusalem and the protection of Israel and Your chosen people. In Jesus' name. Amen.

Map of Asia.
Cartarium\Thinkstock

East Asia

Asia has an enormous population of Christians particularly in South Korea and China, but it is also home to some of the most restrictive governments in the world. The Christians in Asia must always be on guard while practicing their Christian faith.

North Korea

North Korea's authoritarian dictatorship under the paranoid Kim Jong-un is secretive, sinister, and highly restrictive. North Korea heads Open Door's "World Watch List" as the number one persecutor of Christians for the fourteenth consecutive year. According to one website, "North Korean Christians aren't simply killed for their faith in Christ. They are pulverized with steamrollers, used to test biological weapons, shipped off to death camps or shot in front of children, while newborn babies have their brains crushed with forceps in front of their mothers. Crimes against humanity reminiscent of Auschwitz and Treblinka to which the world declared 'Never Again!' more than 60 years ago are being perpetrated today against the North Korean Christians."[280]

North Korea heads Open Door's "World Watch List" as the number one persecutor of Christians for the fourteenth consecutive year.

Christians hide their faith, sometimes even from their children when they are young, to keep from being arrested, tortured, and sent to labor camps for long years under horrific conditions. Death is usually the result of their imprisonment. We don't have clear details of the persecution against Christians because North Korea's government keeps the country completely isolated from the rest of the world.

280. North Korean Christians.com, http://northkoreanchristians.com/christianity-north-korea.html.

China

China, with its population of 1.37 billion, has a rapidly growing Christian community that numbers over 100 million people today, predominantly in Protestant denominations. It is estimated that 47 million of those Christians are Pentecostal believers.[281] In spite of those numbers, religious freedom is still restricted by the Chinese communist government. In response to the rapid Christian church growth, China has been cracking down on house churches and arresting influential Christian leaders, such as Pastor Zhang Shaojie, who was falsely convicted of gathering people "in order to disrupt the public order," fined and sentenced to twelve years in prison.[282]

Beginning in 2014, the Beijing government launched a new attack in the large Christian province of Zhejiang by demolishing Christian churches or tearing down and burning church crosses that once marked the skyline of the cities. Over 1500 crosses have been destroyed to date.[283]

Indonesia, Malaysia, and Brunei

Indonesia, the largest Muslim country in the world, has proven to be surprisingly tolerant of religious freedom, with the exception of radical Islamic groups which continue to target religious minorities, including Christians. Malaysia, still well-known as a liberal and tolerant Islamic country, is slowly becoming more militant and considering the addition of Sharia penal law in one of its federal states. In the small nation of Brunei, which has been ruled by sultans for more than six hundred years, Sharia law was instituted in 2014. Like Malaysia, as the current sultan leans more and more toward conservative Islam, the Christians,

281. Allen, *Global War*, 5.
282. Daniel Wiser, "Chinese Persecution of Christians Reaches Highest Level in a Decade," *Washington Free Beacon*, April 27, 2015, http://freebeacon.com/issues/chinese-persecution-of-christians-reaches-highest-level-in-a-decade/.
283. See Brendon Hong, "China Is Tearing Down Crosses," *The Daily Beast*, August 1, 2015, http://www.thedailybeast.com/articles/2015/08/01/china-is-tearing-down-crosses.html.

who make up 16 percent of the population, are facing increased harassment and persecution.

Vietnam

Vietnam's communist government leaves little room for freedom of religion. A number of Christians, particularly Wycliffe translators, have been executed by the communists with some regularity since the 1960s just for being Christian. Similarly, in Laos, any Christians who refuse to participate in Buddhist practices are seen as foreigners and a threat to the government.

Myanmar

In Myanmar, Christians face extreme persecution from Buddhist radical monks and the Burmese army which operates with a high level of violence against Christians and minorities. In 2015, two female Christian teachers in their early twenties were working with the Kachin Baptist Convention in a remote village in northern Myanmar. They were volunteers bringing education to the neglected Kachin children. In the middle of the night, Burmese soldiers snuck onto the church grounds, gang raped the two young women, and beat them to death.[284] In spite of protests, the Burmese government continues to turn a deliberate deaf ear to the abuse and murder of its Christian population.

Central Asia

Bangladesh

In Bangladesh, the rise of radical Islamic groups and their pressure on the government is a growing threat to freedom of religion. Hossain Ali (65), a former Muslim who converted to Christianity, was hacked

284. See Czarina Ong, "Christian teachers raped and murdered in Burma," *Christian Today*, January 23, 2015, http://www.christiantoday.com/article/christian.teachers.raped.and.murdered.in.burma/46572.htm.

to death early in the morning on March 22, 2016 by Islamic militants in Garialpara, Kurigram, Northern Bangladesh. While Hossain was coming back from his morning walk, three assailants on motorbikes approached him, threw a small bomb and then attacked him with sharp weapons. Hossain Ali died within minutes. Hossain had converted from Islam to Christianity in 1999. After his conversion, his wife tied him up and held him captive in their home for three days. His relatives pressured and persecuted him, yet he refused to forsake Jesus. His faithfulness inspired his entire family to eventually embrace Christ; his martyrdom will inspire the Christian community to stand strong in Jesus.[285]

India

In India, the threat is not from radical Islam but from radical Hindus who have forbidden any proselytizing in provinces throughout the heavily populated country.

In January 2014, a Christian pastor, Orucanti Sanjeevi, was brutally beaten in his home in the southern state of Andhra Pradesh. Hindu extremists knocked on the door of the pastor's house at about 8:30 p.m., claiming they wanted to pray with him. When his wife opened the door, they hit her with an iron rod and then rushed into the house. They stabbed the pastor, beat him with clubs and hit him on the head with the iron rod. Sanjeevi sustained severe injuries to his liver, intestines, and spleen and died within two days.[286]

More than 150 violent acts against Christians have taken place in the last few years in the increasingly hostile nation. As radical Hinduism steadily increases, the Indian government is looking the other way, encouraging these Hindus to step up their attacks on religious minorities including Christianity. The violence includes death threats, forced

---

285. Brianna Nieshe, "Grieving the Death of a True Martyr in Bangladesh" Open Doors, March 31, 2016, https://www.opendoorsusa.org/christian-persecution/stories/tag-blog-post/grieving-the-death-of-a-true-martyr-in-bangladesh/.
286. "Hindu Extremists Accused of Killing Pastor in Andhra Pradesh," *India Morning Star News*, January 30, 2014, http://morningstarnews.org/2014/01/hindu-extremists-accused-of-killing-pastor-in-andhra-pradesh-india/.

reconversions to Hinduism, and mob attacks.[287] This is another confirmation that if radical Islam disappeared from the earth, Christians would still be martyred for their faith.

Uzbekistan, Kazakhstan, Tajikistan and Turkmenistan

The Central Asian countries which were once a part of the Soviet Union have all maintained their authoritarian stand against Christianity. The harsh dictatorships in Uzbekistan, Kazakhstan, Tajikistan and Turkmenistan are becoming increasingly hostile to all things Christian. In March 2016, a man in Uzbekistan was arrested for distributing "extremist literature" after secret police raided his home and found his Bible and Christian books.[288]

Russia

Russia is located in both western Europe and eastern Asia. We will include it here. For decades, atheistic communism held a vise-like hold on Christianity in the Soviet Union. When the Soviet Union broke up, many doors to Christian evangelism were opened wide. Unfortunately, those open doors are closing again. In a shocking move in June 2016, Russia's Parliament voted to restrict all evangelization to church buildings recognized by the Russian government. The law prohibits sharing faith in homes, online, or anywhere, except in those churches. In spite of pleas

In a shocking move in June 2016, Russia's Parliament voted to restrict all evangelization to church buildings recognized by the Russian government.

287. Jonah Hicup, "Hindu extremists threaten to kill Christians," *Christian Today*, September 1, 2015, http://www.christiantoday.com/article/hindu.extremists.threaten.to.kill.christians.in.india.if.they.utter.the.name.of.christ/63567.htm.
288. "Christian Accused of Extremism," Open Doors, April 19, 2016, https://www.opendoorsusa.org/take-action/pray/tag-prayer-updates-post/christian-accused-of-extremism-for-owning-bible/.

from Christian leaders and human rights groups, on July 8, 2016, Vladimir Putin signed the bill into law.

Protestants and religious minorities small enough to gather in homes will be affected the most. Konstantin Bendas, the deputy bishop of the Pentecostal Union, said in an interview, "In June, a local police officer came to a home where a group of Pentecostals meet each Sunday. With a contented expression he told them: 'Now they're adopting the law, I'll drive you all out of here.' I guess we should now fear such zealous enforcement."[289]

Prayer for Asia

Heavenly Father, we lift the countries of Asia to You. There are billions of people living in those nations today. Many of them are Your children and long for the freedom to worship You in spirit and in truth. Lord, please set them free from their captivity. Hide them under the shadow of Your wings from the enemies of God who are seeking to destroy them. We pray that You would comfort them with Your Holy Spirit and strengthen them to stand for Christ without wavering. Give us Your heart for our suffering brothers and sisters in Christ, Lord. Please show us how we can help them even if we can't reach them physically. In Jesus' name, amen.

---

289. Kate Shellnutt, "Russia's Newest Law: No Evangelizing Outside of Church," *Christianity Today*, July 8, 2016, http://www.christianitytoday.com/gleanings/2016/june/no-evangelizing-outside-of-church-russia-proposes.html.

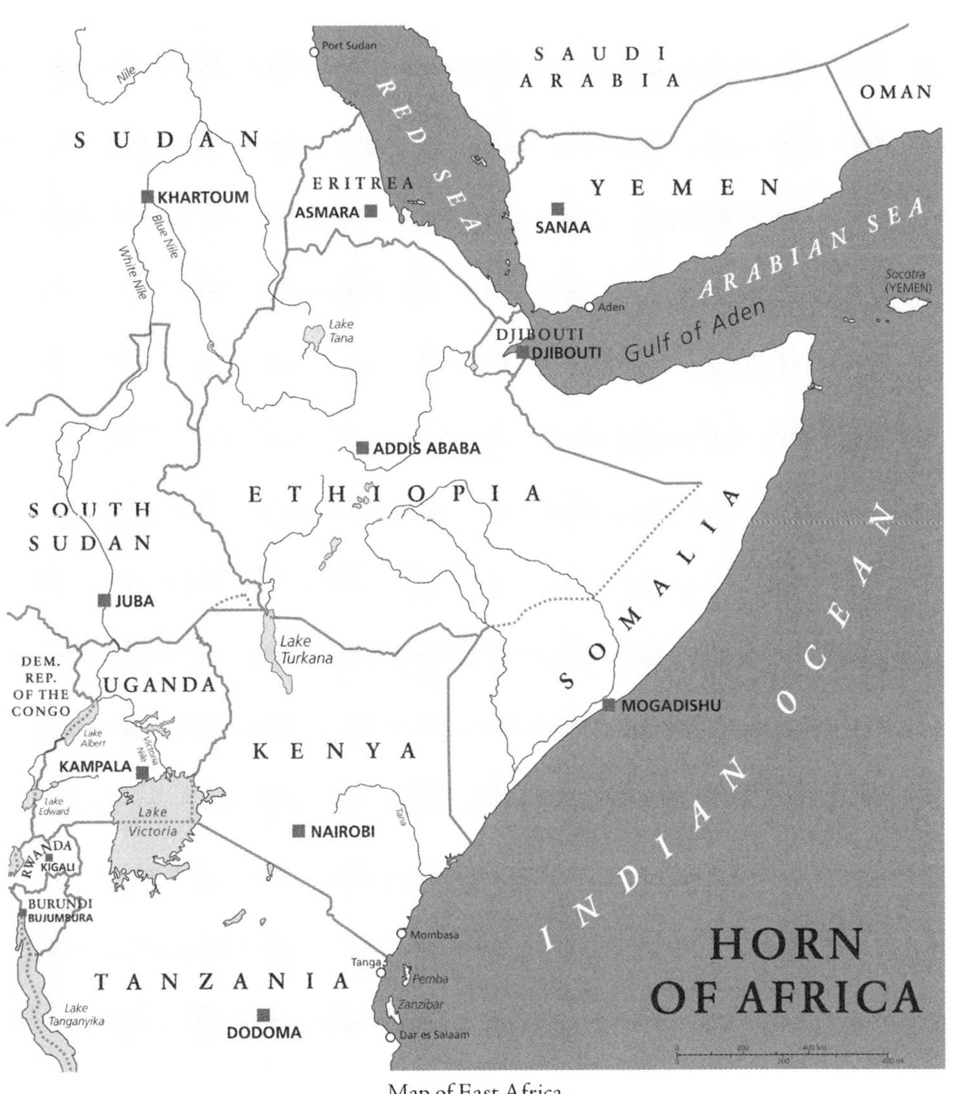

Map of East Africa.
PeterHermesFurian\Thinkstock

East Africa

According to the Pew Forum on Religion and Public Life, at the beginning of the twentieth century, only 9 percent of the population of Africa was Christian; today that count is 63 percent—which means there are approximately 380 million Christians in Africa today! And those numbers are increasing annually. Unfortunately, in spite of the large numbers, Christians experience persecution and death in many African nations. Some of it is at the hands of radical Islamists, other times it is totalitarian dictators who demand complete control of the ideology of their citizens.

Kenya

In Kenya, Christians have been in the majority for years, yet the Muslim minority uses terrorism to gain power. Before dawn, on April 2, 2015, Islamist militants burst into a Christian prayer meeting at Garissa University in eastern Kenya, shooting students who were on their knees in prayer. The masked gunmen, Al-Shabaab militants who had crossed the border from nearby Somalia, quickly stormed the university dorms, taking hostages and spraying escaping students with machine gunfire. The attackers took 700 students hostage and separated them by religion, allowing the Muslim students to leave and executing the young people who identified themselves as Christian. One hundred and forty-seven students were murdered in a single morning.

Ethiopia

In Ethiopia, the ruling party has blocked all channels for freedom of expression and assembly, and has also tried to control all religious institutions. Ethiopians who leave their Muslim faith and turn to Jesus Christ as Savior face severe persecution for converting. In April 2016, a woman named Workitu, living in the region south of Addis Ababa, endured regular physical abuse from her husband for accepting Jesus Christ. Soon after, word came that she was beaten to death by her husband and a neighbor. Shortly after their mother's death, two of her sons embraced Christianity, as well as one of her closest friends.[290]

Eritrea

Eritrea is a small east African nation on the coast of the Red Sea, formerly a part of Ethiopia. Eritrea is known to have one of the worst human rights records in the entire world. Open Doors has ranked it third on the World Watch List for 2016 and has named it "the North Korea of Africa." It is estimated that 2.5 million people (nearly half of the population) are Christians. It is one of two African countries designated as a "Country of Particular Concern" (CPC) by the US State Department because of violations of religious freedom. Horrific stories of torture and death of Christians have leaked out of the country.

Eritrea has a network of prison camps; one known as Me'eter is basically a concentration camp that holds many Christians imprisoned for their faith. Prisoners are forced to live in crude metal shipping containers with barely enough room to sit down. The metal in the hot desert temperatures rises to 115 degrees in the daytime, turning the containers into ovens that bake people alive.[291] Thousands of Christians have been imprisoned without trial, including Pastor Haile Naigzhi, who is still in an Eritrean prison today.

---

290. "Christian Woman Martyred in Ethiopia Leaves Strong Witness," Open Doors, April 19, 2016, https://www.opendoorsusa.org/christian-persecution/stories/tag-blog-post/christian-woman-martyred-in-ethiopia-leaves-a-strong-witness/.
291. Allen, *Global War*, 3.

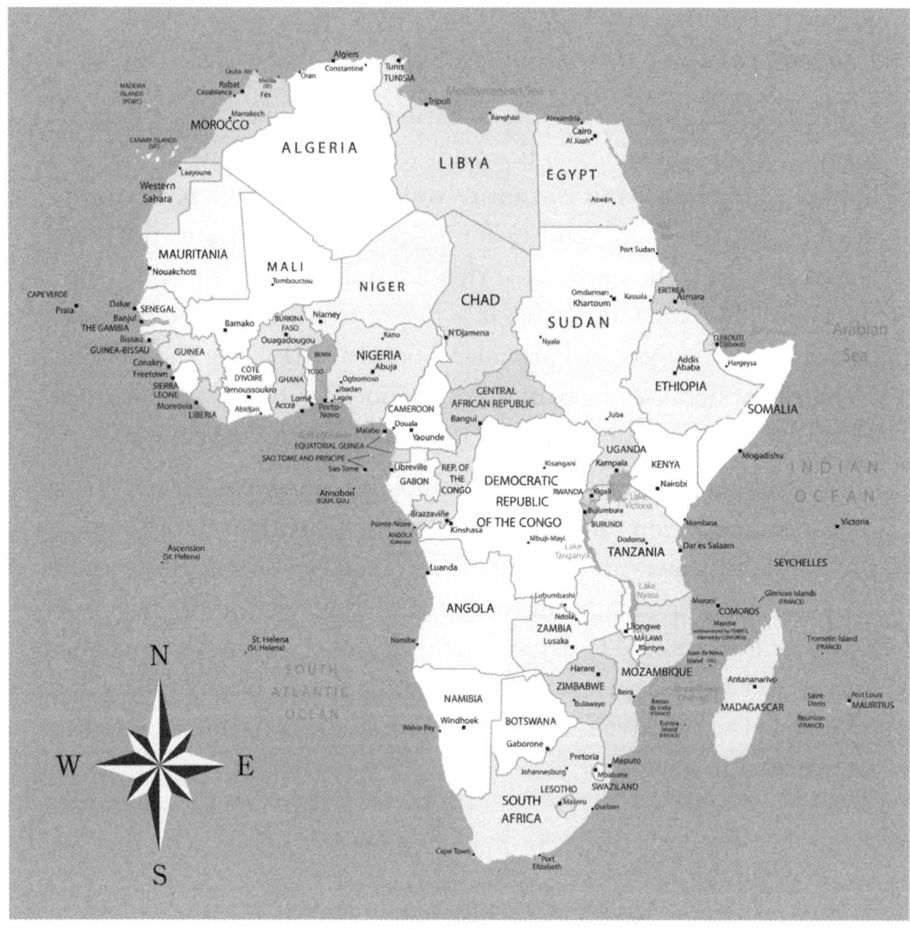

Map of Africa.
roripond\Thinkstock

West Africa

Nigeria

Nigeria, home of more than 80 million Christians, has been targeted by the Islamic extremist group Boko Haram since 2009. In July of that year the group attacked Christian targets in five days of riots that killed 700 people. Since that time, Boko Haram has been responsible for approximately 20,000 deaths in Nigeria and the displacement of 2.2 million people and is currently considered "the deadliest terror group in the world."[292]

Boko Haram gained worldwide notoriety in April of 2014 when the militants abducted 276 schoolgirls from the primarily Christian village of Chibok. (More than fifty eventually escaped.) A month after the kidnapping, Boko Haram released a video showing the girls all wearing Islamic dress. Today, there are reports that a number of the girls who refused to cooperate with their captives have been murdered. Other reports have emerged that the girls were "married off" to their militant captors. Boko Haram continues its murderous raids in Nigeria, intent on disrupting all Western or Christian education of Nigerian students and to create an Islamic state in the country.

North Africa

Libya and Tunisia

After the overthrow of Colonel Gadhafi in 2011, Libya is now seeing the rise of the Islamic State. The country is unsettled and violence is common, including the opening account of the 21 Coptic Christians who lost their lives through simultaneous beheadings. Nearby is the nation of Tunisia, home of the flourishing Christian church in the first

292. Katie Pisa and Tim Hume, "Boko Haram overtakes ISIS as world's deadliest terror group," CNN, Novermber 19, 2015, http://edition.cnn.com/2015/11/17/world/global-terror-report/.

centuries, and the location of Perpetua's martyrdom in the Carthage arena. Today, the pressure on Christians is becoming intense. Suicide bombings are on the increase in that nation.

Sudan

Along with Eritrea, Sudan has been designated a "Country of Particular Concern" by the US State Department. Its ethnic-cultural landscape is complicated, and Christian persecution is severe enough to be branded ethnic cleansing. Freedom of expression and religion are highly restricted.

Egypt

After years of turbulence, Egypt's new, more authoritarian government has established some stability in the country, but less religious freedom for Christians, including Egypt's large Coptic minority. During the "Maspero Massacre" on October 9, 2011, thousands of Coptic Christians in Cairo were peacefully protesting the government demolition of a Christian church. Suddenly the peace was shattered. Witnesses testified that two armored personnel carriers crashed the scene, crushing protesters to death, while Egyptian soldiers fired wildly at the congregation, and riot police threw tear gas. Twenty-seven Egyptian Christians were killed and more than 300 were injured. The Egyptian government attempted to cover up the violence with false state news reports.[293]

293. "Egypt, Don't Cover Up Military Killings of Coptic Christians" Human Rights Watch, October 25, 2011, https://www.hrw.org/news/2011/10/25/egypt-dont-cover-military-killing-copt-protesters Islamist.

Prayer for Africa

Lord, we pray for the countries of Africa and the Christians who live on that continent. Your church is growing rapidly in Africa and countless millions now proclaim Jesus Christ as Lord and Savior. We know that Satan will attack the church that is prospering. We pray against the enemy's vicious terrorism of the African church. We pray that the Christians in those nations will unify with one voice of prayer to fight Satan in heavenly places. We join our voices in prayer with them as well. Lord, give our Christian brothers supernatural wisdom and strength. Change the hearts of those in government in Africa to protect the religious freedom of those who call upon Your name. In Jesus' name, we pray. Amen.

Central and South America

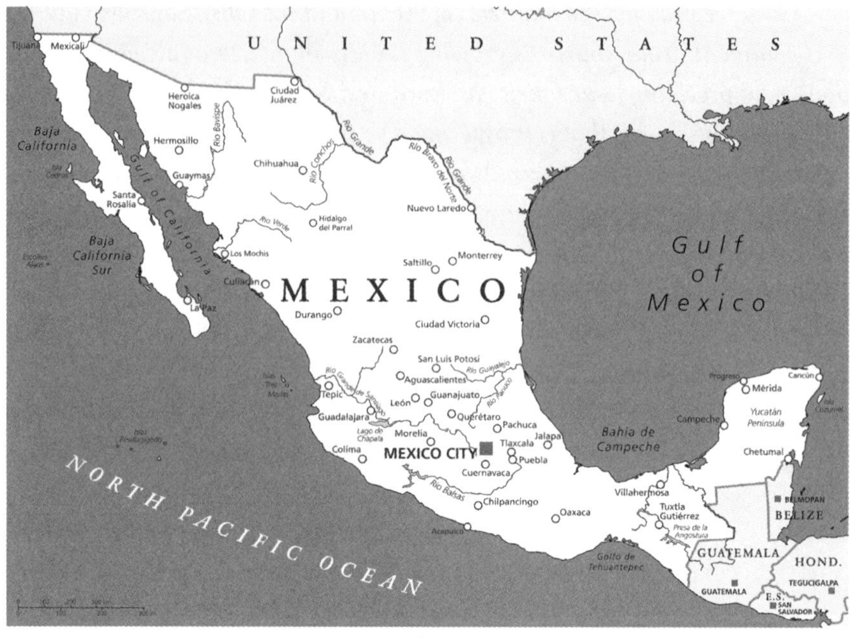

Map of Mexico.
PeterHermesFurian\Thinkstock

Mexico

In Mexico, organized corruption and crime affects every part of society and attacks Christians who stand up against the immorality of drug cartels and crime syndicates. But the majority of Christian persecution in Mexico comes from the rise of new tribal religions that blend Catholicism with the pagan beliefs of indigenous tribes. Christians who refuse to accept these tribal religions are forced to leave their homes and families. In March 2016, Lauro Nunzo, an evangelical Christian, who had been kicked out of his village in Oaxaca after publicly professing his faith, was attacked and imprisoned when he returned to visit his family. Earlier, in January of 2016, thirty evangelical Christians were banished from the village of Chiapas and their homes were destroyed so that they wouldn't return. Mexico's constitution grants freedom of religion, but the Mexican government will do little to protect the evangelical Christians.[294]

Colombia

The violence is heightened in Colombia where large areas of the country are under the control of "criminal organizations, drug cartels, revolutionaries, and paramilitary groups."[295] All inhabitants are at risk from the conflict and guerrilla warfare, but Christians are specifically vulnerable, especially when they speak out against organized crime and in support of human rights. In September 2009, after a church service in the Montelibano hamlet, three armed and masked men broke into the pastor's home and shot him in front of his wife and six young members of the church. His name was Rafael Velasquez, and he died instantly.[296] Anywhere from twenty-five to thirty pastors are murdered by armed guards in this

Map of South America.
Idogesto\Thinkstock

294. Perry Chiaramonte, "Mexico's Christians Face Beatings," FOX News, April 18, 2016, http://www.foxnews.com/world/2016/04/18/mexicos-christians-face-beatings-forced-conversions-at-hands-hybrid-faiths.html.
295. See https://www.opendoorsusa.org/christian-persecution/world-watch-list/colombia/.
296. "Colombian Pastor Assassinated," Christin Solidarity Worldwide, September 14, 2009, http://www.csw.org.uk/2009/09/14/press/908/article.htm.

country every year. More than 300 Protestant pastors have been murdered throughout Latin America in the last decade.[297]

The Western Church Can't Remain Silent

"I challenge the Christians of the world to pray for their persecuted brothers and sisters, to act on their behalf and to live out the life of Jesus in this needy world around us. Only then will we see a radical change take place in the lives of people. Only then we will see the love of Christ replace the hatred of this world."
—Brother Andrew, founder of Open Doors

Right now the Western Christian church is free of life-threatening persecution. By God's grace, we will remain that way. But we are not a separate body from the persecuted church. We are one in the Holy Spirit. *"If one member suffers, all suffer together; if one member is honored, all rejoice together"* (1 Corinthians 12:26 ESV).We can't stand by silently, only grateful that it isn't our family or church facing the unmerciful sword of persecution and death.

I Want to Challenge You

Our brothers and sisters who have walked the road of persecution and death in the past were overcomers. As you read their stories from different countries and times in history, you may not agree with every choice that they made, or every Christian doctrine that they were willing to die for. But the crucial thing is that they drew a line in the sand, a line that they were unwilling to cross in defending their faith in Jesus Christ and the inerrancy of the Bible. The same is true of the persecuted church today—they are overcomers in Christ.

---

297. Allen, *Global War,* 104.

Now, I'd like to raise a challenge for you—and for myself. If we are faced with the same decisions in these difficult days, what will our response be? Where will we draw the line in the sand and say, "this far and no further!" for the sake of the gospel? We must make the choice ahead of time so that we will remain faithful to Jesus Christ "to the end." And we must remember that we are never alone. Jesus Christ has promised that He would never leave us nor forsake us. (See Hebrews 13:5.) And we will always be surrounded by a great cloud of witnesses who have gone before us, led by our Lord and Savior Jesus Christ.

But the crucial thing is that they drew a line in the sand, a line that they were unwilling to cross in defending their faith in Jesus Christ and the inerrancy of the Bible.

> *Therefore, since we have so great a cloud of witnesses surrounding us, let us also lay aside every encumbrance and the sin which so easily entangles us, and let us run with endurance the race that is set before us, fixing our eyes on Jesus, the author and perfecter of faith, who for the joy set before Him endured the cross, despising the shame, and has sat down at the right hand of the throne of God.*
>
> (Hebrews 12:1–2 NASB)

So What Can We Do to Help the Persecuted Church?

What is our role as the body of Christ in "safe" countries? What should we do to reach out with the love of Christ to our suffering brothers and sisters in Christ?

Even while we honor these Christians for their courage in the face of torture and death, we must not ignore their plea for help.

1. **Pray and pray again**; pray earnestly realizing that the lives and safety of your Christian family depends on it. Join online prayer groups that are associated directly with the organizations that I will list below. They will give you monthly updates on the things that require the most prayer.
2. **Learn all you can** about the global war being waged against Christians today! Read the newsletters and the websites of those who are serving the persecuted church today. Join them in their specific efforts to help. (Organizations are listed below.)
3. **Share what you have learned** with the world around you. You may have a large platform for your message, you may be in Christian ministry, or your sphere of influence may be just family and your own circle of friends on social media. Whichever arena God has placed you in, share the plight of the persecuted church. Join together in prayer groups or action groups as the Holy Spirit leads you. Donate your money, your time, or your spiritual gifts. Pray that God will help you to make a difference!

Christian Organizations that Serve the Persecuted Church Today

There are many organizations that can use our support in this global war against Christians today. These organizations' newsletters and websites will keep you informed about what is happening around the world. They each have a different way that they reach out to those in their ministry sphere.

Open Doors

Open Doors, "Serving persecuted Christians worldwide," is an evangelical ministry that operates in over sixty oppressed countries. Open Doors was founded in 1955 by Andrew van der Bijl, a Dutch evangelist better known as Brother Andrew. He spent years behind the Iron Curtain sneaking Bibles to the underground church in the Soviet bloc countries. In addition to providing relief assistance to those in places of persecution, Open Doors also publishes the annual World Watch List which rates the top countries guilty of anti-Christian persecution throughout the world.

 www.opendoorsusa.org

The Voice of the Martyrs

The Voice of the Martyrs is a non-profit, inter-denominational Christian organization that was founded in 1967 by Pastor Richard Wurmbrand, who was imprisoned for fourteen years in Communist Romania for his faith in Christ. Voice of the Martyrs provides practical relief and spiritual support to oppressed Christians worldwide. There are many outlets for assistance through their organization: filling Action Packs or medical packs, adopting a Christian refugee that you can support and pray for, writing to persecuted Christians who are imprisoned in their homelands for their faith, participating in prayer vigils, and donating money for the cause of the martyrs. Whatever you choose to do, your time and talent will be multiplied by the Lord.

 www.persecution.com

The Center for the Study of Global Christianity

The Center for the Study of Global Christianity at Gordon-Conwell Theological Seminary in South Hamilton, Massachusetts, provides cutting edge statistical information on how our Christian brothers and sisters are faring throughout the world. Their website is an excellent source for Christian resources including a biblical encyclopedia that can help you understand the scope of Christianity's challenges today.

 www.gordonconwell.edu/ockenga/research/index.cfm.

Christian Aid Mission

Christian Aid Mission (CAM) is a sixty-year-old organization and generally considered to be the first organization to assist and promote native missionaries overseas. CAM serves as a non-denominational foreign mission board assisting more than 500 ministries overseas with tens of thousands of native missionaries in the field. These ministries are currently serving more than 1,000 unreached people groups in more than 100 countries around the world. Their focus is to reach the unreached where there are few Christians, where Christians suffer because of poverty and persecution or where foreign missionaries are not allowed. Although many of their associates must move secretly in hostile nations, they are bringing a great deal of support to the suffering church in Syria today.

 www.christianaid.org

Asia News

Asia News is a Catholic News Agency which documents daily accounts of anti-Christian persecution against both Catholics and Protestants in third world countries. They have up-to-the-minute reports on the persecution currently happening in Pakistan and India.

 www.asianews.it/en.html

The Pew Forum on Religious and Public Life

The Pew Forum on Religious and Public Life in Washington, DC, is the only organization listed that is not a Christian organization. Their studies are rigorous and fact-based and they provide statistics on religion in the United States and around the world and how it is affecting both society and government. Most Christian organizations find the Pew Forum data very reliable particularly on religious persecution around the world.

 www.pewforum.org

Teaming up with these organizations or developing an outreach program of your own can bring much-needed relief to those who are standing in faith and dying for the Christ we serve. Remember, there is no separation between the persecuted church and the free church—no separation for those who call upon the name of the Lord Jesus Christ to be saved. We are both loving and serving the same God. It is time to stand with them and ask the Lord what we can do to make a difference in this growing world of persecution and hate. By the leading of the Holy Spirit, you and I can both be used to help the suffering church.

> *"For I was hungry and you gave me food, I was thirsty and you gave me drink, I was a stranger and you welcomed me, I was naked and you clothed me, I was sick and you visited me, I was in prison and you came to me." Then the righteous will answer him, saying, "Lord, when did we see you hungry and feed you, or thirsty and give you drink? And when did we see you a stranger and welcome you, or naked and clothe you? And when did we see you sick or in prison and visit you?" And the King will answer them, "Truly, I say to you, as you did it to one of the least of these my brothers, you did it to me."* (Matthew 25:35–40 ESV)

ACKNOWLEDGMENTS

I have been blessed in *God's Generals: The Martyrs* with the skillful help of some very special people. I would like to thank Julie Singleton and Elizabeth Sherman for their assistance with research and photos. Thanks also to Judith Dinsmore, my in-house editor at Whitaker House, for her research, photo discoveries, and dedication in launching this latest *God's Generals* volume.

Special thanks to my editor, Victoria Mlinar, for her invaluable assistance with editing, writing, and research for this book on the great Christian martyrs. It is always a blessing to work together. May God receive all the glory for these martyrs' testimonies of faith!

There were many Christian organizations who have shared their stories with us and with the world. The body of Christ owes a debt of gratitude for their dedication in supporting the persecuted church. We have acknowledged them and their faithful ministries wherever their stories appear in the book.

Finally, thank you to Bob Whitaker, Jr. and Whitaker House for publishing the God's Generals series on the heroes of the Christian faith. May this sixth volume, *God's Generals: The Martyrs,* be a blessing to the nations!

ABOUT THE AUTHOR

From a young age, Roberts Liardon was destined to become one of the most well-known Christian authors and orators of the twentieth and twenty-first centuries. He has, to date, sold over 15 million books worldwide that have been translated into more than 60 languages. Having ministered in over 125 countries to members of the public and world leaders, Liardon is recognized internationally and has experienced great success as an author, public speaker, spiritual leader, church historian, and humanitarian.

Roberts Liardon was born in Tulsa, Oklahoma, the first male child born at Oral Roberts University. His career in the ministry began at the young age of thirteen, when he gave his initial public address. At seventeen, Liardon published the book, *I Saw Heaven*, which catapulted him into the public eye. The book sold over 1.5 million copies and by the following year, he had become one of the leading public speakers in the Christian community all over the world. This established him as a leading Protestant church historian, a role he carries with honor to this day. God spoke to Liardon and inspired him to write and produce a book series and DVD series entitled *God's Generals*. Its mission is to chronicle the lives of the leading Pentecostal and charismatic leaders. It was an immediate success and became one of the bestselling Christian DVD series in history. In 1990, Roberts Liardon moved to Southern California and founded his worldwide headquarters in Orange County. Here he started one of the largest Christian churches and Bible colleges in the region.

Roberts Liardon Ministries helps millions of lives through the power of the Holy Spirit. Liardon is a significant contributor towards building God's kingdom, with the belief that relationships is the key element that bonds the staff at Roberts Liardon Ministries to people around the world. Each year, millions are touched through this worldwide ministry, a genuine resource of victory for the entire body of Christ.

Roberts Liardon continues to speak to this generation of believers, and reaches out to those who are eager to read and learn relevant messages that draw the heart closer to God. For over thirty years, he has continued to complete a demanding speaking schedule along with writing books and mentoring a new generation of world leaders to effect change for the church and society.

From his ministry, Liardon established, financed, and sent almost five hundred men and women to various nations on the globe to help those less fortunate and spread God's Word across the world. Through his ministry's Home2Home project, he has expanded his services to people in various countries, where he provides ways for people to bring positive change to the world. Liardon does everything he can to assist local communities lead better and more fulfilling lives. He has spent time in Namibia, Africa, where he received permission to go into the schools and educate people on the effects of HIV/AIDS and its prevention and protection through abstinence and medication.

Liardon continues to manage and expand his international headquarters in Orlando, Florida, and his office in London, England. Find him on:

www.facebook.com/RobertsLiardon

www.twitter.com/RobertsLiardon

www.instagram.com/robertsliardonofficial